"A Hell of a Place to Lose a Cow"

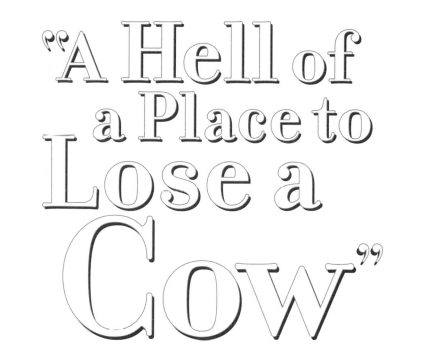

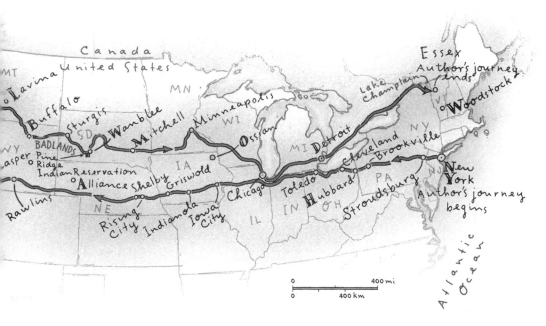

"A Hell of a Place to Lose a Cow"

An American Hitchhiking Odyssey

TIM BROOKES

ADVENTURE PRESS

NATIONAL GEOGRAPHIC
WASHINGTON, D. C.

Published by the National Geographic Society
1145 17th Street N.W., Washington, D.C. 20036

First Printing, July 2000

Map Artwork by James Noel Smith.
Interior Design by Kathleen Cole.
Printed in U.S.A.

To everyone who picked me up.

CONTENTS

"Let's go for a walk," he proposed. "When you walk, you are much more accurate than when you're sitting down. It is not an idle idea that you should pace back and forth when you try to relate something."

Carlos Castenada

"As I have always held it a crime to anticipate evils I will believe it a good comfortable road untill I am conpelled to beleive differently."

Captain Meriwether Lewis

~

CHAPTER 1

A Barometer
of Goodwill

The three months that changed my life began on July 1, 1973, when I first saw America. With my traveling companion and soon-to-be-enemy, Richard, I flew over from England on a student charter flight, four guitars being passed up and down the cabin, some of us by sheer habit sleeping under rather than in our seats, all of us drawn toward America like dazzled, half-blind moths. Myself, I was seduced by a vast poster in the window of Oxford Travel, a photo of a Greyhound bus bearing on its destination board a single word that encompassed the infinite adventure of America, its wild past, its endless plains, its mystery: BUFFALO.

I was 20. I had $90 in traveler's checks, a job waiting for me in the tobacco fields of Ontario, and a return ticket for the end of the summer. I was in love with an Iowan girl I'd met at Oxford with extraordinary qualities that I'd never seen in anyone else, qualities that I took to be quintessentially American: optimism, vitality, spontaneity, courage, a lightness of heart that illuminated everything she looked at. "The future is pliable," she said, contradicting everything England had taught me. "We can make of it whatever we want." It was 1973, and I believed her.

Richard, the friend of a friend, was tall, skinny, with wild black hair, and full of wild enthusiasm. I met him just once before leaving—a major mistake. "You're going to the States," he cried. "Can I come too?" And that was that; as casual as going to the pub. At 45, I'm starting to see how important that casualness is, how it is the necessary ingredient for both disaster and miracle. It's a gift of youth.

For £90 the British Universities North America Club— BUNAC—arranged our visas, flew us over, and put us up for our first night in the United States at the Royal Manhattan Hotel. Everything from that summer now seems like a damaged home movie, vivid short sequences spliced together bridging unknowable lengths of missing footage, but the New York sequence seems the most intact. We arrived after midnight to find the walls of Kennedy Airport covered with posters depicting a skeleton with a syringe climbing in through a window. "KEEP DRUGS OUT OF AMERICA. COOPERATE WITH YOUR CUSTOMS OFFICIAL." A squat, grizzled customs man pawed at my bag, which contained a change of socks and underwear, a nylon rain jacket, a sleeping bag, a single-volume complete works of Shakespeare, which I had to read before the autumn term began in October, and my asthma drugs. I was terrified that the last of these would be mistaken for heroin and babbled out an explanation to the agent.

"Azzma, huh?" he grunted. "That's too bad. " He shoved the bag back at me. "Next."

Dazed, our BUNAC mob were led outside and loaded on a streamlined bus with back-slanted aerodynamic-looking windows. Even muttering at the curb, the bus looked faster than prim, upright English buses. It was after 1 a.m. when we made our way into Manhattan. The city seemed to be uniformly awash in a curious dead light, not the expected big-city jazz of neon but a lifeless midnight sun. Hookers lounged on corners. We watched agog as a car the size of a swimming pool created a parking space by ramming the car parked in front, then the one behind. Everything I'd heard about New York was true.

The Royal Manhattan Hotel, skulking somewhere down in Lower Manhattan, put us up in a triple. The third bed was already occupied by a young guy from Sierra Leone. He told us that he had lost his money and passport and was trapped in a ghastly bureaucratic limbo, spending his days at the Sierra Leone embassy and his nights at the Royal Manhattan, unable to go home or go anywhere else in America. The streetlights burned in through the flimsy paper shades, and the room was astonishingly hot. On television, American hotels had air-conditioning. We opened the window, and the surf of traffic pounded over us. Somehow, we fell asleep. At one point I woke to a room full of pulsing lights and a weird *WheeoowWheeoowWheeoow* sound. I thought the flying saucers had landed. Toward dawn Richard felt the young Sierra Leonean groping at one of his hands tucked between his legs, hoping to fondle him, perhaps, or steal his watch.

In the morning, we found that the Leonean kid had vanished and we had missed our complimentary continental breakfast. We hoofed it down to the hotel ballroom for orientation, an obligatory BUNAC activity. BUNAC theoretically worked as a cultural exchange—and if we did not attend orientation, we were told, we would not get our visas. It turned out that orientation was simply a movie made in the fashionable if confusing quadruple split-screen format showing a bunch of kids traveling around America in a VW bus, to a soundtrack of bluegrass banjo.

"Any questions?" called the student organizer; then we were out on the streets.

The streets were the strangest part of Manhattan, cracked and steaming, bordered here and there by vacant lots being used as primitive car parks. The famous skyline—at one time, the silhouette of the future—was ragged with rooftop shanties and leggy water towers. New York City was both epic and tragic. It seemed to have been invented as a fantastic idea, the idea of the century, rather than as a place where people could actually live. I was petrified, excited, appalled—but not in the least deterred. America was the world's amusement park, and New York was simply, as billed, its scariest, most death-defying ride. The rest of America would be...well, I had no idea, really, but four years of hitchhiking had taught me that whatever it was, I would conquer it. Besides, not knowing was what it was all about—hitchhiking, the trip to America, the world.

Richard knew someone in Boston, I knew someone in Evanston, Illinois, so we split up, agreeing to rendezvous in Des Moines, Iowa. Having heard that it was illegal to hitch in New Jersey, I caught a bus to Stroudsburg, the first stop across the Pennsylvania line. As I was wandering from the tiny general-store-cum-bus-station through a neighborhood of maple trees and neat wood-frame houses toward the interstate, trusting my sense of direction, I passed a postman kneeling beside a mailbox, emptying it. He looked up at this total stranger, this kid wearing a backpack with a Union Jack flag tied to it, carrying a cheap classical guitar in a plaid vinyl case, and called out, "Hiya, buddy!"

Coming from a country so reserved toward strangers, so constrained in its affections, I was astonished. For years to come, when people asked me why I had emigrated to the United States, I told them about the postman in Stroudsburg and a vision of an America of morning sunshine and dew barely off the unfenced lawns, of egalitarian cheerfulness and a future as full of unbounded possibilities as the continent itself.

Hitchhiking was always magical to me. When I was 17 I left my family's home in Worcester to hitch down to London, where my older brother was at college. I went via Stratford-on-Avon, miles out of my way, just because that was where the first lorry driver that picked me up was going. As I walked across the Avon bridge, I saw a large green road sign in the distance bobbing steadily nearer, a sign that showed the roundabout ahead and the roads springing away from it like a compass radiating directions. As the sign grew larger, I was filled with a growing sense of horizons and of awe, of the novel sense of unlimited choice. I could go anywhere from here. It was as if all the lines of latitude and longitude converged at that crossroads, and as soon as I set foot on the magic crux I would be catapulted clear out of the realm of my narrow, tame experience into places unimaginably exotic.

Insofar as I had a plan for my life, it had something to do with hitchhiking. I came across the Japanese proverb "It is better to travel hopefully than to arrive," and took it as my mantra, holding it in my mouth like a piece of fruit, the word "hopefully" provoking a little saliva each time I repeated it. I didn't know what arriving would be like, but I thought I could guess from my father, slowing down as he passed through his mid-40s, putting on weight, irritated more and more easily by change and novelty, developing an almost irrational suspicion of closed doors. What if we could travel all our lives, I thought, and never arrive?

At first, miraculously, everything went according to my planless plan. At the end of the summer of 1973, I flew back to England. With a naivete so great that it amounted to both genius and utter idiocy, I applied for teaching jobs at the colleges and universities in states I had hitched through, just so I could say, "Last summer I traveled through Iowa City/Berkeley/Seattle and was very taken with the place." My naivete, though, opened locked doors: Even though I was still an undergraduate, and every college teaching job in the U.S. routinely attracted a thousand or more applicants with master's degrees or doctorates, I got a job at the University of Vermont.

You'd think that after such startling vindication I might have held on to my Zen navigation principles. Somehow, though, over the next 25 years, they slipped away. By the spring of 1998, I'd had two books published and two rejected, had taught countless introductory writing and literature courses at the University of Vermont, had surgery on both knees, had become the father of two wonderful daughters, had survived two less-than-wonderful divorces, had founded and lost a magazine, I had coached championship soccer teams, my hair had gone gray, and I had shaved off my beard. By the standards of the day, I had grown up. Yet if this were true, I wasn't much of an advertisement for the adult life. I'd spent a decade or more trying to be a good husband and father, trudging grimly through the valley of the shadow of debt. I had a mortgage, I paid child support, I had credit card debts. I was working 50 or 60 hours a week, exhausted by the chronic clutch of anxiety. When I found myself night after night washing dishes under a fluorescent tube, eyes burning, my wife and the girls already asleep, or climbing the stairs with yet another basket of laundry to fold, I found myself imagining that I was hitchhiking beside some highway out West—desert on both sides, mountains like red teeth nibbling the huge horizon, the road itself peeled back and open to the sky.

If this was a midlife crisis, it wasn't just mine. The whole of America seemed to have lost its youthful imagination and vigor. Art and music were stagnating in a spiral of recycled ideas, politics had sold out to business, everyone was downsizing. A new millennium was approaching, but nobody seemed to be looking forward to it with much hope. A new, meaner spirit seemed to have taken root. The end of the Cold War had brought neither peace nor the long-hoped-for peace dividend. Instead conservatives had turned their attack from communism abroad to liberalism at home, to such effect that even while our kids were rediscovering bell-bottoms and tie-dyed shirts, their once-radical parents were renouncing the most exciting time of their lives as a series of youthful indiscretions, abandoning the faith.

I was damned if I would give up that easily, and between fantasy and anger I formulated a plan: Go back on the road. Compare it to my previous trip. Find out what America was really like now.

I toyed with the idea for months, then approached NATIONAL GEOGRAPHIC magazine. What if I were to retrace my 1973 journey, starting at Stroudsburg and heading west to Chicago, Des Moines, Boulder, Salt Lake City, Reno, San Francisco, Portland, Seattle,

Vancouver, Calgary, Winnipeg, Toronto, into the tobacco fields and then back through New England? What if I tried to track down some of the people I'd met a quarter century earlier, find out how their lives and America had changed since those days when, for me at least, America was so vital, so full of life and hope?

The GEOGRAPHIC called me on my 45th birthday to say yes. They would pair me up with a Polish photographer named Tomasz Tomaszewski, a stocky guy with an impish grin, a degree in physics and a rich, self-taught command of English who had been active in the Solidarity movement. He had shot pictures (and been shot at) all over the world, but he had never lost his fascination with America. I'd write, he'd shoot pictures. Every couple of days I'd call his cell phone and we'd rendezvous at some cheap motel and swap notes. We'd wax philosophical about America from our vantage point as outsiders, exchange droll European ironies, maybe travel together every so often. We'd have a road trip.

To my surprise, everyone I knew, including Barbara, my wife, thought I had gone mad. All the men and almost all the women had hitchhiked 20 or 30 years ago, and given a sliver of encouragement, they would launch into their road-trip stories, their eyes lighting up, their faces glowing—yet everyone ended with "I wouldn't do it now, of course...."

"Why not?" I'd ask, and at once the clouds would roll over their foreheads. Sure, everyone hitchhiked back in the sixties, they said, but now America was a far more dangerous and terrifying place. Fear had edged in like dusk, and the land had filled with dark shapes: religious cults with private armories, Nicaraguans marching up through Texas, neo-Nazis, psychotics with shotguns in fast-food restaurants, satanists in the daycare center, pipe bombs in the mail and more psychotics in the mail room, poisoners and perverts, teenage drive-by gang shooters, rapists in pleasant parks and on leafy campuses, sharks in the shallows, and chainsaw killers up the dirt roads: monsters for every age and every political persuasion. It was common knowledge that all hitchhikers were murdered—that was why nobody hitchhiked anymore—or, conversely, were murderers, so drivers were too scared to have anything to do with them. Several people advised me to take a gun. "Nobody in their right mind will pick you up," one friend warned. "You'll be a target for every wacko and werewolf from here to San Francisco."

I was stunned by their vehemence. My God, I thought, this is the America they think of when they make political decisions. No wonder they vote for mandatory sentencing, and buy the wife and kids car phones for Christmas. Or handguns.

Bollocks, I said. America is actually safer now than it was 25 years ago. I cited some of the latest violent-crime statistics: Between 1990 and 1995, network coverage of murder rose by 336 percent, even without including the O. J. Simpson case. Over the same period, real murder fell by 13 percent. Even the roads are safer: twice as many vehicles but, even so, fewer injuries and deaths.

Facts didn't matter. People clung to their fear as if to an electric fence. The entire country seemed to be suffering from a kind of patriaphobia. What happens, I wondered, when we become afraid of our own country? When we were teenagers we went out on the road to disprove our parents' anxieties, I thought; maybe now that we are parents we should go back out again to disprove our own.

CHAPTER 2

Anywho

Like most hitchhikers, I began planning my route by sticking little flags in a mental map: Places I Can Crash (a word I hadn't used in two decades). Gail, my first wife, in Seattle. Barbara's ex-boyfriend Andy in Utah. The trip began to seem like Harold Pinter's play *Betrayal,* in which each scene goes back in time, taking place earlier than the previous one. Maybe if I were on the road long enough, I'd turn back into a teenager.

There were eight people I wanted to find whom I'd met en route in 1973 and hadn't seen since. To track them down I whistled up www.anywho.com, a digital bloodhound. Anywho, which I'd never used before, turned out to be a scary commodity. When I tested it out on myself, it not only knew my name, address, and phone number (which it would dial at the click of a mouse), but choosing the map icon threw up a detailed map of the little valley I live in, with my house highlighted and arrowed. Yikes! Technology might be making my job easier and the past more accessible, but I wasn't sure I'd want to be so easily accessed.

Uncomfortably, I turned Anywho's nose toward Mitzi Porges. I met Mitzi—a tall, brilliant art student, all blond hair and angular cheekbones—when she was hitchhiking through Europe in 1972 and dropped into Oxford to see her childhood friend Steve Block.

Offering Anywho the name Porges in Evanston immediately produced Mitzi's parents. Alberta Porges, Mitzi's mother, said yes, of course she remembered me, and told me I should stop in if I passed through Chicago. Mitzi, she said, was in Oakland: The art student had become an artist and art critic. When I visited her in 1973, she took me around the Chicago Art Museum. Now she was writing guided audio tours for museums all over the world. She seemed to have inherited a life already waiting for her.

I called her, and we began to catch up, but the conversation seemed to consist of two currents—one warm and familiar, the other eerie and unreal. Our mutual friend Steve Block, she said, was now teaching at Princeton. Steve, a hyperactive kid with a Jewish afro, taught me how to play "Ain't She Sweet?" and "Has Anybody Seen My Gal?" on the guitar, and when his draft notice arrived, he and I burned it in the frying pan. When Mitzi and I hung up, I called up the Princeton molecular biology web page, and there was Steve's photo. He had thickened a little around the waist, but still had the same slightly evil, Pan-like grin. "My research interests lie in biophysics, particularly with the problem of cell motility....My lab has pioneered the use of optical tweezers (laser-based optical gradient force traps) and other advanced methods...to make physical measurements of macromolecular assemblies, such as the torsional stiffness of bacterial flagella..."

How did we ever acquire such gravity?

Other names came drifting out of the phone as more or less familiar voices. The two brilliant, radical sisters I stayed with in Vancouver were now married with children, and less radical. Larry van de Maele, the son of the tobacco farmer I'd worked for, was now living down the road in London, Ontario. His wife, who had never met me, insisted I visit. Two others seemed to have vanished off the earth. All the same, I found this rediscovery very reassuring: a time that seemed as remote as a dream was being verified by independent witnesses, and it felt as if part of me, too—a part that I particularly liked—was also being authenticated.

But of all the people from my 1973 trip I wanted to meet again, the most elusive was Kathy, the love of my young life, and the reason I'd come from England in the first place.

She was an enigma. On one hand, she was the woman who changed my life. I could show you the photos: blond hair, ski-jump nose, radiant. More importantly, she made me open my eyes. It was as if, after spending all my young life looking down, I glanced up and found a realm as vast and deep as the night sky. My favorite times with her weren't about sex, which was still new and uncertain ground for me, but about discovery. On her narrow bed, looking up into the dark ceiling, our arms round each other, it was as if everything in the universe had spun out from that tiny box of a room and all we had to do was send out a line of thought and it could reach anywhere.

On the other hand, I was also furious at her. After I had bought my ticket, planning to spend the whole summer with her, she dumped me. I never knew why. But there was still hope: when I came to America, she said, I must visit her in Des Moines, which I did. We had four days together. I spent a quarter of my traveling pittance on a dress for her made of silk scarves. One evening she drove us down to a lake to eat watermelon (which I'd never eaten), and we watched fireflies (which I'd never seen) dance like fairies in the enchanted darkness. When, against impossible odds, I got the teaching job in Vermont, she wrote to say how wonderful it was, that she'd love to come and visit, and was there somewhere her boyfriend could stay? I wrote an angry letter, a hurt letter, and a sad letter, but she didn't reply to any of them, and I hadn't seen or heard from her since.

Now, in the back of my mind, was the hope that somehow on this nineties trip I'd find out what had happened to her, and between us. In a sense, she was the whole story—not just my reason for being in America but my reason for being myself.

Anywho was baffled by Kathy. Her mother had written me a letter in 1976 saying that Kathy was marrying an Episcopal minister named Cramer, or Kramer, but all the Kathys and Kathryns and Heins and Cramers in Iowa were either disconnected or the wrong person. No sign of her parents, Marv and Peg Hein, in Iowa, nor in Minnesota, where they'd owned a summer cabin. Colorado College, Kathy's alma mater, claimed never to have heard of her.

I called the Episcopal diocese of Iowa, who said that they did indeed have records of Kathy married to an Alfred Cramer, but that he had remarried in 1988 and moved out of state. No mention of what had happened to her. Maybe she'd remarried and moved. Maybe she'd died, I thought, suddenly struck with horror. I called the *Des Moines Register* to try searching for her in their obituaries, but by now, they said, the records were too old to be readily accessible. This business of rediscovering the past started to seem no longer a game, and the eerie authority of Anywho looked shallow and threadbare: If she had died, what would it have to offer about her? Information is just information. The map is not the territory.

On the shelf in my office I still have a letter addressed to a detective agency, containing a check for $75 and the few details I knew. Just before I mailed it, I decided to try one last lead, and called the Episcopal archdiocese in New York. "Alfred Cramer?" the secretary asked. "Just a moment...Yes, he's in Vermont."

Anywho gave me two numbers for Alfred Cramers in Vermont, both in the southeast of the state, possibly work and home. I left messages on both machines. Within two hours, I got a call. This is pretty weird, I admitted to him, but I'm trying to track down a mutual friend. I believe you knew Kathy Hein?

"Kathy?" he cried. "Bless me! Well, well, well. Yes. I was married to her. Do you hear the piano in the background?" Beethoven, played quite well. "That's our son."

He gave me her phone number in Texas. She had remarried, he said, and lived in Austin. I walked around all day with my heart in my throat. What would I say when I called? Why would she want to talk to me? Would she think of me as an old friend or a stalker?

At about 5:30 that evening, the phone rang.

"Tim? This is Kathryn Lewis. You may remember me as Kathy Hein." Her voice came unchanged out of the darkness.

"Kathy!" I cried. "This is wonderful. So Al Cramer told you I called him?"

"Al?" she asked, puzzled. "No, I haven't talked to him in months."

"How on earth did you get my number, then?"

It was very odd, Kathy said. Her husband had taken a call from someone at Colorado College who said that a Tim Brookes was try-

ing to get in touch with her, and they had his number if she
wanted it.

Wait a moment, I said. When I called them they said they had
no record of you at all. I spoke to two or three different people, I
e-mailed, they said they'd never heard of you.

"That's not the strangest thing," she said. "When I called the
college, nobody there knew anything about you, and nobody knew
who could possibly have called me. They kept saying, No, we don't
have his number. We don't have any record of anyone of that name
calling. I kept begging them to check again, and they kept saying
no, until someone happened to glance down at a desk and saw
your name and number on a Post-It note on the desk. Nobody
knew who had written it down, or how it had got there." The universe seemed to be conspiring to put us back in touch.

I told her about my road trip; she understood immediately
what it was all about. She herself had recently started wondering
about her time in Oxford. She had managed to track down her
girlfriend from those days, and had been wondering what had
become of me.

"I wish I could make it as far south as Texas on my trip," I said,
"but I can't see how I'll have the time."

"Maybe we can meet somewhere nearer you," she offered. Her
new husband worked for the *New York Times*, she said, and they
were coming up to spend a couple of weeks in the city.

"Well, that's possible, I suppose, but it would have to be pretty
soon. I'm starting my trip from New York on July 20th. When are
you planning to get there? "

"Wait a moment," she said, "I've got it written down somewhere. Here it is. July 19th ."

CHAPTER 3

Clothing Technologies

In 1973, the only gear I bought was a sleeping bag and a rain jacket from an army surplus store for under $25. Now I was in the contradictory position of hitchhiking on a generous expedition budget. I rubbed my hands together gleefully and ran off to the climbing/camping/hiking shops that have sprung up all over Burlington like tents on Everest.

After five minutes in Eastern Mountain Sports, though, I was paralyzed. They had different socks for light, medium, and heavy hiking. They had sneakers that were more like boots and boots that were more like sneakers, and two dozen different types of sandals including some with grooves that would draw water (or sweat) away from the soles of my feet. They had backpacks with dozens of pockets, and an entire range of stick-on pouches for the accessories that couldn't fit in the pack. Nothing cost much less than a hundred bucks, and when I'd finished I might as well buy a Range Rover to chuck them all in.

The EMS outfitter urged me to buy *Medicine for Mountaineering and Other Wilderness Activities* and *Everyday Wisdom: 1001 Expert Tips for Hikers*. All I wanted was insect repellent and a snakebite kit. The outfitter frowned. The conventional wisdom about snakebite kits, he said, was that they didn't really get much of the venom out, and you were better off trying to get to a hospital. If you got to the hospital in time, the bite didn't matter; if you didn't get to the hospital in time, nothing mattered.

I wasn't a very good shopper. I turned down the cutting-edge lightweight microfiber zip-away pants because they made me look like an unemployed circus clown, and I could imagine a Nevada trucker taking one look at them and beating me to death with a tire iron. I did buy a microfiber shirt ("This uses clothing technologies that are barely two years old") for close to 60 bucks because it had a neat invisible vent in the back that kept you cool and more importantly could be washed at night and would drip dry by morning. I went with the sandals that also worked in water and the ecosensitive bug repellent, but I reached a point of diminishing greed when the Gore-Tex rain jacket cost more than my entire trip in 1973. The very idea of good equipment collides head-on with the tradition of hitchhiking. It's not just that hitchhiking is a function of poverty and relies on a certain sympathy for the poor, ragged sod beside the road; it's that ostentatious displays of wealth—say, six-color backpacks and self-inflating sneakers—would make me a target. I imagined getting mugged just for my incredible Dri-Stride light-hiking socks ("...the magenta line indicates the buffer where our patented, anatomical design interface produces the comfort benefits...").

The best stuff was all bright and peppy. I wanted something good but unobtrusive, a state-of-the-art superlight 48-pocket backpack that looked as if it had been dragged behind the bus all the way from Casablanca to Marrakesh. In the end I bought a bottom-of-the-line pack in black and royal blue. "Good choice," he said. "When you're all packed and ready to leave, come back and we'll fine-tune all the straps."

The plan for the expedition was that Tomasz and I would carry cell phones. Though I balked at first, having never owned a one—and couldn't imagine anything more daft than standing with my thumb out while talking into a cell phone—after a while I began to see that the idea had possibilities. If I was on an interstate and saw the highway patrol coming, I could quickly dial 911 and call in a ten-vehicle accident in the other direction. I could have pizza delivered. If I got really desperate beside the road I could dial 900 and have phone sex. Good deal. I stuffed the phone into one of my daughter Maddy's thick socks for protection, and it became the Sock Phone.

I bought a tent, but I had no intention of camping. Camping was permanently tainted for me by the summer of 1975 when I finally lived out the dream of driving around Europe with a girl-friend and sharing a tent. This fantasy of lust and freedom turned out to involve a mosquito-prone tent, shockingly hard ground (this was the days before self-inflating sleeping pads) and a relationship going sour by the mile. A tent to me means sleepless nights, the whine of insects hungry for blood, nylon walls closing around my throat. I'd rather sleep in roach-infested motels and crash on people's kitchen floors.

At the last minute, I bought a large newsprint-quality paper pad and a black magic marker for making destination signs. I toyed with the idea of taking a complete Shakespeare again, but decided on something more suitably American: the journals of Lewis and Clark. And the day before I left, a packet arrived from my brother in England containing a Union Jack flag to tie to my backpack. Unfortunately, the only one he'd been able to find was about six feet by four feet. I could have used it as a blanket.

My father, who was in the Army Reserves, had taught me how to pack, so I shoved everything small and loose—inhaler, EpiPen syringe, antacids, cortisone cream, antifungal shampoo, inhaled steroids, antihistamines, Tylenol, Lemon Zinger tea—into my sneakers. They became my "Pharmacy Shoes: The Perfect Apothecary For The Middle-Aged Walking Hypochondriac." I ended up using all the antihistamines, as every motel cleans its carpets with stuff that would take the paint off the space shuttle, but otherwise I never needed any of my drug supply.

The night before I left, I was delighted to find that everything fit into the pack, just about, and that I could actually lift it off the ground. But the only way I could keep the pack on my back was by unclipping a serious-looking strap apparently designed to hold my shoulder blades together, and at six the next morning, when I swung it up to my shoulder, I nearly fell off the porch. It was like wearing a house.

CHAPTER 4

The Road to Jericho

There is no definitive history of hitchhiking, but the first recorded hitchhiker is Philip the Evangelist. Philip was walking the desert road from Jerusalem to Gaza when he was passed by an Ethiopian "man of great authority"—the Queen of Ethiopia's treasurer, in fact—riding in a chariot. The Ethiopian was reading aloud from Isaiah as his charioteer drove him along. At the prompting of the Holy Spirit, Philip called to him: "Do you understand what you are reading?" The Ethiopian invited Philip to ride with him and explain the text, which he did to such good effect that the Ethiopian asked to be baptized. They never saw each other again: The Ethiopian "went on his way rejoicing," and Philip made for Caesarea (Acts 8:26-40).

What I find fascinating about this story is that the spiritual benefit falls to the one in the vehicle, not the one on foot. The wealthy man may possess the vehicle and the opportunity to be generous, but in the Bible, the wise one is the poor man, the one on foot, and similar figures—gods in disguise as beggars—appear in many of the world's religions. Hitchhiking may seem to be simply about kindness in the giver, but this story, if we take it as a parable, suggests that the giver receives, too, though it's a gift he didn't expect, and certainly not from the anonymous pedestrian, the stranger in the dust.

In early July, when my trip was only a few days away, for no obvious reason I drove home through Essex Junction instead of taking the back roads, as I usually do. Standing by the road on the way out of the town, wearing a puffy ski jacket, jeans and a small pack, was a hitchhiker.

I pulled over. I wanted to quiz him on how easy or hard he'd found it to get rides, how far he'd come, what people were like to hitchhikers these days. Besides, what terrible karma it would be not to pick him up, right before I hoped for the same kind of generosity from others.

"Where are you headed?" I asked.

"Great!" he said. "I'm doing great. Just went into Burlington to help someone out. Haven't had a drink, don't worry. Thanks a lot for stoppin'." He leaned across and shook my hand. "It's my birthday," he said. "I'm 40 years old. I'm still young. I've got my life ahead of me."

His breath smelled of beer and fruit-flavored Lifesavers. My heart sank. I asked him how long he had been waiting for a ride. Somehow the question led him elsewhere, and he gestured at his rosy face.

"I been takin' medication for my thyro," he explained. "Makes my face get all puffy, and I get all hot and cold."

I sympathized. I had thyroid problems myself once, I told him. The strange thing about the medication, he said, was that it meant he'd never get drunk. "I could take any man from round here and drink a case of beer with him and not get drunk."

He thought of something. "Do you ever drink a beer?" he asked, as if he were merely curious. Yes, I said, I liked a beer with my dinner.

Suddenly he was very interested. "Would you like one now?" He reached into his small pack.

I declined hastily, saying something about cops and open-bottle laws. He nodded wisely, and settled back into his seat.

I asked him again about his journey. He said it had taken him three hours to get from Jericho to Burlington; he had done well. My heart sank again. *Three hours to do. . .what, 15 miles?* I tried to find out what he had been doing in town, but he slipped past the question as if dodging a shadow, and was off somewhere else. I remembered something I'd been told by a friend who worked in a bike shop. "You get a lot of mentally ill people coming in," he said, "because they're not allowed to drive cars, but they can ride bikes." Or hitchhike, I thought gloomily.

"Did you lose your driver's license, or do you just prefer not to drive?" I asked.

He shook his head. "Never had one," he said. "I'm 40 years old. I've got my whole life ahead of me."

"I turn off just up here," I said, pointing ahead to the light.

He was galvanized into action. "Could you take me on to Jericho?" he pleaded. "I can pay for your gas." He pulled a bunch of small bills from his pocket. "That's where I live. I'll pay for your gas."

I calculated quickly. It was no more than 15 minutes out of my way. "Sure," I said. He pressed money on me. I waved it off; he offered again. I declined again. We were through the light and making for Jericho—and a strange thing happened. As soon as

I was beyond my rut, my commuter track, driving at this odd customer's behest, the day suddenly seemed lighter, as if I were sneaking a quick vacation.

He was embarrassingly grateful. He shook my hand several times, and talked some more about his thyro. I told him about my hitchhiking plan, and he drew back in astonishment. "Well, if you can do that, you must be Superman," he said. "You must be Superman."

Within minutes, we were in Jericho. He pointed to the church as we passed it. "I'm affiliated with that church," he said. "Minister's a good man. I been shovelin' his steps all winter. He pays me 75 cents."

He kept shaking my hand. "You're a good man. You're a good guy." He lived behind the bank on the left, he explained. Maybe he told me he lived with his parents, or maybe I just guessed it.

I waited for the oncoming traffic, then pulled up in front of the bank.

"Hey, thanks a lot," he said, shaking my hand again. "I'll see you in heaven."

By now something had happened: I felt light-headed, and a little off-balance. My glibness was being worn away. "That's the plan," I said, half joking, but he would have none of it.

"Thanks again," he said, shaking my hand one last time. "I love you, brother."

CHAPTER 5

Searching for That Wonderful Tribe

July 20 — New York City

At 6 a.m. on July 20, 1998, backpack swaying alarmingly above my head, I lurched up the driveway to a taxi that would take me to the airport. By 10 a.m. I was ringing the bell outside the apartment where Kathy was staying. Footsteps came to the door, the lock turned, the door opened and I saw a middle-aged woman—a stranger.

It was Kathy, but it wasn't. At 21, she hadn't worn makeup or jewelry, and her hair and skin shone. Now she wore heavy silver bracelets and had the slightly dry look of someone who has spent too many years in the sun. She asked me to call her Kathryn; no one had called her Kathy for years.

She was equally nonplussed to see me. At 20, I had a full beard and chestnut hair down to my shoulders, but the man that she saw was clean-shaven and greying. When she produced a sketch she'd done of me playing the guitar on the sands of South Wales in 1973, only my forearms and my long, pointed nose looked familiar. She and I could have sat next to each other on the subway, and we'd never have known each other. In that door-opening instant, I got the first inkling that my entire project was sunk: No matter how intimately I had known the America of 25 years ago, I wouldn't recognize it now.

We talked in the apartment, in Central Park, in a restaurant over lunch, and back at the apartment. The stories came flocking back with warmth and color: searching every greengrocer in Cornwall because she discovered I'd never tasted a mango (a mango, in Cornwall in 1973!); camping out in Wales and nearly freezing to death, ending up in an all-night laundromat. Gathering mussels on the beach below King Arthur's supposed castle in Tintagel, then accidentally leaving them under a seat in the rental car so it smelled so ghastly we barely dared to return it. Dropping books and papers to hitch down to London; trying to find the Tate Gallery, getting lost but knowing that wherever we went we were always finding things, and finding ourselves. Getting up at two in the morning and walking down to the Thames to watch the swans by moonlight. Kathy told me that her mother had recently discovered a stash of old Oxford photos. "In all of those pictures, we were posed something like the Beatles in *A Hard Day's Night*." She laughed. "Every picture I have...making pyramids. There wasn't a straight photograph in the bunch."

We were both laughing giddily, finishing each other's sentences. "So what happened to you after you went back to college?" I asked, and then time began again, the path forked.

Her sunny, American optimism had evaporated once she was back in America. Back at college for her senior year, she fell into a black depression. Trying to find her way in the darkness, she got entangled in some confused relationships; within a couple of years she was a Des Moines mother, in graduate school, and working. "In that year in Oxford I was never lonely," she said. "When I left to go back to the States, I was very lonely. I was always searching again for that wonderful tribe, that group of hilarious, spontaneous, bright friends, and I never found it."

After nearly twenty years, she divorced, then remarried, and her life began again. It was as if she had surfaced like a submarine long overdue, rocking and bobbing uncertainly while the crew threw open the hatches for fresh air. What she had gained from that long detour, she said, was two wonderful children, and her own successful graphic design business; I didn't ask her what she thought she lost.

As she talked, she became a separate person. The grievances that I'd held against her seemed ridiculously petty against the long, slow wavelength of time; but by the same token my own presence in her life seemed incidental. The more complete she became, the less I mattered. The shared past dwindled to a small, bright point.

I asked her why she had dumped me. It was too much, she said. Both of us were younger, more fragile, and less experienced in love than the other thought; both of us were looking for the other to lead the way. I wanted her to be my America, my new-found-land, my spiritual guide. She couldn't carry that load. Nobody could. She had dropped me because I was just too much weight.

The afternoon, too, seemed to be getting heavier under the burden of my expectations. I wanted her, once again, to give me answers, yet if we met now, for the first time, we'd probably have nothing to say. The past was visible, all too clearly—but it was under glass twenty-five years thick. It was like those tantalizing visions of the Holy Grail offered to the Round Table knights who were good, but not perfect: This is all you get. You're lucky to be granted a glimpse of it, and that glimpse in itself may energize and inspire you, but you can never have it.

The reunion was almost over: we had to meet Tomasz to shoot some pictures, and then Kathy, her husband (who seemed to be deliberately keeping out of sight), and her daughter were going out for the evening. We took a cab to Times Square, where Tomasz showed up with his grin and his camera. Kathy and I goofed around, back doing those *Hard Day's Night* poses again. We had touched on that third rail of shared silliness—then it was over, we did the good-friends hug-and-kiss-on-the-cheek thing, and she was gone.

She became my guide after all. She showed me that I couldn't go back, that I would find my own path, through America, through everything. Just as I did then. She cut me loose again. At the time I didn't see that, though. The teenage boy in me had been brought back to life, and he was crushed, all over again. To hell with the past, I thought. You can't get there from here.

The following morning I woke up in a hotel in Chinatown that was surrounded by shattered streets and sidewalks, with garbage bags piled up in their dozens, and corrugated storefront shutters spattered with paint as if by small-arms fire.

Tomasz met me at the breakfast table. He raised an eyebrow. I explained.

"To tell you the truth," he said ironically, "I was surprised to see you yesterday in such a good mood."

I shrugged helplessly.

"You idolized her," he said. This was the second time I'd met the guy. Was it that obvious?

"I've always tended to idolize women," I said gloomily.

He shrugged and grinned. "Everybody does."

"That's right. The Polish are notorious romantics too, aren't they?" I said, thinking of Chopin, and of the Polish Army trying to stop Hitler's tanks with cavalry charges. He chuckled.

Breakfast done, Tomasz went off to find his rented car, and I went off to find ... well, everything, really.

CHAPTER 6

Been a Long Time Since I Did the Stroll

July 21 — Stroudsburg, Pennsylvania

The Port Authority bus station was a dam rupturing: smartly dressed men and women poured out of every door, flooding the sidewalk in both directions, surging onto the street, scowling and waving for taxis. I picked my way through them in shorts and backpack, fighting the tide.

A guy built like a running back, head shaved, one gold earring, collapsed into the seat next to mine. He told me that he was a merchant marine and had driven 40 hours straight to catch the bus. He'd been around the world seven times. After a while, he said, every port and island had started to look the same. Now he just ran coastal routes. He had a house in the Poconos but was thinking of moving to Nevada to escape taxes. He fell asleep minutes outside of the Lincoln Tunnel, leaving me wondering what kind of omen this was: The first person I met was a world traveler who was sick of the world?

On the other side of the aisle sat a young African-American businessman whose cell phone went off, embarrassing him, as we turned onto the interstate. A quarter century ago, a half-empty bus left I-80 and bumped through rundown, dusty Newark, home of race riots. On one grubby street I had seen a single slender tree enclosed in a metal cage, as if to keep it from escaping. A van had passed, advertising "Electrified Water—Every Glass Full of Health." America's doorstep now seemed slicker and faster, the road in better fettle, bearing twice as much traffic as it raced past huge malls and billboards:

SNEAKER STADIUM
CIGARS: 450 KINDS IN STOCK
INNOVATION LUGGAGE

Not so much a road as a shopping channel.

The bus station in Stroudsburg still doubled as a store, though. I looked for signs to I-80, maybe half a mile away, past white wooden houses under maples barely changed since 1973. There were no mailmen around, but an elderly gent coming out of the *Pocono Record* office nodded and smiled. I found the interstate roaring through the valley like an asphalt river. I shrugged off my pack, hung out my thumb, and settled into my spot by the guardrail as if I had never left it. I was doing nothing, and I was doing exactly what I wanted. Anything was possible. I had arrived.

Within five minutes, two young guys in a red muscle car pulled off the interstate and paused opposite me at the head of the ramp. "Need a ride?" one called out. "Yeah!" I called back, though I couldn't imagine that they were going back onto the highway, having just pulled off. He screamed an obscenity and gave me the finger. *Guys*, I thought, *do you have any idea what a cliché you are?*

Almost at once, a blue Buick Skylark that seemed to have missed its exit off the interstate came to a halt at the bottom of the on-ramp. Must be lost, I thought. It paused, then began to reverse up the ramp. It had Virginia plates. Must be seriously lost, I thought. To my amazement, the car stopped beside me. *No! Surely not!* The window rolled down. The driver leaned across the passenger seat. It was Tomasz.

"How did you get here so quickly?" he asked, grinning in bewilderment. It was the first sign that he was used to a leisurely, time-consuming prowl, looking for the right conjunction of subjects and the perfect light, whereas I was moving at the speed of the interstate. Our coordination was already starting to fall apart.

We shook hands as if this, rather than our clownish photo-shoot in Manhattan, were the real start of the journey, and he headed off into Stroudsburg to look for small-town America. He had barely completed the complicated and illegal task of reversing up the rest of the ramp, peering around and disappearing down a maple-lined street, when a pickup pulled over and an ex-Marine, now driving for UPS, picked me up. I was on my way.

Thinking of the long trip ahead, I asked him if there were other hitchhikers on the road, or whether I was as much of an oddity as I felt. "Oh, I see a few," he said. "A couple of years ago I was working as a security guard on a construction site where they were building a mall. I picked up this hitchhiker coming east from California and he didn't have anywhere to stay, so I took him over to the construction site and found him somewhere out of the way to sleep. I always wondered what happened to him, and then, guess what? I picked him up again two years later, heading back west."

He dropped me off a dozen miles later in Tannersville, where a new mall had been carved into the woodland. "Seems like it's happening all over," he said, shaking his head. Then he was gone.

A short ride, but it was still before noon, and above all, the journey had begun. Yes, I thought, pounding the guardrail with the flat of my hand.

Ten minutes later, it was Jeff, a calm, bearded young guy, also driving a pickup. He worked for a lumber company, assisting one of their chief salesmen who was blind—and at once I imagined him feeling the clean rectangularity of a well-planed board of ash or maple, smelling the rich tang of sawdust. I wondered if, for him, smell had a hint of color—if he could detect the dense redness of cherry, the soft breezy amber of pine.

As we drove west, the Pennsylvania woodland rose and fell in gentle waves. "How has America changed over the last 25 years?" he mused. "I'd have to say that people are moving farther away from God." He cruised through the calm morning sunshine, as comfortable in his faith as he was in his driver's seat. Anyone who disagreed with his church's beliefs was damned, it turned out; discussion was Satan's way of trying to confuse and pervert the faithful. He fascinated me, though. I'd never met anyone quite like him, yet in a way he seemed no different from so many Americans I know: goodhearted but deeply mistrustful of other Americans. His stern faith seemed to be a kind of spiritual agoraphobia.

He turned off after about 30 miles at White Haven, where the interstate had a familiar everywhere-and-nowhere geography: tarmac baking in the midday sun, stubby grass, a gas station where I belatedly bought a map. All I ever saw of White Haven was a yard full of Hi-Reach cherry-picker vehicles looking like mechanical giraffes, next to which I set up my pack. I still felt uneasy beside the road. I expected that I looked like an oddity, or just a fool. I examined my clothes and fiddled with the British flag my brother had sent me. Under the pretense of conducting a scientific experiment, I strapped the flag onto my pack for 20 minutes, then took it off for 20 minutes, then gave up altogether because it was a kind of fraud: I hadn't come from England this time. I'm not really English anymore.

My next ride was in another pickup with a blue-collar guy who had his own industrial cleaning business—scouring out giant boilers and furnaces, cleaning up toxic spills—but we talked mostly about hospice, as both of us had mothers who died in that calm, luminous care.

When he let me off at a rest area after 50 miles or so, it was 1 p.m. At this rate it would take me a week to cross Pennsylvania, which I remembered vividly from my earlier trip as the first hint of the unimaginably vast breadth of America: wooded hill and valley after wooded hill and valley, the greenery interrupted only by giant yellow Sunoco signs. I love the woods, but this was just too much. I could imagine the early pioneers driven mad by struggling up to ridge after ridge and still finding no break, no view.

Overhead, the sky had been getting steadily darker, and a brisk wind had sprung up. A guy in a construction truck leaned out of his cab and said, "You might want to stick around here," meaning the rest area, which at least offered shelter. "There's a severe storm coming. Might get your ass wet."

My only fear, before I left, had been of lightning. Planning the trip I imagined myself out in one of the Great Flat States—Nebraska, say—with one of those horizon-to-horizon purple thunderstorms approaching, and the only vertical item in the entire landscape being me. What should I do? Was I safer on the road or the grass verge? Would the lightning be attracted to anything metal in my pack? Should I carry a collapsible metal pole—like a tripod, or a music stand—so that if the thunder was right overhead, I could plant it 50 feet away as a lightning rod?

"I'd get down on my knees and pray, honey!" chuckled the woman at the National Weather Service, when I called to ask. She thought about it a bit more. "No, I guess I'd dig myself a hole and jump in it." We threw jokes back and forth nervously for a moment, and then she discovered that she had a pamphlet on this very subject right on her desk. She faxed it to me.

It was called "Thunderstorms and Lightning—the Underrated Killers!" and was a fascinating document. Twelve pages long, the pamphlet spent the first nine pages convincing me that storms were much, much more dangerous than I had thought ("The air near a lightning strike is heated to 50,000° F—hotter than the surface of the sun!"), and it wasn't until page ten that I reached "What YOU Can Do!"

In the case of my Nebraska Lightning Nightmare, it boiled down to:

• wait until I feel my hair stand on end

• squat down to make myself a small target, but

• rest on the balls of my feet to minimize my contact with the ground so the lightning passes through me as quickly as possible (The longer the charge stays in your body, the more damage is done.), and

• place my hands on my knees with my head between them, but another authority—was it NOAA?—said to clasp my hands over my head to prevent contact burns to my skull.

No suggestions about packs, keys, or portable lightning rods. Of course, with my bad knees I would probably lose my balance as I squatted, fall over backward, and present the lightning with a perfect target, a rich, ripe place to set its forked foot. Next day I read about a guy in Georgia who ran into a portable toilet during a storm and was killed when the toilet was struck by lightning.

Behind me and to my left the sky turned purple. Lightning struck, first in the distant hills, then closer. Rain smashed against the road in large, ballistic drops. When confronted by the real thing, I was strangely unafraid. I pulled out my rain jacket, which I had packed near the top of my pack, and a black plastic garbage bag, which I had intelligently packed in a small mesh side compartment. I put the jacket over me, and the bag over my pack, which now looked like a large stuffed grape leaf.

The rain began falling steadily. With a bit of luck, I thought, the poor-drowned-rat-sympathy-effect would kick in. Sure enough, another pickup pulled over. I threw my grape leaf in the bed, and jumped in. No sooner had we started than the rain tripled in force, pounding the pickup, bouncing off the road. Traffic slowed to 25 mph.

Nothing creates intimacy like sharing your car with someone. There's an added intimacy when the outside world turns to liquid, running down the windows. He was a retired newspaperman with the *Philadelphia Inquirer*. As we passed a General Motors plant, he told me how GM became the nation's top car company because of World War II.

"All the automobile plants went defense. They even dug up trolley tracks for the steel and put the trolleys out of business, just to get the steel. GM jumped the gun because they knew Truman was going to drop the atomic bomb on Japan, and they started converting their plants back to automobile production six months before the war ended. That's how GM beat out Ford and became number one. Hudson and LaSalle, they couldn't compete. It took 'em a year to retool and die, and—*boom!* American Motors had to merge with Chrysler and was kicked out of the big three."

He was the first person I heard call the stripped tires beside the road "alligators," or "gator skins," and explained that these were faulty retreads: in reconditioning the tire, a new tread is sealed onto the old. As it heats up, the seal can give way, and the whole tread rips off like duct tape. He also spoke the arcane language of highway department signs, with their cryptic terms and abbreviations. This section of highway, with its blue signs "Minimal Restoration" or "13 Inch Overlay Rubblize" was a test section: The state was trying different forms of road surface to see how a layer of shredded tires under the top stratum of asphalt affects the life of the highway, its grip and its dynamics. I never found out what "Saw and Seal Joints" meant, or "Brake and Seat," but it helped to bring alive the road, the least animate feature of the landscape, to show it rippling and changing beyond our limited perception, slower than the grass but faster than the rocks.

He dropped me off at 3:30 p.m. at a rest area near Snow Shoe, Pennsylvania, a little beyond Jersey Shore, which is neither in Jersey nor on the shore. Every ride so far had been in a pickup. An hour later, I got my first ride in an 18-wheeler truck.

In 1973, I got only one ride in a truck, and that was from a guy who had actually been a successful accountant and had dropped out to drive truck for a year to get his head together. The trucker's world had been summed up for me by a graffito I saw on the wall of a gas station men's room in Iowa: ALL THE HIPPIES AND ALL THE COMMIES AND ALL THE NIGGERS IN THE WORLD AIN'T NO

MATCH FOR ONE ALABAMA TRUCK DRIVER. In England, lorry drivers had impeccable working-class credentials and were thus part of the great socialist alliance between students and workers (though this came as a surprise to many of the lorry drivers). In the U.S., they were the enemy.

But this guy was perfectly amiable. "How has trucking changed in the last 25 years? The technology, most of all," he said. Trucks are easier to drive, ride better, last longer (more than half of the trucks his company owns have more than a million miles on them, he said), get better mileage (up to eight miles per gallon, as opposed to three or four) and are more comfortable to live in: he had CB, a cellular phone, and a small television, whose antenna cable draped over my right shoulder, out through the window, and up to the roof of the cab.

The storms were still not over, and I told him my Nebraska Lightning Nightmare. He took lightning seriously. His father was a dairy farmer and had two cows killed by lightning, which struck the outside of the barn, ran inside along the milk pipe and through the milkers still attached to two of the animals. "The cows just dropped," he said.

He let me off in the late afternoon at DuBois. The on-ramp was littered with fragments of rock and concrete, bottles and cans, a dead pigeon. Women in passing cars stared at me as if I were in a zoo. Perhaps I am an endangered species, I thought.

The sun was getting low, nobody looked like they'd be stopping, and I was still in Endless Bloody Pennsylvania. After an hour or more I gave up on the ramp and climbed up onto the interstate, the open concrete stage where it was just the trucks and me. And perhaps a state trooper. After ten minutes, I was picked up by a Penn State student named Erik in a new candy-apple-red Jeep.

He was wearing fashionable bug-eye shades and holding a CD player, which he'd hooked up to the Jeep's sound system. This was my chance to find out what today's twenty-somethings listen to. I cocked an ear.

"Isn't that The Doors?" I asked him, puzzled.

"Yeah, man. They're the best," he said enthusiastically.

He was headed to a county fair to help some friends of his, who were playing in a band, set up on stage. This sounded like fun; I asked if I could come along. "Sure," he said. "That'll be cool." He was just launching into more praise for Doors albums I'd never heard of when he broke off. "Oops," he said. "Oh, well. I just missed my turn. I was supposed to pick up some of the guys back there." Did he want to go back? "Nah. They'll figure out some other way to get there."

The Jefferson County Fairgrounds were carved out of a wooded hillside near Brookville. The band, rather generically called Label, was setting up on stage in a corrugated shoebox in front of a scattering of picnic tables and benches. Half of the musicians weren't actually there because the bass player had forgotten his bass, and had set off on the one-hour round trip to get it. They had also forgotten their bug spray.

"They won't need it," Erik told me. "Mosquitoes are afraid of noise."

While they waited, I explored the fair. Not many backpacks here, not many sandals. The lemonade stand pumped two shots of pure corn syrup into my dixie cup and the juice of half a lemon. The young Army Reserves recruiter hailed me, having seen me earlier beside the interstate. He was at a disadvantage, he explained, because he didn't have any tanks or howitzers for the kids to clamber over. "The [National] Guard has those, but we don't get along with them." So his tactic, he said, was just to corner folks and talk about $40,000 toward the cost of college.

My favorite part of fairs is the animals, and my favorite animals are rabbits and chickens. The Jefferson County fair had an extraordinary chicken with the face of a Pekinese surrounded by a startled ruff of feathers. THE SULTAN, the cage label read. The world must see this chicken, I decided, and I pulled out my camera.

I've never actually done any photojournalism, but Tomasz impressed on me that the first rule is to take good notes so you can write up the captions. No caption info, no photo. I diligently wrote down the details from the cage labels: BUFF ORPINGTON #1118 SEX C (this baffled me for a long time, wondering what the other sex was after M and F), WHITE SULTAN #1118 SEX C, BUFF SILKIE #1119 SEX C-H (even more baffling). I got the soft evening light falling across the cage, the row of cages fading away out of focus to suggest the scale of the event. All that was left was to focus on the bird, point, and shoot.

I focused, pointed, and shot. Nothing happened. Instead of the usual green light, I started getting a combination of flashing yellows and oranges, as if my camera had been designed by an out-of-work traffic engineer. I tried changing the flash setting. OFF was clearly not right for in-tent shots. AUTO seemed to be having fits. The only one to work was something labeled AUTO-S, but that seemed to suffer from performance anxiety, as it gave a series of small, stuttering flashes, and then went off when I had given up on it. Still, this one, however eccentric, at least flashed, so I crouched down by the Sultan and focused.

The Sultan had clearly been bred for show, as it had developed a bizarre feeding-and-display-in-one dance. It drew itself up to its full height, looked around haughtily, abruptly ducked its head and pecked half a dozen times at the corn, then shot back up again and minced a few steps down the cage as if being watched by the MTV fashion editor. This was too good to miss. I focused on its head, pecking around on the cage floor, and pressed the shutter. The fill in flash started blipping. At once, the Sultan shot up and began mincing, the flash went off, and I had successfully photographed its feet.

All right, I thought, and focused on its head. It stopped mincing and froze. I pressed the shutter. The flash began blipping. The Sultan ducked swiftly and pecked at the corn. The flash went off, and I had successfully photographed an empty cage. This went on for about 20 frames, by which time I was frenziedly changing the flash setting every shot and pounding the shutter over and over until the flash went off. I no longer cared about composition, or even if the bloody animal was in the bloody frame: just getting the camera to go off was an achievement. Eventually I ran out of film, thank God. I threw the camera in its expensive little clip-on protective pouch and went off in search of another paper cupful of lemon-flavored corn syrup.

In front of several hundred people in the grandstand, a well-built young woman sang the national anthem. "Heather and 11 others will be competing in the county talent show on Saturday night," said the announcer, and then it was time for the tractor pull.

The Antique Pull, quaint little tractors with slanted pairs of front wheels, went first, then the Farm Stock, the big machines, shooting up more smoke than a steam locomotive as they heaved at their huge concrete sleds. The 4500 class appeared to have pulled without anyone measuring them. One tractor managed a long but very, very slow pull. "I was late for work the other day," said the announcer, who had the unruffled and laconic humor essential for county fairs, "and I *know* that was the tractor I was behind." The waiting tractors lined up around the back of the clearing, idling, giving the place the atmosphere of a cigar bar. One tractor had something wrong with its timing, and blew enchanting clusters of smoke rings out of its chimney, then backfired sharply and shot sparks backward out of its exhaust like a muzzleloader.

Meanwhile, Label had finally assembled, tuned up, and started playing Hendrix's "Red House." Twelve people were watching, their view impeded slightly by a half dozen healthy young saplings that grew between the seats and the stage. Dave "Goober" Renwick sang Eric Clapton's version of "Crossroads," though the words were not quite in the same order as when Robert Johnson wrote them. The bass player, wearing a 99 Gretzky shirt and a baseball cap, played with his back to the audience. The songs tended to peter out rather than end, but there was no doubt that Jim Kassip—if it was indeed Jim playing lead guitar—knew what he was doing. The question was what I was doing, nodding along to the songs of my youth played by kids half my age. I felt both at home and a million miles from home.

They had just started into Led Zeppelin ("Been a long time since I rock and rolled,/ Been a long time since I did the stroll"), and time was bouncing back and forth unnervingly, when I realized that I was exhausted, and that I couldn't imagine waiting three hours for them to finish so I could beg them for a place to crash. I had to get out.

But that was the catch. The cheery folk on the gate told me that Brookville, just down the hill, didn't have any kind of a motel (it says a lot about my attitude toward camping that I didn't even remember I was carrying a tent, sleeping bag, and pad), but there were several just along the interstate at the next exit, no more than four miles away.

The first problem was that no traffic at all was going onto I-80 at the Brookville exit. The second was that evening was falling, and by the time I climbed up to the interstate, it was already dark enough for drivers to think twice about stopping even if they saw me. Oh, well—I'd walk it. Four miles, call it an hour. I'd be there by 10:15, maybe 10:30. I set off along the shoulder, at first with my thumb out, then just trudging over the crown of the hill and down the other side.

It was a pleasant evening, warm and calm. The woods down to my right, deep in shadow, would have made me uneasy at 20, when darkness occasionally terrified me. That all changed when my second wife told me that she was pregnant. To my surprise, fatherhood settled around my shoulders like a coat that had been made years before and had just been waiting for me to grow into it. My fears of the dark vanished as if they had been loneliness unable to express itself.

The highway had a nice broad shoulder, so the traffic was ten or twelve feet away. After a while, I made out the rectangular shape of the next exit sign, across the valley where the road started back uphill. Four miles? It must be less than three. I'd be in bed by ten o'clock.

As darkness fell, trucks seemed to outnumber cars, and they seemed to be coming in convoys: for every singleton, there was a massive cluster of two passing three, a solid phalanx of heavy metal.

After ten minutes or so, I was close enough to the foot of the hill to realize a third problem with my plan. Where the interstate leveled, crossing the dark, wooded heart of the valley, was a bridge—a long bridge, maybe a thousand feet. The bridge had no shoulder.

The trucks, which couldn't see me, were now slamming past two or three feet away. I thought quickly: among all the clothing in my pack, did I have a single item that was reflective? No. I looked over the parapet, which was barely thigh-high. The river was a hundred feet down, and looked shallow. If I hit that, I was dead.

Curiously, I wasn't frightened. I was alarmed, certainly: The seriousness of the situation got my attention, no mistake, but it was clear what I had to do. I started running as hard as I could, the pack lolloping from side to side and threatening to topple me over the edge. I heard the next truck coming up behind me, and at the last moment I squeezed down against the parapet, trying not to stumble off the bridge. As soon as the truck had passed, I jumped up and ran again, stopped again, crouched again, then ran again, sweating hard. By the time I reached the middle of the bridge I found to my dismay that as the trucks passed, the bridge bounced. The traffic seemed to intensify. Sometimes there was so little gap between one cluster and the next, it made no sense to run on, so I just stayed huddled against the parapet, waiting for a decent break. At last the road behind me cleared, and I ran the last 20 or 30 yards, passed the end of the parapet and lurched to my right onto the shoulder, which seemed as wide as a tennis court.

Yet, it was now that I started to worry, because about 30 yards ahead of me, where the interstate began to climb again, a truck had pulled over. It looked evil, its flashers blinking, its engine idling, the cab, of course, in complete darkness. It seemed not parked but crouching. I had seen enough movies: I didn't want anything to do with it. I walked past it like a kid passing a graveyard, believing that if he didn't look, and kept repeating that he didn't believe in ghosts, he would be all right.

I'd got maybe a half dozen paces past the massive front end when I heard a short hit on the horn, not a blast but almost a quiet *ahem*. I turned round, walked back, and looked way up at the cab window. It was dark. There was nothing else for it: I put one foot up on the sill, hauled myself and the pack up to the door handle, and opened it.

The driver, a short, ordinary guy in jeans and shirt, looked across at me.

"You'd better get in before you get yourself killed," he said.

He had stopped to rescue me. This would be the pattern for the trip: I would always be afraid of the wrong things. People would turn out to be friendly; my most dangerous enemy was myself.

I'll call him Bob, as many drivers can get in serious trouble for going against company policy and picking up riders. Nothing has changed since Tom Joad was picked up by the trucker in *The Grapes of Wrath*. "Didn't you see the "No Riders" sticker on the windshield?" asks the trucker. "Sure—I seen it," Tom says. "But sometimes a guy'll be a good guy even if some rich bastard makes him carry a sticker."

Bob told me about the trucker's life, which comes down to the loads you get. Some loads pay more per mile than others—three dollars a mile is good; a dollar twenty-five is not—but a long load that pays only a dollar seventy-five may be more worthwhile than a short load that pays two twenty-five. In this respect, every trucker who works for a company is at the mercy of dispatch, universally pronounced *dis*-patch. Dispatch didn't like him, he said, because he'd complained about this and that, so now he only got shitty loads. He had family in Texas, and once in a while a load went down there, but he never got it. He was thinking of buying his own cab so he could become more independent; that was the only way to go in the long run, but he'd need bobtail insurance (a bobtail is a cab without a trailer; when you work for a company they'll insure you only while you're pulling their load) and the owner-financed deal he was looking at, buying a used cab from a fleet owner, sounded pretty shady: If he missed a single payment, ownership of the cab would revert to the seller.

I offered to buy him a cup of coffee and a piece of pie. He thought about it for a moment. "I wouldn't say no," he said, and we pulled up on the weedy fringes of a huge truck stop lot that looked like a giant warehouse, the trucks all virtually the same shape and size, chrome crates stacked side by side. Inside, all the tables had phones—another innovation since 1973—and a remarkable number of truckers were using them, calling wives and family, calling dispatch.

He told me some of his own army hitchhiking days. Much of his travel had been in the South. I told him I had avoided the South. "After seeing *Easy Rider*, I was convinced that some redneck'd shoot me."

He chuckled. "Won't shoot you," he said. "Might run you over." He was hitching somewhere in the South and was passed by a cop. A couple of hours later the same cop came by again. He called Bob over and said, as cops do, "Son, you got a choice"—but this was an unusual choice. "Either you let me get you a ride, or I arrest you." It seems some wacko had been swerving off the road and hitting hitchhikers. So the cop got on the CB and said, "This is Smokey the Bear. I'm at mile so-and-so. I need someone to pick up a hitchhiker," and explained why. A few minutes later a semi pulled over, and Bob was on his way.

He was less lucky in West Virginia, where a cop threw him off the freeway and wouldn't even drive him to the next exit, but made him bushwhack 150 yards through woods and undergrowth down to a little country road running parallel to the highway. "I was lucky if there was one car an hour, and that wasn't going anywhere because he lived on that road and was just going home." His luckiest trip, he said, was Jasper, Texas, to Bangor, Maine, in 45 and a half hours. If there were a Hitchhiker's Hall of Fame, that would put him in it.

Back in the cab, the CB kept up an intermittent speckled chatter. In that strange dark industrial world of Bob's cab, lit only by his instruments, within the equally strange world of a midnight interstate lit only by vehicle lights and flanked by orange barrels, the CB was the voice of those who worked overtime while the rest of America slept.

"Can you smell burning?" I asked Bob near the Ohio border. He sniffed. "Smells like brakes," he said, though it smelled more like rubber to me. He ran a quick internal check. "Not coming from me," he said, meaning his truck. He got on the CB. "Anyone out there smell burning?" he asked. A no and a yes from other voices, running somewhere close to us in the darkness. The smell kept up. "Must be someone up ahead," Bob said. "Hasn't got his CB on."

For ten or fifteen minutes we continued to smell something burning; every so often the CB would alive with another invisible trucker saying, "Yeah, I smell it too." An ad came on for what sounded like a body shop and tattoo parlor, which I thought must be a wonderful combination business, like a gas station and charm school.

Finally, just into Ohio, Bob's headlights fell on some big vehicle, an SUV or a pickup, towing a trailer with a large inflatable pontoon boat on it. The truck was slowing down and pulled onto the shoulder. The smell was so strong it was amazing nothing had caught fire.

Passing the truck, we plunged through the darkness toward the Ohio line. Bob dropped me off well after midnight at Truck World, just across the state border in Hubbard, Ohio. It was an enormous truck stop, the largest I saw on the whole trip, with its own small motel surrounded on three sides by parked trucks. I staggered in, as filthy as I've ever been in my life, dried sweat on dried sweat on dried sweat. The guy running the motel was a chubby, graying Indian gentleman.

"Please tell me you've got a room," I gasped.

"No," he said.

My jaw fell, aghast.

"Just kidding," he said.

It was a decent room, in that the bed was horizontal. I found dried blood all over my left knee from a two-inch gash. I had no idea how it had gotten there. I fell asleep to thunder and lightning, and the distant rumble of idling diesels.

CHAPTER 7

The Vagabond, When Rich

July 22 — Hubbard, Ohio

f there's one thing that has changed in 25 years, it's truck stops. Truck World had a game room, an ATM, and a booth offering Internet access for a quarter. It also had its own curious highbrow streak, expressed in a series of maxims neatly painted on boards hanging in the restaurant:

LIFE IS A CAFETERIA: HELP YOURSELF

INTELLECT IS INVISIBLE TO THE MAN WHO HAS NONE

And my favorite:

THE VAGABOND WHEN RICH IS CALLED A TOURIST.

Paging through my notebook over eggs and corned beef hash, I found that I had already forgotten the faces of everyone who had picked me up. When you hitchhike, you get to know the drivers who pick you up in a nonvisual way. You plough on mile after mile, looking ahead, the white line flicking under you like a hypnotist's pendulum. All that you see of each other is a glance of profile every few miles. Every time I get a long ride and we stop for a bite to eat, I make sure that I take a long look at the guy's face as we climb out, stretch, and amble over to a restaurant. I've found out things about this guy that I don't know about my best friend, but, if I take my eyes off him, I'll spend the next fifteen minutes wandering from table to table trying to find someone who looks familiar.

I called Tomasz on his cell phone. He was somewhere north, closer to Lake Erie. You've got to see this place, I said.

So he motored over and we ate breakfast together, while Tomasz stared in fascination at a couple of giant, hairy truckers—the exception, not the rule—wondering where they got their tattoos.

He asked me how the previous day had been different from what I remembered of my trip in 1973. Was hitchhiking harder now? Easier? More dangerous?

No, none of the above. More interesting, I said.

This was a surprise to me. After all, novelty had left that first visit permanently endowed with the brilliant visual clarity of a dream. What adventure could compete? Yet, looking back, it seemed to me that I'd just sat there passively and let it all roll by. I had the shallow fascination that only a visitor can afford: I'd come to conquer, not to fit in. Besides, I was traveling with Richard. Hitchhiking with a companion is safer, but leaves you less open to chance. When the two of us were on speaking terms we were a small, traveling England, resisting the Americanness of America; when we weren't, the wait seemed longer and there was half as much space on the side of the road. It was when I was on my own that I felt circumstance peeling me open.

Beyond that, in 1973 we encountered our own kind—to such a degree that I can't remember ever speaking to someone of color on the whole trip. It seems to me now that I had very little sense of other people's kindness and tolerance, or curiosity about how they lived and what they thought. I got one ride from Lincoln, Nebraska, to San Francisco in a VW bus with a bed, eight-track, baby fridge—the whole nine yards—five male hitchhikers, one female driver called Robin and her big white dog Shantih (Sanskrit for "peace"), yet I can't remember anything interesting that anyone said during the entire 1,700 miles. I whiled away most of the time reading an enormous stack of DC and Marvel comics. No wonder it all seemed so golden and carefree. We were like children given an entire continent as our sandbox.

In 1998, I was meeting working America, and it seemed a less privileged, more real encounter. I was meeting people who were nothing like me. I loved it.

So much, in fact, that I decided to head off next to Cleveland, the epitome of blue-collar cities, butt of a thousand jokes. "I think I come with you," Tomasz said thoughtfully. Well, that was easy, I thought. Hitched a ride just sitting here eating breakfast.

Bill DiLillo, my tennis partner in Vermont, grew up in Cleveland. I called him while I was on the road; he alerted his dad, and Tomasz and I were off in the Skylark. We found Tony DiLillo in a dim retirement home on the outskirts of Cleveland that smelled of resignation, with an Indians cap on his settee and a copy of *Inside the Vatican*, a lavish photo book, on the coffee table. "This was shot by a friend of mine," Tomasz said, fingering the gilded pages.

Tony, now widowed, was a strong man only slightly bowed by time. He had been born and brought up in Little Italy. With a little prompting he agreed to join us in the Skylark and show us the neighborhood. He told us about the Italian-American Brotherhood Club, where the political deals were made, with boxing in the back room. "Some of the best lightweights that ever fought fought there."

We dragged west toward the city past mall after mall until the road took a sudden twisting dive, and we were in the narrow, colorful streets of Little Italy. Here, as in other American cities, even the poorer Italians built walled, sunny gardens behind their houses, filling them with peach and pear trees and grapevines. The DiLillos bought rather than grew their grapes, but they did have their own press, and Tony had helped his father press the grapes and make the wine. After six months of fermenting, the wine was ready, and at once friends and relatives would start to drop in. "We always had two bottles of wine on the table, growing up."

Over there was the corner where he sold papers, 65, 70 years ago. "Two cents a paper. I made 25 cents, 30 cents." He showed us Guarino's restaurant—"This used to be a pool hall. I used to play pool in the back"—and the Holy Rosary Church—"That's where I was baptized and got married."

Outside the church, a cheerful stout woman was selling raffle tickets for the Feast of the Assumption, when the Virgin is carried in effigy around the streets of Little Italy. A local drunk—bottle in brown paper bag, only one tooth in his head—was talking big, saying he was going to steal the poor box. "If they have a poor box, I might as well take it. I'm poor."

The cobbled streets and idiosyncratic little brick houses and shops of Little Italy are a prime target for gentrification. "We used to have all kinds of grocery stores, hardware stores, dry goods stores," Tony said. "Now it's all art stores." We passed the cemetery where his wife was buried. "And this is where I will be, when the time comes."

Having nothing much else to do, Tony agreed to spend the next few hours with us. He climbed back into the front seat and directed us through a series of increasingly broad and well-landscaped streets, past the city's palatial civic buildings toward the hot, flat, decrepit industrial downtown and the West 25th Street Market. A cluster of long, narrow, old, brick buildings, the market seemed European rather than American, its cluttered geometry bringing vendors, customers, and produce together in a proximity that suggested a relationship rather than a transaction. In the meat-cheese-and-fish building, for instance, I could smell what everyone was buying, especially the bracing salty halloo of fish, 56 kinds gazing one-eyed from the slabs, their names written up on the blackboard, including some that I'd never heard of, like buffalo and blackfish, the chalk handwriting itself a developed art, and one nearly lost to computer graphics and the uniform printed signs of franchises.

Finally, Tony took us to the most arrant and cynical manipulation of time and memory, what Tomasz called, "This pyramid of nonsense": the Rock and Roll Hall of Fame and Museum. Perched on a fabulous, and fabulously expensive, plot of groomed grass overlooking the lake, it was like an expensive oldies-theme-restaurant-and-gift-shop, but without the food.

No Photography signs hung everywhere. Tomasz disappeared to try to get permission to shoot. Tony and I wandered aimlessly, scowling at Annie Liebowitz's photographs, snorting at the aisles of T-shirts and CDs and gift trinkets. It was Graceland without the kitsch. No juice, no guts, a representation of rock-and-roll without the spirit. If it could really embody rock 'n' roll, it would be an electrifying disaster: Pete Townsend jamming his guitar through its ceiling, Bill Haley's fans tearing up the seats, Hendrix setting fire to it, Grace Slick slipping acid into its water coolers, Jim Morrison exposing himself in it, Brian Jones dying in its pool.

Tomasz came back. No dice. We gotta get out of this place, I thought, even if it meant missing the Flying Elvises, due to parachute down on the Hall on August 8.

We dropped Tony off at his gloomy retirement home, and headed off into the unknown. As soon as we were heading back east along two-lane blacktop in search of Amish territory, the country seemed to shrink and flatten. I began to wonder why I was already bored, when Tomasz pulled off the road at a garden statuary business, fascinated by an 18-foot fiberglass giraffe. I was walking along between gnomes and bambis, when a wasp stung me. My hand must have brushed it in midair, because by the time I felt it and looked down, the insect had gone. I found one of a dozen assorted ornamental ponds and laid my hand under the cool running water. It wasn't especially painful, and after a few minutes it seemed like the perfect way to spend this hot, dull day—sitting on a low wall, letting the water run over my arm.

Amid the pleasant open fields of Amish country, we stopped to visit a cheese factory. I'd love to do an *Across America by Cheese* book, except that I'm almost completely uncritical. Doughty Valley: very nice. Middlefield Swiss: very nice, if a bit sweaty after five hours in a car. Full of romantic potential, though: "Excuse me, ma'am. I'm doing a story on the Cheeses of Madison County. You wouldn't happen to have a glass of lemonade to go with this chunk of Bakersfield Brie I've been keeping in my shirt pocket?"

Tomasz spotted a beautiful, shy, 19-year-old Amish girl leading her horse to the barn and found out that she was going to a friend's 20th birthday party. We followed the little buggy at ten miles an hour along a series of lanes, the Amish cornstalks with their curious braided crests glowing in the low sunlight. When we arrived, though, the mother of one of the Yankee (the Amish word for all outsiders) girls at the party threw us off the property, made uneasy by our stalker's pace, our intrusion. "People pick on the Amish because they're kind of backward," she said forcefully. "Please leave."

"Saturday night in Toledo is like being nowhere at all," Tomasz read from *Road Trip USA*, which he had bought in an increasingly desperate desire to find photogenic America. But as we skirted Cleveland to the south, trudging through one stoplight after another in the rain, past bank after bank advertising its drive-through ATM and an endless succession of convenience stories offering cut prices on soda and cigarettes, everywhere was nowhere at all.

"I went to the woods," Thoreau wrote, "because I wished to live deliberately, to front only the essential facts of life, and see if I could learn what it had to teach, and not, when I came to die, discover that I had not lived."

But going to the woods no longer works. In some respects, I already live in something of a 20th-century Walden, in my unassuming little house on ten acres in Vermont with a small wood and a beaver stream, but it's no longer the retreat it might have been in 1845, or even in 1965 when the first of the hippies began moving up here from the big, rotten apple. Planes from Burlington airport climb the violet morning sky, the New York train moans from across the ridge, the world rushes in by Federal Express truck, telephone and modem. Those of us who moved to the woods did nothing to solve the problems of the greater society and everything to hasten them by removing our money, our intellectual capital, and our goodwill. In the end this came back to haunt us, in the form of an America that sends a new suburb or a Wal-Mart steaming into the fields around us like an aircraft carrier while we howl impotently. It's impossible, these days, to be as isolated as Thoreau, that old proto-hippie—except, perhaps, by being Amish and running the risk of being stared at or stalked. In the long run, we're much better off going back into town, getting elected to the planning commission and making sure that in 50 years time there still are woods, not merely rows of little semi-dwarf crabs and sand cherries planted between Circuit City and Toys 'R' Us.

We crawled toward the outskirts of Sanduskie, Ohio, where the air stank of bitumen, then started looking for a motel with ground-floor rooms that opened directly onto the parking lot so Tomasz could back the car right up to the room, and not carry his equipment more than 15 feet. He traveled with three cameras (four, after he bought an old Brownie at a junk shop), tripods, lenses, special suitcases—probably more than 50 pounds of stuff in all. Once he was shooting in Spain, he said, and his entire back seized up from lugging so much weight around.

The air inside the hotel was acidic; whatever chemical they had used to clean the carpets was still hanging around, and at once began to go to work scouring the linings of my sinuses. Tomasz tugged at cigarette after cigarette as he worked out the day's expenses. I tossed and turned for two hours, feeling wretched, not knowing why. At one in the morning I woke from a half-sleep with the revelation that I had done nothing all day of my own free will. I had not been a vagabond: I had been a tourist.

To hell with it. I'd go and have a swim in the motel's tiny pool. I woke Tomasz to see if he wanted to come too. He stared at me in disbelief, through one eye—"What the . . .? Am I dreaming? What time is it?"

On the flagstone walk sat a large toad. The toad, I seemed to remember, was a Hopi symbol of wisdom. I squatted down and looked at the toad, which looked at me for a moment. Then I padded off to the pool. The gate in the three-foot-high chain-link fence was locked. This was the funniest thing I had ever seen. I hopped over it, watched the parking lot lights swaying on the almost still water, and slipped in.

CHAPTER 8

"Public" Being a Dirty Word

July 23—Sandusky, Ohio

"A*gh,*" Tomasz groaned from under his bedcovers. "You are one of those born with the propeller in the arse. You have to move all the time."

It was true. I wanted to get moving, as I always like to in the mornings, to get the day on the road. "Morning is when I am awake and there is dawn in me," said Thoreau. Over a quick breakfast, I chatted with a couple from Erie and their two preteen daughters. They were all on their way to the amusement park at Cedar Point, which the father had last visited 20 years ago. Must have changed a whole lot since then, he said, they added all sorts of rides. What's your favorite music? I asked the girls. "The Beatles and the Beach Boys," they answered.

We arched north through to the shores of Lake Erie in the hope of a photo, but everything was buried in fog. "Drop me at a rest area on I-80," I told Tomasz. The overcast sky and the dulled green of the alluvial fields made me feel trapped. As we made our way southwest, Tomasz told me that by his calculations he had narrowly missed death 14 (I think) times. In El Salvador, he was in a helicopter with eight soldiers. The pilot, who was drunk, hit a 700,000-volt power line. Luckily, it wasn't live—there had been an earthquake, and the grid was down—but the chopper still came down. Four were killed instantly, the others died later, one of whom had had both legs cut off above the knee by his metal seat. It was an hour and a half before help arrived.

Then there was the Coast Guard flight he was supposed to be on, but he got delayed on his way to the airport and it left without him. Forty minutes later it crashed, killing everyone on board. Or the time he was shooting a story on the St. Lawrence River for NATIONAL GEOGRAPHIC. He hired a light plane to do some shooting, got on very well with the pilot, and agreed that he would come back later to shoot more pictures. Shortly afterward, a mutual friend hired the same plane and the same pilot. The plane crashed, killing both of them. Or the time he hired a helicopter with a very young Indian pilot who neglected to mention that this was his first flight since getting his license. They flew into fog. The pilot panicked. They ended up landing blind—and discovered they were in the courtyard of a factory. They had missed a solid metal gantry by a very small margin. When a more experienced pilot arrived to retrieve the chopper, he was afraid to try taking off, and decided to remove the rotors and truck the chopper out. I made a mental note never to travel with Tomasz in anything other than a car.

He drove a few miles up I-80 and dropped me off where he could also get gas, cigarettes, and more coffee. Gasoline vapor wafted over from the pumps. I petitioned truckers in their cabs and got a series of silent head-shakes. The morning had become hot and sweaty under a dull, glazed sky of no color at all. A cop, racing past on the interstate, honked angrily and pointed: hidden behind a parked truck was a sign saying, NO HITCHHIKERS. This had been my fear before I left: that after three weeks I'd still be stuck in Ohio.

It was over an hour before a courteous, elderly gentleman pulled over in a Lincoln Town Car, possibly the only Town Car in the world at that moment with three bricks in the trunk. He was George Persinger, and he was restoring Toledo Cathedral. Every brickyard, he explained, produces a slightly different brick. One of his jobs for the day was to take the bricks around every yard in western Ohio until he found a match for each of them.

We drove into Toledo with George explaining to me that dirt doesn't penetrate limestone, so you can scrub it clean with a wire brush, but it penetrates sandstone to a depth of up to three-quarters of an inch, so it needs sandblasting. And that decorating a ceiling with gold leaf isn't as expensive as it sounds: an ounce of gold, beaten to the thinness of leaf, should cover an acre.

He was one of a family of 18. "All we've ever done is mason work," he said. He's been doing restoration work since he was 25, and it goes far beyond bricks and stone: In the cathedral he'll raise tile, put up netting to keep pigeons off the statues, replace wood sheeting with cedar to resist rot and insects, replace wiring, heating, ducting, insulation....In one place, he found that the heating ducts had never been hooked up, so for years the vapor in them had been simply piped into an attic, where the condensation had rotted all the sheeting. "I spent 24 days in that attic," he said.

We circled the cathedral, and he showed me the nearby storage building, guarded by a Rottweiler, where they keep $50,000 worth of copper for the flashing and gutters. "This isn't the best end of town," he said dryly. The other day someone had broken out all the windows of five parked cars, and then the following day had come back and done the same to thirteen more. A diocesan report on the cathedral wrote: "Locks on doors seem to be jimmied regularly.... In our choir door entrance, two stained glass panels have been vandalized...one entirely and one with bullet hole."

He parked on a leafy street on the good side of the cathedral, and met his sons Tim and Chris, who reported on progress, then all three took me on a tour. The stone steps had previously been mended with up to six inches of caulking, which traps water, instead of mortar, so the rain had worked gullies all round the caulk. That all had to be replaced. Between the stones of the cathedral itself, someone had used caulking covered with a thin veneer of sand instead of mortar; George got out his penknife and scratched at it, and the solid-looking joint made a dull rubbery noise instead of a healthy scrape, leaving the gray caulk exposed.

He opened the main door, and in the darkness of the interior, all I could see were several blue stained glass lights from a window somewhere on the far side of the building, swimming like celestial fish.

He threw on some lights. It was a fine building, smaller and younger than the European cathedrals I'd known, but majestic, well proportioned, and decorated to the hilt in the Catholic fashion. I counted dozens of different marbles in one flight of inlaid steps alone. At the same time, the full scale of the restoration job became apparent: 150 light fixtures to be cleaned, repainted, the cheap plastic fittings replaced with brass "candles," the cracked marble above the heating registers to be replaced. Limestone was shipped in from France, marble from Italy. The pulpit—all wood, pins rather than nails or screws—and made of wood from the Black Forest had to be entirely rebuilt, and, up on the ceiling, a tide line showed where the first few sections had been cleaned and repainted (from a scaffold, like Michelangelo) while the rest remained dull. I had a sense of parallels, of a faith built soul by soul, a cathedral built stone by stone.

The walls and windows, especially above the votive candles, were so black with soot that the parishoners didn't know they were stone. Such restoration changes entirely the emotional tenor of worship. The stained-glass windows before cleaning were solemn; afterwards, they were joyful.

George's son Chris was stripping and repainting wooden carvings and reliefs. "They get that from their mother, who's very artistic," George said. The boys have been doing restoration work since they were in high school. He sent them off to do work at Mary Wood College in Scranton, Pennsylvania. "I told them, 'Get in the truck and drive it around, so they know you're at least 16,'" he chuckled.

One of George's brothers was now on the job, too. "I know I can trust them," he said. "I could call in someone who says he's been doing something for 50 years, but that still doesn't mean he's going to do it right."

Before we left, George chatted to one worker who had just come down from the roof. He had been way up in the battlements, trying to work loose a large piece of carved stone in a space so tight that he could only use his fingertips.

"Show me your hands," I asked him.

He held out the large, rough hands of a mason.

"Turn them over." Two of his knuckles were grazed and oozing.

He grinned. "Most days I skin a couple of them," he said cheerfully.

Despite my resolution to travel in the present rather than the past, I did decide to make for Evanston, Illinois, just north of Chicago, where Mitzi's parents, Karl and Alberta Porges, still lived.

On the map, Chicago seemed to extend in a blotch of suburbs and townships from South Bend, Indiana, halfway to the Iowa border. Major cities are always a headache to hitch through: on the way in you're always being dropped off in some out-of-the-way suburb; on the way out nobody knows where you want to go, so you're faced with what John Dos Passos described as "the walk out of town with sore feet to stand and wait at the edge of the hissing speeding string of cars where the reek of ether and lead and gas melts into the silent grassy smell of the earth."

Besides, I was falling behind schedule, haunted by my fear of never getting farther than Ohio. George offered to take me to the Greyhound station, where the manager behind the ticket desk warned me not to throw my receipt away. My credit card number was on it, and someone might root through the trash, find the one and use the other. We must be close to some level of desperation, I thought—and sure enough, two women arrived to harass him loud and strong over something that happened the previous day. This was the bus as public transport, "public" being a dirty word in America.

The bus driver was a short, sharply dressed young African American whose name was James E. Carter. As soon as he pulled us onto the highway, he ran through his own version of Greyhound's house rules in a cool amused tone.

"There will be no smokin' or drinkin' on the bus, and no snortin', injectin' or hallucinatin'. If you smoke or drink, I'll pull over at the next service area and put you out. If you're snortin', injectin' or hallucinatin', I'll pull over at the next service area and *I'll* get out." He skillfully paused for effect. "Just messin' with you. My name is James. I'm not the driver for this trip. Your driver for this trip is our heavenly father."

Soon the greasy sky of Ohio was gone, and we were in Hoosier farmland. A hawk circled over a swamp. I saw my first triple trailers, and James advised us to set our watches back to Central Time. In the fields, long insectlike irrigation crawlers were parked alongside the roadside fences, not needed at the moment because of the recent torrential rain—three inches in an hour, the same downpour that had hit me in Pennsylvania. The corn was as high as an elephant's thigh.

We pulled off for a fast-food break at a service-area restaurant. "If this bus should peel off and leave you," James warned us dryly, "it might take six hours for Greyhound to find you and pick you up."

We clambered off and back on with our Styrofoam lunches, turning the bus into a dining car. A woman with a Tennessee twang, sitting across the aisle from me, confessed, "First time I've eaten today."

She was traveling with a young boy, who was sitting in the seat behind me. She was loving and attentive; he was well behaved. They were from near Elkhart, Indiana. She was his aunt, or perhaps his grandmother. They had been on the bus for more than 23 hours. "Where are you coming from?" I asked. "Barre, Vermont," she said happily. Barre is an old quarrying town, remarkable mainly for its place in the history of industrial safety. It was in Barre that the Italian anarchists, stonecutters, and skilled monument carvers held out against the bosses because of the lethal conditions in the cutting sheds, where marble and granite dust filled their lungs, slowly killing them.

The boy, whom she called TJ and who was just going into sixth grade, had done a school project on Vermont. Fell in love with the place. So they took a week's vacation, two days each way on the bus, three nights and two days in central Vermont, seeing Barre, Montpelier, a granite quarry, and a mall.

Did they see the mountains? From a distance. Lake Champlain? The state house? No. "We found all kinds of things on the Internet," she said, "but in the end we didn't get round to any of them." He wanted to buy a CD to add to his collection of three, but they ended up with everything but: T-shirts, ashtrays, mall souvenirs of Vermont. Then back on the bus. Now he wanted to go back when there was snow on the ground and learn to ski.

To me there was an epic quality to their trip—two days on the bus each way! It made hitchhiking seem spoiled—but there was also something sad. When they arrived in Vermont, how on earth were they supposed to get to the Green Mountains, or the lakes, or even the Ben and Jerry's ice cream factory, now the state's top tourist attraction? It's a small state; but even so, nothing is within walking distance. And if you wait for a train or a bus, you'll die waiting. The mall makes perfect sense. It's one of the few American public spaces designed for pedestrians.

I spent the next hour chatting with a young Baptist—a nice kid, clearly, as he had chatted to TJ about CD's, in flagrant violation of the teenage rule that you never talk to kids younger than you. He was coming back from Connecticut: he'd just up and gone off to see a girl he knew, a friend. Twenty-four hours on the bus each way. "It gets cold on the bus at night," he said. Cleveland had terrified him. When the bus took a layover, he had made it only as far as the crust of humanity at the entrance of the Greyhound station, where guys had begged money or offered to sell him drugs, and women had offered to sell him something more. His parents had been hippies and hitchhikers, he said, so maybe he inherited their wanderlust. The greatest time of his life, he said, was last summer when he went with a group from his church, more than a dozen of them in a van, telling stories, singing songs, sleeping all over each other, all the way to Mexico to help build houses for the poor. Yet it might not happen again. The church might throw him out, as they had done to a girl he knew, for secretly listening to his rock-and-roll CD's.

"What should I do?" he asked.

"Well, what do you believe?" I asked back.

He couldn't say. Instead he repeated what he had been taught, and as he spoke he seemed to lose his youth and his vitality. You either believed the true faith, he told me glumly, echoing Jeff the lumber salesman, or you were damned, and the true faith was as follows....

He's a good kid, I thought, but his church is going to lose him.

A narrow stack of skyscrapers rose over the horizon, and freeways struck at us from all directions. It must have been somewhere near here, back in 1973, that the truck taking me from Wilkes-Barre to Evanston broke down beside the Edens Expressway, and, knowing virtually nothing about automotive repair, I crawled underneath, waggled a few wires, and fixed it.

The bus extricated itself from the interstates and chugged into the South Side of Chicago as if into the Third World. The overpasses were rickety, the pavement shattered, the small buildings the urban equivalent of tarpaper shacks. Billboards advertising $50 divorces and bankruptcy lawyers sprouted among them like weeds. Every fourth building, it seemed, was a storefront revivalist church, and I found myself thinking of the Toledo Cathedral. Respect for materials is a close cousin to respect for spirit—which is perhaps why the devastated landscapes of South Chicago were a sign of injuries to the spirit and why there were so many revivalist churches.

Before long James was on the mike again. "On your right, you'll see a very tall building. That's the Sears Tower. For those of you wanting a fine view of Chicago, it has an observation deck on the 103rd floor..."—a well-timed pause—"If that's a little too high up for some of you, a little farther over you'll see the John Hancock building, with the two red antennae. That has an observation deck on the 60th floor. If that's still a little too high for some of you, you will now see on your right the Greyhound building. That has an observation deck on the first floor."

The sad moment had arrived, he announced, when he must part company with us. "Greyhound hires only professional and handsome drivers. Ladies, if over the last eight hours you've fallen in love, become infatuated or been seized by passion, please, please, please control yourselves when leaving the bus." He offered thanks to the Light of the World for a safe trip.

I stepped into the tiny subway station and was immediately out of my depth. I needed to take three or four different-colored lines, apparently, but there was no map immediately visible and no sign of how much this would all cost me. By the turnstiles, a chuckling knot of three guys spotted me and beckoned me over in a small explosion of welcome. A short round one, who seemed to be the station manager in the sense that this tiny tiled antechamber was his stage, gathered money from my hand, fed it into a ticket machine, and fed the ticket through the turnstile while introducing a taller, skinny guy as "The Mayor."

"Pleased to meet you, your Honor," I said, recognizing one layer of irony and sensing others. We shook hands, and I was ushered through the gate toward the trains—but at once I heard calling behind me, and The Mayor (whose name, I gathered, was George) was running to catch up with me and volunteering his services to walk me through the kaleidoscope of lines that I apparently needed to take. As we walked, he launched into a story so fluid and convincing it couldn't possibly have been entirely true, or entirely false. Could I guess where his accent was from? he demanded. He bet I couldn't because he had worked in 17 states doing track repair for the railways, and even when he was down in Atlanta they thought he was from Georgia, or something....They called him "The Mayor" because he was always giving food or money to those who needed it, his daughter was getting her Ph.D., but he had been downsized, but that was okay. The only problem was that now he lived 67 miles away and his train was leaving in half an hour and he needed $17 for the fare....He glided with me from Clinton to Belmont and from one subject to the next with the fluent fiction of the rural auctioneer. Here was my platform, with the three guys playing drums, percussion, and guitar; here was my train. I gave Mayor George $10 for his guidance and his entertainment, and considered it money well spent.

"All aboard, step up, step in, doors are closing." And the train slid off, above ground now on its carnival erector set of rusted scaffolding, impossible to take seriously. The most enchanting feature of the Chicago's elevated trains is that they are so clearly an afterthought, passing barely ten feet from the windows of the little brick houses and the third- and fourth-floor balconies and decks set out with chairs, barbecues, even a hammock, as if the train were a sunset over a lake, with trout leaping for flies.

I was making for Evanston, where Karl and Alberta Porges still lived, and where I spent my first Fourth of July all those years ago, astonished and vaguely disturbed by the weird draft-the-kids militarism of the parade and the unself-conscious flag-waving, just when the country seemed to have come to its senses and decided to back out of a war nobody wanted anymore. Astonished also by the spaciousness of green American suburbia, the gray squirrels— rarer in England—running through the yards. As the light began to fail I found Judson Avenue, named for the redoubtable Philo T. Judson, the first treasurer of Northwestern University, and was surprised all over again. This is no ordinary suburb but a regatta of magnificent wooden houses with deep porches, fronted by tall, mature trees and with no less than ten paces of grass between the sidewalk and the road. Even this was a little threadbare, Alberta said, since the Fourth of July tornado last year, which had brought down so many trees the city had to come and cut her out of her own house.

Both Alberta and Karl were bent over in considerable back pain, and moved with difficulty, but even so Alberta made me the best meal I had eaten in five days. Afterward she and Karl fought to tell me the history of Evanston, whose first house was a tavern on the Green Bay Trail but ironically became the home of the Women's Christian Temperance Union, which promptly made it a dry town. "Chicago" was an Indian word for a foul-smelling swamp plant, skunk cabbage, or wild garlic. Every agricultural product, in the days before railroads and refrigeration, had to be both portable and imperishable. Hogs were cured into ham, corn was distilled into bourbon, and logs were made into rafts or barrels. The settlers floated the rafts down to New Orleans, broke them up, sold the logs, and then walked back to Illinois.

Karl, recently retired from a career in nuclear physics, told me of a college roommate who had hitchhiked around the world in the late 1930s. He set off at the beginning of summer, rode the rails to San Francisco, worked across the Pacific as a stoker, worked in Japan as an English-language reporter, and rose to become a fashion editor; bought a ticket on the Trans-Siberian Railway, took a ship from Gdansk to New York, and arrived in Cambridge a week before term restarted.

My days are parabolic, I wrote in my notebook. *In the morning I'm young and optimistic; by evening I'm the middle-aged man falling to earth, missing his family. If I were 20 I would be making awkward and futile attempts to get laid. I seem to prefer middle age.*

CHAPTER 9

In the Silverware Drawer

July 24—Evanston, Illinois

I woke up with my left knee in agony. This was the knee operated on two years ago. While lying on the table, cheerfully stoned from the spinal, I heard the surgeon curse, and knew that things were not going well. The pain, I thought, was probably caused by tissue, swollen from several miles of hiking on Chicago's hard streets, pressing on a nerve. If so, I should rest it, and with luck the swelling would subside in a couple of days, I told myself firmly, trying to ignore the voice of middle age—constantly alert for signs of that final crash into decrepitude—yelling, *It's finally happened. The cartilage has ripped right out.*

I decided I'd call Tomasz and hitch a ride with him for a bit. Did this constitute cheating? Well, yes, of course, but I had six weeks to make it around America, and in any case, perhaps I should accept the luxuries of middle age along with its liabilities.

It was a glorious morning, leafy and quiet with the sun falling through sprinklers, so I left a thank-you note, tiptoed out of the house, and limped into Evanston. I was up so early the only place to have breakfast was a Starbuck's. I despise Starbucks, which has succeeded in making the most iconoclastic of public spaces, the coffee-house, both pretentious and generic. As I sat in the window nibbling on an expensive muffin and keeping one eye on my laundry going round in the laundry across the road, one espresso drinker timidly approached another. "Good morning! Heard you the other night, the Beethoven Ninth. Really liked it." Heard as in attended the concert, it seemed. The musician, clearly one of the star soloists, immediately launched into an appraisal of his own fine performance and bemoaned the trials of working with the numbskulls surrounding him, including another soloist ("she's renowned for her hissy fits"), whom the concertgoer had praised, but not including James Levine, whom the soloist called "Jimmy." A blond girl crossed the street, a coffee in each hand, to where her blond friend, sunglasses atop her head, was waiting in a Mercedes.

When my laundry was dry I refilled my pack, shuffled to the station, and took the El into Chicago, where everything was three and a half painful blocks away. At Union Station—vast, magnificent and empty, a cathedral to a forgotten religion—I was told that trains don't go to Des Moines, or Iowa City, or in fact most anywhere. Then more limping to the post office, apparently designed for track-and-field events, where it took me four or five minutes just to reach the escalator. I caught sight of my knee in the oceanic plate-glass window, and the double glazing made the bulge look grotesque. Then another three and a half blocks to the Greyhound station. A tall, thin guy looked me up and down: "Man, I sure hope you ain't plannin' on goin' far," he said.

After some unsuccessful punching at the sock phone, which I had already discovered to be useless when I was out in the country near mountains, or if there was a cloud in the sky, I found a pay phone and got through to Tomasz. We agreed to rendezvous in Iowa City, which I remembered fondly as the place where I first had a Reuben sandwich. He sounded more cheerful: He had found a building near Peoria completely covered with hubcaps. "It is quite fantastic, I think." Later he would shoot a replica of Stonehenge made out of junk cars—"This is really very interesting. History as junk as art."—the Liberace Museum, and a coffin maker who customized caskets in the shape of furniture.

This is a European's America, glittery and bizarre, but also flamboyantly free from tradition, common sense, the tyranny of good taste. When I first saw it, I felt a strange mixture of emotions, half-mocking, half-fascinated by the excess of light and energy, the outsized hypertint. Now, Tomasz's friendly mockery just made me uneasy: I felt as if he were making fun of me, too, for staying here and digging in rather than for laughing and leaving.

In the ticket line ahead of me at the bus station, a beautiful young woman with broad shoulders and a tight, worried jaw carried her huge Nike bag as if it weighed nothing. In my imagination she was a college track star. Nowadays, when I see gorgeous women running, I look at them longingly, envying their knees. Across the crowded hall was a middle-aged woman who might have been the depressing surprise of some tabloid "World's Biggest Bust!" come-on, wearing cutoffs and a huge Florida State T-shirt, her breasts pouring out and down, out and down until they finally stopped somewhere below her navel. She was a pyramid on chubby legs. For the 750th time my water bottle fell out of its handy little net pocket on the side of my pack, was retrieved by a kindly stranger who could actually bend down, and I decided that whatever the experts said about the importance of rehydration, the bottle was going in the trunk of the Skylark, to join the tent, the sleeping pad, my writing portfolio, and a few other odds and ends. I was getting lighter all the time.

A young Italian couple with a child were having trouble with the Greyhound authorities: tickets but no seat. The mother, holding a pink heart-shaped mylar helium balloon on a stick, poked at the stout African-American Greyhound employee and shouted *"Fark* you!" The father was wearing denim shorts so low I could see the top three inches of his white underwear, over which the strap of his money belt hung like a tail. In the end the the Greyhound employee stayed calm, and the Italians got on, handshakes and smiles all around.

Part of me admired the Italian woman for speaking her mind, not caring who turned a startled head or what anyone thought of her. My soul tosses in mid-Atlantic. Half of me, the half I think of as American, is confident and outgoing, but half is middle-class English, brought up on politeness and self-concealment, and I can easily imagine a fatal collapse of initiative, a sudden shriveling of spirit, and then I'd be spending the rest of my life saying, "Of course, sir. Certainly, madam." My habit is to sort through my thoughts like a butler going through a drawer of silverware: Some may be worth considering, perhaps polishing a little, but some...well, it would be unthinkable to present them. Most unthinkable would be simply to say what I think on the spot. What is the source of the world's suffering? asked Gaston Bachelard the French philosopher-postman. It lies, he decided, in the fact that "we hesitated to speak.... It was born in the moment when we accumulated silent things within us."

We passed a hitchhiker, the first I'd seen on the trip, sitting next to I-88 on a small pack, thumb up, barely noticing the traffic, looking weather-beaten and stoned. In the old days, these would have been attractive qualities to some; he might have been thought mellow, mysterious, perhaps even sexy, well traveled, at peace with the universe. Perhaps he was.

As we neared Davenport, the Midwestern sheet of cloud broke into smaller and smaller clusters, until we were under the Iowa sky I remembered: cornflower blue, full of light. The corn here was as high as an elephant's ear. You know you're in Iowa when you see a billboard advertising windows installation, and it actually means windows, not Windows.

The driver, Barbara, had a book on tape, *Petals on the Wind* by V. C. Andrews, which judging by the box would comfortably last her from Chicago to Fairbanks. She was chubby and nervous, talking out loud to herself when she couldn't find her way through Davenport. I was ready to look down my nose at her until she got into a conversation with a blind girl sitting in the front seat, claiming that she spoke seven languages—and to judge by some of the offhand observations she made about German and Russian, she did.

I read for a while, too, and began compiling a list: Top Ten Things Lewis and Clark Encountered in The First Six Weeks of Their Expedition That I Haven't So Far:

BEAR

WOLVES

FRENCHMEN

BUFFALO

QUICKSAND

CURIOUS PAINTINGS AND CARVINGS ON LIMESTONE INLAID WITH

WHITE, RED, AND BLUE FLINT

THREE VERRY LARGE SNAKES

300 LBS. OF GREASE

TICKS (thank God)

BOILS (ditto)

DEASSANTARY (ditto)

But my pack needed still more lightening, and in Iowa City Lewis and Clark would go into the trunk of the Skylark.

When the bus dropped me off, I happily sat down on the sidewalk, my back against a wall. A guy with graying hair curling down over his ears bicycled past me. I was clearly in a college town, and felt immediately at home.

Tomasz picked me up a quarter of an hour later and gave me a wan smile. "I must say, this is one of the hardest assignments I have ever done. I am getting up at six in the morning when the light is still quite good; I am driving for twelve hours a day staring out of the window of this car looking for pictures, and I am finding nothing. So far I drive maybe 2,000 miles and I have maybe one frame, that's all. Normally I would spend two, three weeks in one place looking around, talking to people, before I start shooting. That is the only way to find something of quality. But this driving, looking out the window, is impossible. It's madness. I am permanently exhausted."

He had been living off a diet of hamburgers, coffee, and nicotine. Poor bastard. I would take care of him. I'd even help with the driving.

From the two-lane blacktop the undulating wilds of Iowa were not nearly as flat as they had seemed from the interstate 25 years ago. Quiet folds of greenery lay tucked into the small, neat river valleys cutting through the farmland. Tomasz shot the small, terraced huts of a pig farm silhouetted on the grassy hilltop against the late afternoon sun. We pulled over in North English, one of the tiniest villages in this or any state. A woman outside the convenience store saw our Virginia plates. "You've got to be lost if you're in North English," she remarked cheerfully. And yet even in this tiny, peaceful spot, the newsstand selling the *Gazette*, "The Newspaper of Eastern Iowa," was trying to attract readers by advertising that the paper would carry "Unsolved Murders Sunday Through Wednesday." Two guys in bib overalls, leaning on the bed of a pickup, looked in our direction. If we were in a movie, I thought, this would be the first hint that shotguns were just out of sight, chainsaws waiting to be tugged into action.

By the end of the day we reached the small town of Indianola.

Tomasz and I were cracking jokes with desk clerks and waitresses like young traveling salesmen let loose on their first territory. ("I wouldn't accept that credit card if I were you. It isn't even in English..." "In those pants you look, if I may say, *radiculous*...") We ate at a Country Kitchen, and met the hands-down national winner for Best Waitress Humor—blond, middle-aged, cheerful but nobody's fool.

Two guys, one in a John Deere cap, asked her what the catch of the day was. "Crocodile, I think," she offered straight-faced. They looked blank.

She watched while Tomasz insisted I sit with him in the smoking section. "Tell you what," she said helpfully. "I'll bring you a coupla straws and you can stick 'em up your nose and round the corner into non-smoking."

I suggested we could attach the straws to some kind of tube running over to the salad bar.

"Great idea," she said. "That'll probably get us into the Country Kitchen newsletter."

Or the web page?—

"Yeah!" she shot back," Hotcakes dot com."

Letting my dinner digest, I browsed through the local *Recreational Review*. Wipers and white bass, I learned, were to be caught below the dam at Saylorville by casting jigs tipped with minnows. At Saylorville Lake, the catching of crappie—pronounced "croppie"—had slowed down due to high water, the result of the storms that had hit me in Pennsylvania, but there were still a few being caught along the rocks at the marina, along roadbeds and in parking lots that had been covered by the floods. This, not unsolved murders, was the real news of the region.

CHAPTER 10

Dysgeography

July 25—Indianola, Iowa

It was fair season. The huge Iowa state fair, with its celebrity country singers and hot-air balloon launch, was still a couple of weeks away, but the Warren County fair was opening barely a mile down the road. We parked on the vacant grass while the sun was still slanting low over the trees, before anyone was there to charge admission. This is my favorite time at a fair. Farmers and their wives and kids were setting up, coaxing the sheep and goats into the stalls; three handsome Swiss cows were staring thoughtfully toward the back of the grandstand; wood shavings in the horse stalls were still clean and smelling sweetly of cedar; and the 4-H kids were setting up their exhibit, "The Dos and Don'ts of Baby-sitting," illustrated with Barbies. Not yet the sticky smell of elephant ears, nobody yet charging $2 for lemonade that is half water, half corn syrup; not yet the louche carnies offering BB rifles with bent sights and plastic darts that barely stick; no chicks-on-the-Harleys posters nor hats proclaiming "51% angel, 49% bitch."

The merry-go-round with the American flag was shining, its empty chairs, slightly rusted, shifting on their chains in the breeze. The carousels and miniature trains were silent; the fast-food carts, locked up, smelled of nothing. Only the flags and the fringe stirred on the red-yellow-and-blue canopy over the toy motorbikes and rockets. It all seemed hokey yet miraculous, as if our chief accomplishment as a species was to produce a series of artifacts so angular and bizarre. A great, dignified cottonwood leaned over the video arcade tent.

"Pretty quiet this morning," said a passing farmer wearing blue jeans, blue cotton shirt, and a blue baseball cap. "Couldn't get much better, could it?"

Outside the 4-H tent an elderly woman was taking no guff from an elderly guy. "I got taters at home that weigh a pound and a half, pound and three-quarters," he grumbled, as if affronted by the pitiful specimens on display inside.

"Well, go get 'em, then," she replied briskly.

Kids hosed down white-faced cattle. A trailer went by full of black-faced close-shorn sheep looking like a bench of magistrates trapped in a freight elevator. A woman beside the Farm Bureau stand told her friend a bad-weather catastrophe story regarding the recent rains: "Thank goodness I had my old flivver instead of the decent car."

For the rest of my trip I'd remember how healthy and attractive the children and young teenagers all looked, how unself-consciously cheerful. Indianola came to represent that old-fashioned heartland calm, the evidence that sun, local food, and hard work in the open air might not be the secret of life, but they'd do until the right answer came along.

Steve Beckley, who owned a Buick franchise but had moved out to the country to become a gentleman farmer, helped his daughters Laura and Stephanie and their boy, Christopher, unload the animals: Nubian goats, chickens, Peking and Cayuga ducks. Christopher held a duck called Boomer as if he were holding a set of bagpipes.

Steve recommended the figure-eight racing—in other words, racing where the track crosses over itself and a collision is a good possibility every lap. "The funniest thing are the women. They get so revved up about it." Once last year there was a crash, and the race marshals put up the red flag, "but they wouldn't stop. They had to block the track with old tires or those gals'd have been racing all night long!"

We climbed into the Skylark and headed west, Tomasz looking from side to side for photogenic curiosities. He found a man mowing his lawn with his poodle on his lap, and shot half a roll—always a sucker for dogs, he explained. Back in Warsaw he and his wife founded an organization that takes in strays, and currently house over 150. We stumbled onto one of the bridges of Madison County, which Tomasz insisted on shooting, art imitating art imitating art. But the bright promise of the morning clouded over and turned into another car day; and a car day in the Great Flat States is like dying slowly of oxygen depletion—very like my case, as Tomasz alternated between cigarettes and pipe.

There's nothing like a road trip for making enemies. Traveling with Tomasz was actually a breeze compared to traveling with Richard, who by the time we reached Boulder had abandoned his energetic, sunny self and had sunk into a black melancholy. He had dark hair and dark eyes, and day by day seemed to shrink into a cave beneath his eyebrows from which he stared out, at first moodily, then bitterly, emerging every so often to deliver a muttered sarcasm. Traveling with Richard might have been an education, a chance to try out new tactics for dealing with people I didn't like but was stuck with, but I just kept going, thumb out, hoping things would get better. As I was still doing years later when I was married and things didn't seem to be working.

We stopped at a rundown middle-of-nowhere gun shop, whose owner gave us the usual line: media prejudice and government interference were ruining business, but he added that competition from the likes of Wal-Mart and K-Mart were hurting small dealers like himself. One of his sons took me out front and showed me a genuine antique, parked right by the road because they didn't know what else to do with it—a cast-iron King fairground shooting gallery, badly rusted. Step on up and shoot the ducks gliding across on a cog belt, or the eagles or bull's-eyes! Hit the smoking pipes or the little stars, and make them spin. What about ricochets? I asked. Apparently the .22 bullets would have been made of powdered metal, disintegrating on impact with a solid ping. There probably wasn't even a prize, he said, just satisfaction—and compared to that, trying to win a cheap soft toy with an air rifle with bent sights does seem a poor substitute.

Griswold, Iowa, had an eerie, abandoned quality: nobody in sight, a half dozen cars parked on the main street, shop windows vacant, silent, bleached, and dusty. Only a bar and a bank looked new. Tomasz decided to try some shots in front of what looked like a dilapidated hotel. It was actually a daycare facility, according to the small, handwritten signs, but there were no signs of life.

Later I called Shirley Ward, owner of the Sleep Well Motel and president of the Griswold Chamber of Commerce, to ask her why the town was in such sad shape. Part of the reason was the flood, she said. They got 13 inches on June 14. "The crick overflowed, it flooded out my whole motel, it flooded downtown, and people's basements. I'm still dealing with the effects of the flood. We had FEMA and the Red Cross and the Small Business Association in here, and let me tell you, some of those organizations are not all they're cracked up to be." The flood closed the bridge on 92, and "thanks to certain persons not getting the applications in properly," she said darkly; it would be a year or even two before the bridge was open again.

Other, deeper causes: the opening of a Wal-Mart in Council Bluffs, 40 miles away, had an impact on the town businesses, adding to the general economic decay. "My personal opinion is that the city council hasn't done a damn thing to help it....They do not cooperate with the Chamber of Commerce to get things going on Main Street."

I wished her luck. "Okey-dokle," she said, and went back to the tough business of revitalizing Griswold.

Kerouac, like us, passed through Council Bluffs, where "the great wagon parties...held council there before hitting the Oregon and Santa Fe trails. And of course now it was only cute suburban cottages of one damn kind and another." I wish! Our road was a dead gray artery of gas stations and car dealerships, with the wind tossing a million flickering blue-and-white plastic pennants separating moving cars from the sticker-priced, queued cars facing the road.

Tomasz's daughter, Maryna, inheriting her parents' taste for adventure, had just left Poland to visit China for a month. As we hauled ourselves through Council Bluffs, Tomasz tried to call her in her hotel in Beijing, having spent the previous ten miles trying to subtract time zone by time zone and calculate whether it was tomorrow morning yet. He stood at a phone booth outside a gas station bellowing *Hello? Hello?* across the world to a hotel functionary who spoke no English. I slumped moodily in the car, suffering a strange dysgeography, thinking that this ghastly urban landscape by Route 92 in south Omaha with its gray half-finished, untenanted concrete homes and a steady stream of cars up and down the hill by the gas station was in China.

Tomasz came back over to the car and examined his coffee in disgust. "We are entering 21st century and we still drink this horrible brown liquid," he grumbled, having not yet learned, it seemed, what Amoco coffee tastes like.

As we dragged west in steady drizzle along Route 92 through a series of small, desolate Nebraska towns, the concrete slab cracked and weedy, little sign of business to be done or pleasure to be had, the whole country seemed bleak and shattered. We ground to a halt at York, a service excrescence growing on the artery of I-80. The Super 8 motel advertised a donut bar but didn't have any vacancies. "It must be because of the donut bar," Tomasz observed wearily, reaching for another cigarette. My lungs were burning. In a week the Skylark would be uninhabitable. When he turned it in, back in Washington, the rental agency would probably just sell it for scrap.

As evening falls, I wrote in my notebook, *I always feel farthest from home.* I was exhausted. The people of York, or Shelby, or Griswold were probably perfectly happy—far happier than I. I was bored, and suffering from oxygen deprivation. The very idea of playing journalist, of going on the road and reporting back about the state of the States, seemed ridiculous. The America I found was an America I was creating. Staring out of the window into the darkness, I saw my own reflection.

CHAPTER 11

Missile Silos Would Make Great Condos

July 26—York, Nebraska

The next morning it was drizzling, but I was up at six. After two days in a bus and Skylark, I was more than glad to be on my own, limping out onto the weedy roadside in the early morning rain.

The traffic materialized out of the wet mist under the overpass, roared past, and vanished in the drizzle to the west. Rain beaded on my expensive rain jacket, and every few minutes I'd shake my arms and shoulders to throw off the drops. My shorts were more of a concern: Once I was inside a car, they would dry in a few minutes, but already they were clinging and clammy. Yet not a soggy molecule of me wanted to be anywhere else.

In less than half an hour a truck pulled over, and I ran-hopped 60 yards to catch it. It might be a hoax, and my knee wouldn't take many little sprints like this, but not many truckers would waste all the gas and brake lining involved in stopping just to jerk me around.

I'll call him Chris. He worked for a trucking company in Cincinnati, and was hauling 18,000 pounds of assorted electrical components through Wyoming and Utah to Boise. What a stroke of luck, I told him. My wife's old boyfriend lives in Ogden, Utah. Chris looked at me and raised an eyebrow.

"No, it'll be fine," I said. "I already e-mailed him, and he said I should drop by."

"O-kay," Chris said doubtfully, working up through the gears.

Through gray, damp Nebraska, Chris talked about trucking and weather hazards. Once he came along I-80 soon after a tornado and found pieces of a barn on the road and pigs rooting around on the median. Another trucker he knew, driving late at night near Grand Forks during the Red River floods, came across a three-story house in the middle of the road. In snow, he said, he may have to use chains, but they're a pain in the ass. A semi usually needs eight sets, and putting them on can take an hour and a half in good conditions. "It can take two and a half to three hours under your trailer with snow dripping down your neck." And then another hour to take them off.

Like three-quarters of the guys who had picked me up so far, Chris had done a stint in the armed forces, where he'd done a fair amount of hitchhiking. But it wasn't only from standing beside the road that he'd learned the value of patience, and the futility of worry. Once, for example, his squad was ordered to report for transport in the middle of winter, and had sat in sleet for an hour, waiting for the bus. "What are you going to do?" he asked me rhetorically. Complaining wasn't going to make the bus come any quicker. "If you can wait it out for the duration, you've learned what patience you'll need later in life."

The Army had also taught him to take care of himself, which may be one reason why he wasn't afraid of picking up hitchhikers. If anyone wanted to steal his load, or anything in his cab, he was planning to take the Buddhist route. "If they want it bad enough, they can have it. You can always get it back—you got it in the first place."

Mind you, he wasn't entirely without protection. He had a remarkable communication device, a kind of 21st century pager. It was essentially a small computer hooked up to an antenna in a bubble on the roof of the cab, which connected via satellite to his company headquarters in Cincinnati. It not only sent out all the dispatcher's messages and various communications from the company, like a cross between e-mail and a newsletter, but it enabled him to send messages back—and given that the company employed more than 1,000 drivers, that was a lot quicker than a phone line, and less likely to get backed up with calls. Two more features: The satellite pinpointed his position so he and the company always knew where he was to within 30 feet; and he could also send a shorthand distress signal that would be automatically relayed, along with his location, to the nearest police station.

Hitchhiking shows you only the narrowest ribbon of country, and one disadvantage of this long ride was that I wouldn't be able to see a place I'd noticed on the map and fascinated me: Massacre Canyon, near McCook, Nebraska.

Massacre Canyon was where, in August 1873, the last major intertribal Indian battle between the Pawnee and the Sioux took place. A group of 300 Pawnee warriors and 400 women were on a buffalo hunt along the banks of the Republican River, in Sioux territory. They camped on the north bank of the river on August 4, and the next morning a band of Sioux, which outnumbered them four to one, happened upon them. The first to die was Sky Chief; after his death the Pawnee raised a white flag and a rider rode it toward the Sioux, but his horse was shot from under him. The Pawnee fled into the canyon where the greatest loss of life took place as the Sioux rode down the walls and fired upon them. As the Pawnee were attempting to cross the river at the bottom of the canyon, the U.S. Cavalry arrived and the Sioux fled.

The incident at Massacre Canyon marked an end, not just of an era but of a history. Within two years, the Pawnee would be herded onto a reservation in Oklahoma; as an active, independent people with their own culture and traditions, they effectively ceased to exist. This is what nowadays is called "ethnic cleansing." Within three years the Sioux would be crammed into roughly a third of South Dakota, their sacred territory in the Black Hills, but when gold was found there, they would be shunted again, onto three much smaller reservations. There would be no more inter-Indian conflict because there would be no more Indian nations; and there would be no more fighting over buffalo grounds because there would be no more buffalo. In 1800, there were more than 60 million buffalo in the U.S. and Canada. By 1900, there were fewer than a thousand.

As soon as we forked north on I-80, leaving I-76 to cut southwest into Colorado, everything changed. The agriculture at once became more varied, the endless corn giving way to fields of different colors: dun-colored bare earth, spring-green shoots coming up in a haze, golden stubble...Then we were in a country that was all bare hills and undulating grassland. The rain stopped at the same time, the sky cleared, and the dappled shadows of a flotilla of small clouds rose and fell across the dimpled plain. The skyline near Potter, Nebraska, was broken by a huge howling coyote sculptured in sheet steel.

As soon as we crossed into Wyoming, we saw the first cattle, the first artesian wells, the first nodding donkeys. Power lines stapled the horizon, cattle clustered around wells and feed bins, and to our surprise there were ore and coal trains everywhere, a half dozen in no more than 20 minutes. The on-ramps were now gated so that the interstate could be closed for snow, then cattle grids appeared by the gates. Both the railway and the highway were periodically lined with snow fence sections looking like flimsy bleachers. "Nothin' to stop it for miles," Chris observed laconically. We saw first an antelope at a stream, then a spotted deer on a hilltop.

Bluffs appeared on both sides of the valley, then pines on the bluffs. The West was starting to look western, and even to adopt a certain cultural self-consciousness, as if aware of its obligations. We saw our first stetsons. Truck stops rented audiotapes of westerns: *Lady of No Man's Land; Treachery at Triple Fork.* Wonderful rock formations like piles of chocolate chips grew above the small rivers.

Chris had a stronger sense of history than most of the people who picked me up; world events had an odd habit of reaching for him. He missed the war in Vietnam, but his English teacher brought a Vietnam veteran into class—a daring thing to do in Bible Belt

Arkansas, even in 1975— who told them about the war in graphic detail. "He told us this story of when he was in a foxhole with his lieutenant. All he saw was a bright flash of light, and next thing his lieutenant wasn't there," said Chris, and for the first time, some of the class began to ask themselves questions.

He also had a clear view of the end of the Cold War. "North of Tucson, in a city called Catalina, there was a Titan base, or silo, right across the street from this little shop my friend owned. Trucks came in; they opened up the top of the silo, and a crane came in and picked up the warhead. They picked it up, put it on a flatbed, secured it, and carted it off. They went ahead and drained the second section of all the propellant, took it up and laid it down on a cradle, and did the same to the final section. They left the silo open with the sections on cradles for 30 days so that the Soviet satellites had a chance to come by and verify that they were putting nothing back in, and that it was dismantled. They took the sections to Davis-Monthan [Air Force Base], cut them up, took the rocket engines out, and the Soviet observers were watching at Davis-Monthan for part of the time when they cut them up. It was the first time the Soviets were on a base in the States. We saw the Aeroflot that they came in on. Then they took all the rest of the equipment out of the silo, back-filled with rubble, concrete, sealed 'er. Let the Soviets verify that for 30 days.

"I always thought missile silos would make great condos," he added as an afterthought. "Put a dome over the top and you could have one hell of an indoor garden."

Yet, the end of a war isn't always what it seems. Just as the end of the Cold War robbed American conservatives of their favorite enemy, forcing them to turn their fury on domestic liberalism, so the end of the Vietnam War defeated America's brief flirtation with leftist politics. The antiwar movement declared victory and went home, and at once my generation lost its coherence and lost its way. I don't think we've found it since.

Chris agreed. "1973 was a time of hope," he said. "I think a lot of people have lost hope—that tomorrow will be better, that the weekend will be nice," Chris said as we approached the Continental Divide. Everybody had come to want things to be larger than life; our faith in the value of the ordinary has been lost. "My grandfather's idea of a good day was waking up, having a cup of coffee, scratching his dog behind the ears, and being able to go out and see horses. And that's not bad. We get oversold on larger-than-life. Life has gotten real simple for me lately, and it's going to get simpler. I've done the rat race." Chris liked gardening, he said, and pottery, and he'd like to know the constellations, so he'd have something to look for in the night sky.

As we began the long, slantwise haul up the Continental Divide, he told me of being estranged from his father for most of his adult life, then reuniting. I told him about the ghastly summer of 1982 when in the course of three months I tried homesteading, got married in secret, developed a fear of flying, and began to go gray. The journey was slipping into balance: Instead of driver and hitch-hiker, we were fellow travelers. We found ourselves in a strange high desert, with reptilian ranges stretching off out of sight on both sides. Scrub brush, a few cacti, and tough clumps of grass more brown than green. A billboard for Jubitz, a big-deal truck stop, announced, "Rejoice! Only 1,094.2 miles!"

"It's in Portland, Oregon," he explained. "Beats me why someone hasn't taken a shotgun and shot the hell out of that sign."

For me, this was a part of America where the myths had not yet been kicked out by brusque reality. Nowadays the word "California" no longer means to me what it did in 1973, when it was a place wholly without substance outside the imagination, and when I burst out singing "I'm going to see the folks I dig,/ I'll even kiss a Sunset pig,/ California, I'm coming home" as we crossed over in Robin's VW bus from Nevada on I-80. Oddly enough it really did feel as if by coming to California we were coming to the home we ought to have, as opposed to the old-and-cold-and-settled-in-its-ways isle that I would soon leave for good. The West, too, wearing its young but vivid history on its sleeve, seemed more myth than map. Laramie, Rock River, Elk Mountain, Fort Steele, Red Desert, Table Rock, Bitter Creek, Point of Rocks, Green River—the names themselves a chronicle of discovery, of hope and disappointment. Butch Cassidy worked in a butcher's shop in Rock Springs—hence the "Butch," some historians think—and the Hole in the Wall itself is a natural gateway through a red canyon wall on Buffalo Creek, just away to the north of the interstate. I had no desire to see the replicas of old jails or boot hills, advertised at every turn in the road, or even the real ones. For the time being, I wanted to carry on savoring the soft explosion of astonishment that I was actually here in the place of myth, the land of *Gunsmoke*.

It was around this time that Chris pulled over for gas and got out of his cab. As I was idly flipping through his road atlas, I found his gay pornography.

I barely saw it—a large playing card, perhaps 4-by-6 inches, bearing a black-and-white photo of a guy in a leather cap and a leather jacket open to reveal his bare torso. I shut the road map and dropped it on the floor. Half of me remained perfectly calm. The other half panicked.

The panicking half ran screaming around my head, yelling, "Do something! Do something!"

The calm half said, "Think about this. The guy has shown you absolutely no ill will. You're actually bigger than him. Besides, does it really make sense to throw away a good ride?"

The panicking half, meanwhile, had gotten in touch with its inner homophobe and was not going to let him go. Chris might have good reason not to want the trucking fraternity to find out about his private life. If he knew what I knew, and felt threatened by the possibility of being exposed, who knew how he might react?

After several minutes, Chris got back into the cab and set us back on the road. By now I was calming down a little and had reasoned that I was learning some valuable things about fear, and about violence. For one thing, this was not a credible fear. I have gay friends of both sexes and never feel threatened by them in the least. No, this was an old worm, a deep, deep serpent of fear, one that hadn't surfaced for decades, and it had taken the extra vulnerability of hitch-hiking to bring it to the surface. This was an interesting journey of self-discovery: I wondered what other worms might surface before the trip was over.

And yet this don't-ask-don't-tell policy, hatched at the behest of yammering anxiety, was ridiculous. Within 50 miles or so I realized that I was getting exactly what I deserved. I had left myself to gnaw in silence on my fear, thereby guaranteeing that I would never know even whether the photos were in fact Chris's or, more interestingly, what it was like to be a gay man in the trucking trade. Besides, he and I had steadily been getting to know each other better, and now that stopped dead. I was now cautious and a little distant. My fear, my loss.

By early evening Chris had used up all his legal hours for the day and needed to take a sleep break. He pulled over at the Flying J Travel Plaza in Rawlins, Wyoming, and after a bite of dinner he went off to sleep in the truck's cab. I ordered more coffee and began writing up my notes. At the table behind me, a group of truckers were telling hitchhiker horror stories—this guy getting his load stolen by someone he'd picked up, that guy getting killed. Intellectually, I thought yes, well, this is the climate of fear, everyone afraid of everyone else, but deeper down I was laughing in a mixture of amazement and relief. These truckers, these tough-looking characters, were afraid of me. After ten or fifteen minutes of this I got out of my seat and squatted down at the end of their table. "I couldn't help overhearing what you were talking about," I said, "and I thought you should know I'm one of those killer hitchhikers."

They broke into embarrassed laughter. "No, man," "We didn't mean you, man."

They asked me to join them. The most vocal was Jason, a young blond guy with a military mustache and a habit of making his points emphatically with a finger leveled like a rifle. Next to him sat a marmalade blonde who may have been his wife. Across the table sat a magisterial dark-haired guy, quieter than the others and perhaps in his early 40s, who drove high-end removals for top executives, and a short, round, balding guy in his 50s who offered a series of cheerful, rude remarks and dirty jokes. From them I learned that an entry-level trucker such as Jason might make $30,000 a year, but if you were carrying cars or doing removals, you could easily make four times that amount. The schoolmasterly trucker acknowledged modestly that he had made well into six figures the previous year.

Freedom of expression is a trucker's job benefit, almost part of the job description. Everyone said exactly what was on his or her mind—a spirit fostered by the constant use of CBs, perhaps—and accepted everyone else's right to free speech. The roly-poly guy, who would have got on my nerves at once, was tolerated like a wicked uncle; his coarse cracks were taken in stride by everyone, including the woman, who was gloriously unoffended by everything, and while she clearly loved Jason had no hesitation in telling him exactly what she thought of him when an occasion arose.

They restated the trucker's creed—Everything You Own Came By Truck—with a certain militancy born of knowing that America looks down on its truckers. Jason told me the story of driving 18 hours overnight through a blizzard to deliver a shipment to an auto parts store. He had to get a signature for the delivery, so he went around front and into the store, which had just opened. The clerk was serving a customer, who asked for a part he'd desperately been waiting for. The clerk looked it up on the computer, and said it had just come in; it had been part of Jason's load, in fact.

"Thank God!" the customer cried out. "Thank you so much for getting it in."

"What the hell did he do?" Jason yelled at the customer, pointing at the clerk. "He finished work last night at six o'clock and went home to bed! Why don't you thank the trucker who drove all night in a frickin' snowstorm to bring you that part?"

"Who is this guy?" demanded the customer.

The clerk said, "He's the trucker who drove all night in a frickin' snowstorm to bring you that part."

As the guys were packing up to leave the table, they asked me if I wanted a ride, but they were all headed East. Jason gave me his name and address, and as an afterthought told me that I really ought to check out the annual Harley-Davidson rally that took place just down the road from his place, in Sturgis, South Dakota. It started around the second week of August, he thought, but the partying went on for the whole month. Bikers were part of my anxiety, and I had dared myelf that before the trip was over I'd go into a biker bar and start interviewing. Sturgis sounded like a biker bar with a quarter of a million bikers. "It's wild, man," he said. "You gotta see it if you're seeing America."

Then I was on my own—but that was all right, too. No hitch-hiking trip is complete without being forced to stay up all night in a truck stop somewhere, waiting for a driver to wake up or just waiting for dawn, eyes stinging, nose itching from cigarette smoke, folding your arms and putting your head down on a Formica table. "Thirty-nine years old and I had four back injuries," complained one trucker. "Last one put me out for five months. Last week and a half I been eating a bottle of Tylenol a day." The big-screen TV in the drivers' lounge had been out because the satellite dish had been hit by lightning—from the same storm system I had been tracking backward across the vast flatlands of America. The steady background sounds were country music on the PA system, the grunts and thuds of kung-fu games from the video parlor, and, all night, the prerecorded announcements from the ablutions hostess: "Shower number 237 is now ready. Shower number 238 is now ready."

~

CHAPTER 12

A Frontier Planet

July 27—Rawlins, Wyoming

Gray-green ranges lounged like iguanas on the horizon; mesas like elephants' feet lined the dry valleys. The entire landscape, coming off the divide into western Wyoming, was barren except for oil and gas flares, chemical plants, and soda mines. It was utterly without shade as far as the eye could see; and when we reached the horizon, we'd find another barren and bizarre landscape as far as the eye could see, then another, then another. Completely beyond human scale. It was not only hard to believe this was the same country as Vermont; it was hard to believe it was the same planet. Winding down beside the interstate was the longest train I've ever seen—150 cars just in the section I could see. I never did see either the beginning or end. It was a forever train.

Then another chemical plant, and another.

"Where do their kids go to school?" Chris wondered. Exactly. How far do the people who live and work here have to commute?

Where's the nearest public library? Where is civilization? This was a frontier planet. Who would willingly come here, except miners, thieves, and whores? "The world's largest deposits of trona, the rock that produces the industrial chemical soda ash, are west of Green River," says *Roadside Geology*, but this makes the region sound as if it's a rational landscape: Here are the minerals, so here we mine. The fact is, this was some of the most inhospitable land I've ever seen, dry, savage, impossibly alkaline. Off to the left, a badlands area looked as if a giant had hacked up the ground with a cutlass.

Just as strange as these natural sights were the man-made ones. Many of the small towns had no landscaping at all, presumably because water is too expensive, so the front yard of the boxy modular home was just fenced-in sagebrush. The whole place seemed to have been dropped from midair. There was nothing to make the houses seem settled and woven into its landscape, to suggest a shared history. In one town—Green River, I think—the only place where I saw grass (thanks to a spattering of sprinklers) was the cemetery, which we like to think of as the place of rest, as a final home.

For several hundred miles we'd seen signs for what looked like a hotel called Little America. Between Green River and Evanston, where the desert had flattened out a little but was still as bleak and uninviting as ever, there it was: a small cluster of brilliantly clean, new buildings (supersize convenience store open 24 hours, laundry facilities, ATM, U.S. Post Office, 24-hour auto-and-truck-repair garage, and a service station) surrounded by a cluster of valiantly watered trees.

"This traveler's oasis," reads the brochure—the photos all shot in a tight close-up to hide the fact that beyond the fringe of trees, around the pool, lies nothing but soda—"was conceived by a local sheep rancher who became stranded overnight in a blizzard, miles from nowhere. He dreamed of creating a place of warmth & comfort on that spot with a cozy fireplace, comfortable beds, good food and congenial atmosphere." Little America was the ultimate service area; it even had its own interstate exit sign, as if it were a town. Yet it was so alien to this strange, barren land that it was, in effect, its own country, a little America, a foothold on a forbidding continent.

I was struck by the vulnerability of the place. Everything must have been trucked in from hundreds, even thousands of miles away. No use could possibly have been made of indigenous elements, unless they served the guests heaping piles of baking soda for breakfast. How would this "oasis" hotel survive hard times? Several months later I was driving through the Anza-Borrego Desert, west of the Salton Sea in southern California, and saw other adventures in desert investment: an abandoned motel, a driveway winding off to the weedy beige waste, a pair of ornate gateposts with nothing but sand beyond them—the sense that a civilization had sent its emissaries here but they had been shipwrecked on the dry shores. Most of the West, I'm convinced, is a series of valiant (and often crooked) attempts to put humans where humans were never intended to be, a few successful, most not. Little America looked like a ghost town waiting to happen.

It turned out that Andy, my wife's former boyfriend, lived just up the hill from the McDonalds where Chris dropped me, on the northern fringes of Ogden. I didn't want to be a burden to Andy, so I thought I'd rent a car. I had the massively misguided notion that I might drive out to Dinosaur National Monument and be back by the time he got home from work, forgetting that this was the West, and two inches on my pocket road atlas was actually 200 miles. The nearest car rental place, however, was at the airport, which turned out to be virtually in a different state. I called a cab.

While I waited, studying the decor in McDonalds, I noticed an ad for the Ogden Eagles, a semi-pro football team that was scheduled to play that night. For more information, call 737-9024. Good deal. I'd never seen small-town football. I copied down the number.

The rear side window of the cab I took to the airport was decorated with two stickers: a fake bullet hole and a notice—"Warning! Driver Only Carries $20 Worth of Ammunition." The ride cost me $25.

Utah's Second Busiest Airport featured the Best Lil' Airport Terminal in the West, home of the Taildragger Cafe and Budget Rent A Car. Budget Rent A Car was not in. According to a note at the desk, he had gone to the other Budget branch to return a vehicle, and should be called at a number that was illegible. I tried calling various number combinations on the sock phone, but by now the wretched thing was routinely telling me that the number I had dialed was not available to me, or in a fit of higher mischief was telling me that I should enter my secret access code, and when I entered it told me that I should disable the secret access code and try again without it.

I gave up on modern weaponry and used the pay phone, standing in the airport's tiny lobby and looking across its small, empty forecourt up at the dry, almost vertical Wasatch Hills, the final range of mountains beyond which Brigham Young stopped his long trek, pointing at the vast lake ahead of the Mormons and saying, "This is the place." Then they discovered that it was salt, and stank, but all the same they built their new capital by the Great Salt Lake, like an illustration on the cover of a science-fiction novel.

I called both Budget and Hertz and was told they had no cars for at least a week. I called the Ogden Eagles' number and was told that it had been disconnected. Suddenly, the sock phone rang. Nothing could have surprised me more: it was like being attacked by a fried egg. It was Tomasz, whom once again I had left behind, meandering through western Nebraska. At once our conversation was interrupted by the sound of a phone on the line, ringing so loudly neither of us could hear the other. I called Tomasz back using the pay phone, and after a while we worked out that our plans to travel in tandem were bollixed up almost beyond belief: we had the entire state of Colorado between us. He wanted to take me to see Bryce Canyon, which he had seen on his first visit to the U.S.; I wanted to see Las Vegas, which I'd missed the first time around. We agreed to meet next day at Beaver, Utah, near where I-15 going south through Utah meets I-70 coming west from Colorado. Hitchhiking more than 200 miles to a rendezvous is always tricky; I decided to take the bus.

Now all I had to do was call the cab company back and pay another $25 to take me back to Andy's, where I had started. The cabbie had his fiancée in the front seat with him, keeping him company. Both were African American. They'd moved to Utah from the Bay Area, which was getting just too dangerous, they said, but they were finding that Ogden was a hard place to fit in. Well, Utah is a very white state, isn't it? I asked. No, it's not just a matter of color, they said. They knew white newcomers to Ogden who said the same thing. Well, what was there to do in the evenings? They looked at each other and laughed. Not much, it seemed, especially if you were an outsider. "I just drive up into the mountains," she said, pointing up at the Wasatches towering right in front of us, "find some jazz on the radio, lie on the hood of my car, and look up at the stars."

Andy had the strangest address I'd ever seen: 608E, 2650N, Ogden. Once again, I felt as if I were on another planet, navigating by grid references alone. Not so far wrong, he explained when he turned up an hour later and found me asleep on his front lawn. The whole of Utah (and parts of eastern Idaho, Arizona, and Nevada) lives by Mormon geography. Street addresses are based on a grid that in turn is based on one's position relative to the intersection of Main and South Temple Streets in Salt Lake City. It all seemed faintly Arabic to me. I imagined road engineers putting in a new development turning toward their latter-day Mecca, squinting through the theodolite and writing "15700 South" on the clipboard.

I'd never met Andy. When I called Barbara and told her I was going to be dropping in on him, she reeled. "My worlds are colliding," she said. Andy was in his early 30s, with a goatee and long blond hair pulled back in a ponytail, talked in that slow valley drawl, attentive and playful with his young daughter. He taught computer art, and was an exquisite connoisseur of contemporary Americana. He was both hip and retro. For example: Every year he and a group of friends hold a golf tournament—not that Andy actually can play the game, or would do anything so tiresome as go to a country club. No, they drive out into the desert and play at night, using luminous balls on one of the dry salt lake beds. The surface is so flat, a good drive will send the ball half a mile. It's near an Air Force base, and one year a military satellite picked up their lights and interpreted them as a landing strip for drug runners. "Before we knew, it there were helicopters and all kinds of shit chasing us around the desert."

He was exactly the person I needed to tell me what I should see in Las Vegas. The thing I had to understand, he stressed, was that the casinos had evolved from cheesy gambling dumps into hotels-cum-theme parks. I had difficulty picturing this, so as we hung out in his kitchen, looking out on the tidy Mormonic front yards of suburban Ogden, he ran down a few of his favorites.

The Stratosphere: "I haven't done it yet. There's so much to do in Las Vegas, you always run out of time. Anyway, this guy built this big tower, definitely the tallest thing in Las Vegas. It's got a revolving restaurant and a casino and all that stuff, but the really funny attraction is on the very top—you know how they have a needle on top of those towers? They have this thing. It's, like, seats that go up in the needle, and they strap you in there and then they fire you off! You zoom up at, I don't know, five g's, or some crazy thing, and then fall down. And you're just surrounded by air. And there's a roller coaster up there, which I hear isn't all that great, but that also goes along the edge, like, way up high. Apparently this guy is like this Las Vegas legend and he, I don't know, shoehorned this thing in there with some kind of leveraged money that he got somehow. Anyway, it's going bankrupt. That's what I hear."

The Luxor—he giggled in delight or disbelief, I wasn't sure— had a concrete Sphinx. "It's really cheesy." Circus Circus, it seemed, had its own amusement park inside a pink glass dome. Treasure Island had a show in front where they sank a ship every hour. New York, New York was the only place in Las Vegas where I could get really good coffee, "But I can't imagine it'll last too long. Everything in Las Vegas is made to be disposable. In a few years it's going to be so dirty and dusty and hideous, it'll be a nightmare in there."

Caesar's Palace had statues of Bacchus and all his attendants, and if I stood there long enough, "the lights dim, there's a big thunderstorm in the ceiling with lightning and stuff, and then the statues all come to life and dance around and sing! We were in town once right after a Grateful Dead show, so there were all these Deadheads in there, camped out. They weren't moving. They were just watching that thing all day."

His only concern was that I might be arriving at the same time as the annual Comdex convention, the biggest computer gathering in the world. "They're all computer geeks, right? So they never spend any money at the gaming tables. All they want to do is go to the titty bars on the outskirts of town and watch the strippers." He laughed. "They'll be lined up ten deep trying to get into those places!"

His final comments, though, were warnings: Some cheaper motels were drug-connection motels, and I'd hear people coming and going all night, shots in the parking lot. And as soon as I got a room, I should check the lock on the door, make sure it works. "The scam is to check out, take the key, and, because the cheap motels don't change their locks, then break back into the room and rob whatever is in it. The electronic locks are much safer."

Fully briefed, I went with him into town to pick up his daughter Abigail from daycare and then to Farr's for homemade ice cream. Farr's offered an array of flavors hitherto unknown to man: licorice, play dough, raptor ripple, named after the local baseball team (in turn named after Utah Raptor, who was left on the cutting-room floor when *Jurassic Park* was being edited), pineapple upside-down cake, grape, ambrosia sherbet, and spaghetti-factory spumoni. This was the kind of Americana Andy loved. I shuddered.

CHAPTER 13

"A Hell of a Place to Lose a Cow"

July 28—Ogden, Utah

My friend the cabbie with the fake bullet hole drove me into town. He, too, had moved here to escape the fear of crime—in his case, in New York. He dropped me off at the Greyhound station at 6:30 a.m. The ticket office was closed. We could pay when we got to Salt Lake City. Greyhound was clearly a lot more relaxed here than back East.

Ogden has had a very peculiar past. Founded as a small Mormon community, it was swooped up and whirled around when the Union Pacific and Central Pacific Railroads met nearby. Ogden became a railroad town. The three blocks of 25th Street between the city and the railroad became a red-light district known as Electric Alley, all the more rowdy as prostitution was legal, or next to it. One of Ogden's more famous madams was hired away by Salt Lake City to set up a brothel there. To Mormon eyes, this was appalling—

but as the religion still condoned polygamy, it suffered a strange impotence: dominant in numbers, but politically powerless.

With the collapse of the railroads after the Second World War—Andy took me down to the switching yards, where only a few tracks were still active on land that had once clearly been laid out for dozens—the town lost much of its income, and much of the area down by the tracks was still semi-derelict. But at the same time, the city fathers had been investing heavily in the city's rebirth, albeit largely along Mormon lines. As a result, Ogden has a downtown that is half yuppie, half Bowery. In one two-block stretch of 25th Street, flanked with new antique street lighting and neat, little saplings like ruffed choirboys, I found a biker bar, pawnshops, a brew pub, a flophouse hotel, a coffee shop (which had to be new, as coffee was not to be found in Utah until recently because of a Mormon prohibition on caffeine), vacant storefronts, antiques shops, a comedy cafe, a beauty salon, a place selling pool tables and dart supplies, a club full of Beatles paraphernalia (bars, too, were not to be found in Utah until very recently, alcohol being as unacceptable as coffee, but private clubs flourished), and a Chinese restaurant, the Star Noodle, with a neon sign so spectacular it had appeared, according to Andy, in several movies. Rumor had it that renovators discovered a network of tunnels under the old downtown that enabled the Mormon elders to visit houses of ill repute; but I was unable to verify either the tunnels or the houses of ill repute, so sadly this must remain a rumor.

On the corner, waiting for the bus, I met a frail-looking middle-aged black guy named Robert. His eyes were bloodshot; he had perhaps a day of white stubble on his chin, and he clutched a plastic grocery bag. He had just ridden into town on a freight train.

"I rode most all of them," he said. "The Union Pacific, Conway, Rock Island, Burlington Northern, Chicago Northwest..." He'd recently come from Newport, Rhode Island, he said, where his ex-wife lived.

Wasn't riding the rails dangerous? He shrugged and nodded at the same time. "You have to know what you're doin'," he said. "You pick up a spike, put it in a door so it won't close on you. But some people out there, they don't know what they're doin'."

He scratched the plastic hospital tag on his wrist. "I just been in the hospital for my kidneys," he said apologetically. "Had to be on antibiotics. Some of them antibiotics'll kill you." He was on dialysis, he said, but at another point he said he took his kidney medicine with him.

I told him what I was up to, and he asked me about hitchhiking by road. When I told him I had started in New York, his eyebrows rose. "Hey, I might try that," he said. He'd once asked some guys about road hitchhiking and they'd said he might have trouble because of his color. "I said [to them], 'I ain't havin' nothing' to do with that. *I* ain't prejudiced'."

Now, writing this, I realize that hitching by rail is also a significant step closer to the dangerous edge—to the metal. You don't have to be white to get a ride, or look reasonably presentable. The train doesn't care about your race, or your clothes; but, then, it doesn't care about you at all. If it slices your leg off, or leaves you trapped in a freight car to die of heat or cold, it won't look back.

"I'm lookin' for a ridin' buddy," he said. "I don't trust some of those guys." I thought maybe he was looking at me hopefully. This is the kind of hitchhiker who is more likely to get killed, I thought, not some tall white guy. His death wouldn't even make the nightly news. He couldn't defend himself. All I could do was give him $5 for breakfast, and then I got on the bus.

When I set out, I had hoped to get to Salt Lake City and relive one of the most amazing moments of my 1973 trip. I was in Robin's VW bus. Two of the hitchhikers had got out in Boulder; the other hitchhiker, Chas, was driving while I rode shotgun. Richard was asleep on the bed. We skirted Salt Lake City around 10:30 at night. As we headed west across the Great Salt Lake, Chas asked, "Have you been to Salt Lake City before?"

"No," I said, "this is my first trip to America."

"You mean you've never seen the Great Salt Lake by moonlight?"

"No," I said, wondering what this was all leading up to.

Right there and then, on the interstate, he killed the lights. All around us, the moon reflected off a billion tiny crystals of salt, and we were sailing on an ethereal sea, glowing soft silver, waveless and insubstantial, as far as the dim horizon, where dark mountains rose like whales.

In the past week, something happened to that previous trip. Far from wanting to retrace it, I wanted to avoid it. First novelty, then the burnishing effect of memory had created scenes that glowed in the darkness like the Salt Lake, part fact, part imagination. They were among my most precious possessions. Why would I want to risk destroying them?

The bus headed south through Provo and slowly climbed between scrawny pines into high, dry country dotted with scrubby sagebrush running up to the distant, arid mountains. I was in the desert.

Or rather, I was in an air-conditioned bus looking out through polarized windows at the desert. I wondered what the air outside smelled like. Maybe it would be like the south of France, dry, hot, and resinous with pine—and perhaps a hint of sage.

We stopped on the outskirts of Fillmore, Utah, and I bought a gas-station tuna sandwich that turned out to be several shades of brown in the process of evolving into a more complex life-form. A grizzled grain-elevator worker from Fargo, North Dakota, chewed next to me on the baking asphalt by the bus. A pickup crawled by, its bodywork apparently made up of parts reclaimed from every other pickup in Fillmore. "That's a five-tone paint job," he remarked.

I was stunned by the light. It was hot, yes, a clean, pure heat that lay on my skin without wringing the sweat from my vitals, but what struck me more was the light. I found myself remembering *Paris, Texas* and *Baghdad Café*, films set in the desert but made by Europeans, and how in each case the opening sequence was drenched in light, as if the desert light were in itself a character and a plot point. The sky was a brilliant blue virtually untroubled by clouds, lucid, as if to encourage clear thinking as well as clear vision. It made the eastern light and European light seem complex and equivocal, untrustworthy. No wonder there's a tradition of coming to the desert to tell the truth, or hear the truth. No wonder, too, that the desert is a filmmaker's medium rather than a novelist's. Every sentence would have to contain the word "light."

The Greyhound stop in Beaver turned out to be the El Bambi diner, a classic aluminum-and-Naugahyde joint standing alone in the noonday desert sun, a Disney deer on its sign. I sat on the low cinderblock wall out front, trying to generate some melanin.

Twenty minutes later, Tomasz pulled up in the Skylark, looking dazed. "I must tell you, this is something completely new for me," he said. "I drive 18 hours to see someone who is neither my lover nor my wife nor my child. This has never happened to me in my life."

As we turned east toward Bryce Canyon, the soil turned a vivid orange-red, the result of oxidized iron and manganese deposited by streams 60 million years ago. Spectacular chimneys and spires climbed away among the pines on both sides of the canyon, while a little stream ran chattering down beside the road. We pulled over to shoot pictures, and I got to talking to a woman from New Jersey, her nails painted in an Art Deco pattern in black on lilac and cinnamon, who had just come from Las Vegas and couldn't say enough good things about the Rio, where you could take part in the show and have your photo taken with the cast.

I wondered again what the desert smelled like, and stepped off the road into the sagebrush. It did smell like the south of France, hot and resinous with pine, with a hint of sage. Maybe I'd finally get to see a rattlesnake. I looked more closely at the red earth around my feet and saw something long, narrow and cream-colored. I picked it up. It was a section of snakeskin. I put it in my shirt pocket and stepped smartly back onto the road.

But this was just the prelude. The canyon road wound along for several miles, not especially deep but utterly beyond belief in its livid redness and the unearthly carvings rising all around us, then climbed a little, dropped us in a small grove of pines with the usual National Park signs, and Tomasz announced excitedly that we had arrived.

What we saw from the guardrail, elbowed by Germans and shouldered by Italians, was the remains of the Paunsaugunt Plateau, part of the Colorado Plateau that ten million years ago was thrust almost a mile up, shattering and fracturing. As it rose, a river now known as the Paria and its tributaries carved swiftly through the rock, leaving a bowl about three miles across and several hundred feet deep filled with thousands upon thousands of slender ridges called "fins" and individual pinnacles called "hoodoos"—yellow, red, brown, pink, beige, salmon, peach, even violet, filled with entrenched shadows, timeless yet breathtakingly fragile. Hawks soared over it; down in its depths, a small party of horses wound between the hoodoos, following a stream long dry.

Here was a place unlike anywhere on earth, so the first thing everyone did was to try to make it like something else. The Paiute legend was that the canyon itself was full of "Legend People," half-human animals turned to stone by Coyote. People around me saw family groups and birds. A German said, *wie Kirchen*, "like churches." But the challenge of this place was to see it without metaphor, to be dumbstruck and just take it in. Not so easy, as a car alarm went off back in the parking lot and tourists squabbled and chattered. I backed away from the railing and tried to stay with my own perceptions, feeling a cool breeze springing up, lying down on a half-tree bench looking up through the pine branches at the scudding clouds. Then watching a beautiful young Italian girl of perhaps ten or eleven, her face framed by long dark hair and a baseball cap, trying to handle the frisky water fountain, drinking with the jet running all over her face and off her chin.

I didn't want to follow the crowd; I didn't want to follow Tomasz's directing, as he tried to set up a portrait shot. No wonder hitchhiking appeals so much to adolescents, or to the adolescent in me: It's full of decisions we make, at our own behest, and the discoveries that come with them. I found myself remembering climbing the Malvern Hills at 16, on my own for the first time, discovering the breeze and the springy turf as if I'd never been up there before, as if nobody had every discovered such a place, or felt such strong and unnamable emotions. I watched in delight as a western magpie laid its head sideways on a puddle to drink out of the corner of its beak. The guy behind me said to his girlfriend, "They're magpies. Heckle and Jekyll were magpies—you know, the cartoon characters."

After a while I confronted Tomasz, who shrugged and said, "If you don't want me to shoot you, I won't shoot you. You can do what you want. What the hell? We are just two guys."

I calmed down, and only then did it strike me that finally, after more than 3,000 miles of driving and God knows how many cigarettes, this was Tomasz's first real day of work. He shot again and again, pausing only to say "This is incredible," then shooting again, then shaking his head. He pulled in an elderly southern lady so he could shoot her and her beige umbrella, then held his camera upside down above his head so he could squint up through the top viewfinder and shoot four college girls in shorts leaning in a line on the rail, their bare legs at identical angles, a study of landscapes within landscapes as he was shooting down at the canyon below them. Ah, America: girls in shorts and T-shirts, their muscular legs promising competence and go-anywhere adventurousness. This stunned me when I was first meeting American girls. They all rode ten-speeds, they could all swim well, they could all drive, they'd all look you in the eye. Of all my reasons for leaving England, this was up near the top.

Tomasz shot a guy looking at the viewfinder of his digital video camera as it panned across the canyon. I looked over Tomasz's shoulder, seeing the view of the view of the view of the view. He had earned this day.

We found a plaque explaining that Bryce was named after a Mormon farmer named Ebenezer Bryce who had settled in 1875 on the flatlands at the foot of the canyon. He sounded like farmers have always sounded: When asked for his impressions of this incredible place, he said laconically, "It's a hell of a place to lose a cow."

Afterward, Tomasz and I strolled into the little tourist village that had been tacked on to Bryce like a necktie on a peacock. Tomasz had his photo taken in full western gear, sitting on a stuffed bull. I had ostrichburger for dinner at Ruby's Canyon Diner. It was tough and a little dry, but that's probably what meat tastes like if it's had an active and fulfilled life.

CHAPTER 14

Red Wind at the Mirage

July 29—Bryce, Utah

"If America were run by Europeans in the European culture," Tomasz asked seriously, "do you think it would be improved?"

We were driving east from Bryce toward Escalante in search of a petrified forest, under a brilliant sky, winding between solitary bluffs and small, raggedly scalloped mountains heaving themselves out of the desert. We had eaten breakfast in the little village of Tropic, at the foot of Bryce Canyon, which had grown out of the farmstead of Ebenezer Bryce himself. Tomasz seemed to have stopped eating altogether and was living on coffee, cigarettes, and his pipe. I worried about him, and gave him all kinds of grief about his diet until he grinned and said, "Shut up and drive." A pickup was parked outside the restaurant; on the trailer attached to it lay the head, skin, and entrails of a cow.

I imagined a gaggle of Brussels bureaucrats looking around at the parched grass beside the road, the slabs of slanting rock studded with rough and hardy juniper, pinyon, and ponderosa pines. The English delegate was fanning himself weakly with the *Sunday Telegraph*, the Frenchman complaining loudly about the lack of decent coffee. Utah seemed to have nothing in common with Washington, D.C, or Indianola, or Stroudsburg, let alone with Europe. "I think they'd all give up or shoot themselves," I said. "It'd be madness."

It was hard to imagine anywhere farther from civilization. The road itself seemed scratched along the desert's margin; the road crews laying hot mix seemed tiny and irrelevant against a landscape so inhospitable, so completely abandoned. They also made me feel guilty: I was here because I wanted to be; they were here because they had to be. Even rubble and weeds have majesty on this scale. *You could not build anything one-hundredth this size*, the desert says. *Your Hoover Dam barely fills one wrinkle in my endlessness. You cannot destroy me, because I am already laid waste.* I had found the physical equivalent of the Bachelard Principle: The landscape that is not afraid to speak. *My geography and history are transparent, unafraid. This is what I am*, not even bothering to add, *Take me or leave me.*

In the end we found no petrified forest, but, hidden on the parched valley floor behind a screen of trees was an artificial lake on which one girl was driving a motorboat and another was water-skiing behind her. O America, burning your natural resources like the runner carrying the Olympic torch, with every other country pounding along behind you, trying to catch up.

We had lunch at Mount Carmel Junction in The Best Western Thunderbird Resort, in which everything was fake except the hanging plants at the front consuming half the region's water supply. Out of the corner of my eye, I thought I saw a long green snake among them. When I looked again, it was a hose.

We were just finishing lunch when a Harley roared past. Not just any Harley, though: this was a Harley trike, with flames painted on the two rear wheel covers, and it was being driven by a woman, with a guy on the back. I immediately thought they might be able to tell us more about Sturgis; Tomasz immediately thought picture. We leaped into the Skylark and shot off after them.

Almost at once, the road began to wind uphill, hugging the mountain. "Pull up beside them! Pull up beside them!" Tomasz yelled. Well, that was my plan, but I couldn't help thinking that once they saw they were being followed by two maniacs yelling and waving at them from a car, then even if I did manage to avoid a head-on collision and even if we managed to get them to pull over, they might kill us. "Faster!" Tomasz yelled, frantically waving me on. After a few moments, when we hit a relatively straight stretch, I managed to pull out alongside them, but to my horror Tomasz, instead of calling out something neighborly like "May we take your picture?" shouted "Pull over! Pull over!" and pointed off the road. To my amazement they did. I pulled up behind them at a safe distance, in case they got off and came after us with a chain and a tire iron. Tomasz armed himself with a few pounds of cameras. I waited in the car, trying to hide under the dashboard.

Their names were Reggie and Sharol, and they were from Royal, Arkansas. He was tall and burly, she was slight, and both were tanned and leathery from the sun. They wore T-shirts from the Broken Spoke Saloon, Sturgis, South Dakota. Both were well into middle age. She worked in a convenience store.

"He's on disability," she explained. "His eyes are going."

"Only reason I'll let her drive," he said, in mock disgust.

They'd set out two weeks previously; they'd been to see Lake Powell and Zion Canyon, now they were heading off to Colorado to see her dad, and some friends. The whole trip would be 5,000 miles before they were done.

The Harley was immaculate.

"Got 2,000 miles on the shine job, mind you," Reggie pointed out, tongue in cheek. They'd bought the bike-to-trike conversion kit from Canada by mail; it had cost them $15,000.

As I asked questions, Tomasz sprang into action, shooting me by the bike, by the couple, with my notebook out, chewing my pen, behind the bike, in the back of the bike behind Sharol, in the back of the bike behind Sharol with Reggie's enormous forearm in a hammerlock around my neck. Then order was restored, and Reggie climbed over the fenders and into his place in the back.

"Could I ask you to please put your arms around her?" Tomasz inquired. Reggie reached around Sharol and squeezed her breasts. She grinned.

"This is a very American thing," Tomasz said afterward—the Thorolds' trip as an expression of freedom, that is, not the squeezing of breasts. What I thought was especially American about them was not so much their outlaw spirit—every nation has its bikers—as their goodwill.

It was at this point that I began to wonder if Sturgis wasn't a kind of Woodstock, in a very specific, chrome-and-leather way, or perhaps what Woodstock might have become if it had been held every year, and admission had always been free. I couldn't wait to get there.

Zion Canyon consisted of two quite different halves. The first was shallow and pink, and the rock on each side of the tiny road, winding between vast boulders, seemed to have been scoured into a series of rippling horizontal grooves, leaving it looking curiously soft and fleshy. After an umbilical tunnel, the road emerged at mid-height into a valley of magnificent mountains and then zigzagged downhill step after step after step, and with each descent the mountains on each side grew still taller and more overwhelming. At the western end of the canyon, someone had put up an IMAX movie theater. "YOU HAVE SEEN THE PARK NOW SEE THE MOVIE."

Every town in southern Utah, it seemed, had its fake western saloon, its fake jail, its fake livery stable. It all had a strange quote-of-a-quote quality, as the architecture they were echoing was itself the desperate false-front pretentiousness of a century ago when every western main street building, and many eastern ones, was little more than a shed with a much taller rectangular frontage to make it seem bigger, grander, and older. In a speck-on-the-map called Virgin, the "Indian store" itself made no bones about being just a big metal box, but out front sprouted a bizarre set of pint-size Wild West buildings, bent and exaggerated like a Warner Brothers cartoon. The fakery reached a glorious peak in a little buy-your-fossils-here bend-in-the-road called Orderville, where outside an odd building like an upturned pot stood a strange white skeleton. "What is that?" I asked the proprietress. "It's a cow, a deer, and a horse," she said. With its fossils and dinosaurs, this was in some respects the very oldest America, yet nowhere did America's history seem less genuine.

Maybe everything seems false when it exists without a context, I wrote in my journal. *Maybe it's just that this is a desperately poor region, and everything has to be turned into a commodity. And to be a commodity, it needs to be recognizable, which is why inside the upturned pot building, the exotic minerals and the delicate, bony fish fossils cost twice as much if they have also been carved into coasters, or bookends, or just geometrical shapes. No commodification without representation.*

We saw Las Vegas from the north, a bowl of smog in a valley of gravel. As we neared the city, an AWACS plane flew overhead, looking for trouble. Both sides of the interstate were littered with so much trash and broken glass it looked as if the entire population of Nevada spent its Saturday nights cruising up I-15 getting drunk and chucking longnecks out of the window. Las Vegas lay like a mirage, offering the promise of fiscal redemption, a beacon for the nation's illusions, but all around was the wasteland of a poor state. It was like being back in the eighties all over again. One stroke of bad luck out here and you'd flame down into the gravel wastes and all that would be left would be the fragment of your humanity, holed up in your wreckage under the merciless sun.

Or at least that was my vision of Nevada—a paranoid concoction of my hatred of fiscal conservatism, my conviction that the place is still run by organized crime, and an irrational fear of the Nevada police, which must have been left over from the *Hitchhiker's Guide to North America.* I couldn't buy into Andy's amiable view of Las Vegas as colorful and fascinating; I was bracing myself for trouble.

Like all sizeable American cities, Las Vegas' characteristic glamor-sights are a tiny portion of an unremarkable whole, most of which was being torn down or built up. The taxis sported ads for—we're talking about the same ad, now—doctors who made house calls and strippers. When we peeled ourselves out of the Skylark at a gas station that tried to charge us twice for the same tank of gas, we were suffocated in a kind of air I'd never tasted before—an evil, hot, angry air. Raymond Chandler wrote a short story called "Red Wind," and I knew at once exactly what he meant.

As soon as I stepped inside the Mirage I could see what Andy had meant about a theme park. Kids, parents, grandparents, singles, and family groups—all had that Disney World look, the head revolving on the neck, eyes wide as oysters, determined not to miss a sight, not the white tigers, not the wolves or hippos, or whatever other jungle attractions the hotel offered. Most hotels don't see that much lobby traffic during a fire. The front desk had a 20,000-gallon aquarium, featuring live sharks and tropical fish. What it didn't have was a desk clerk. I eventually attracted the notice of a small, dapper man impersonating a French waiter, who told me that the hotel was full. I could have told him that.

Tomasz defied death by making two U-turns on the strip, dropping me off at the first hotel that advertised vacancies: the Casino Royale. I liked the Casino Royale immediately because it didn't pretend to be anything other than a casino with rooms on top of it. It was so modest its restaurant was a Denny's. It had no gift shop, so the guy who asked Julie, the desk clerk, if he could buy a Casino Royale sweatshirt was disappointed. It had only four floors, unlike the Mirage opposite, which seemed to have several thousand. The view from my window encompassed a large parking lot flanked by a small, uninviting kidney-shaped pool and a long Pepto-Bismol pink wall punctuated by the word "Casino" in red neon over a small door; on the right, by an unfinished hotel-casino the size of Belize; and between them lay a very tall crane. Behind the crane stood Treasure Island, a new hotel-casino-theme park in the shape of an open book standing upright.

There were no laundry facilities in the Royale. I could have my laundry picked up, but Julie warned me against it: "I had a man send his laundry out and it came to $80." I had the overwhelming urge to watch TV and suck my thumb, but no: I would shower, don my least smelly clothes, and go out to look for dinner and live sharks.

By the time I left my room, though, Las Vegas phobia had started getting to me. All the muscles between my shoulderblades locked so tightly that I felt shooting pains up and down my back and I couldn't turn my head to either side. My first stop was the aptly named Mirage, across the road, where the first sight was a tank decorated not at all like a temple in which a white tiger was lying with its back to the four-deep throng at the glass frontage. It seemed stuffed; everyone near one of the video monitors watched those instead, where the video tiger cubs gamboled and played.

This thoroughfare led (of course) into the main casino, where the hostesses wore short red velvet dresses caught in the clefts of their buttocks. The ATM, if I understood the screen correctly, charged $7.99 for credit card withdrawals between $25 and $50. I became so convinced that I was being watched on camera that I started sneaking into the men's room to take notes in a stall: *Waitresses @ Mirage have little tails.* Every second I expected a security guard to grab my notebook and tear all the pages out.

I found a tropical-theme grill, but froze in my tracks when I saw the three-piece band playing between the fake palms. A girl with the exact expression of a magician's assistant was playing light percussion and shifting her weight back and forward almost, but not quite, as if she were dancing. An aging male model played congas; an aging rockabilly hipster played a steel-drum line on a Yamaha keyboard. All had clearly been dead a long time.

I ate noodles in a Chinese restaurant (all this was still in the Mirage, by the way) with fake ferns and bird-of-paradise flowers, followed by decaf in a coffee-and-pastry shop next to a man who looked unnervingly like Billy Graham but sounded like Fred Rogers. I thought of getting my nails done in lilac and cinnamon at the Spa and Salon, but it was closed, the door guarded by two bronze Dobermans. The whole area was nothing but a mall, the dullest of all human creations. I retraced my steps to the casino...

...where the strangest thing happened. I was strolling between the slot machines and the blackjack tables, trying to look as if I were an undercover agent from the IRS and giving the dealers my best steely gaze to make them, rather than me, feel uneasy, when the whole clanking, flashing, glittering place seemed to pale, as if someone had undone a valve under the carpet that let all the color drain away, and left the room and all of Las Vegas seeming no longer threatening but utterly irrelevant. A guy sat at his slot machine while it paid out 145 quarters like a mechanical orgasm, but his success, and the failure of the college student losing steadily at the blackjack table, just didn't interest me. This place wasn't about dreams and depravity and greed and glitter, it was only about making and losing money, and as such I had already seen it all over America. I found myself thinking of the biker couple from Arkansas, and their 5,000-mile escape, blasting through the southwest to get away from the convenience-store job, and next to them Las Vegas seemed lifeless and unimaginative.

I left the Mirage, whose name now seemed to have taken on yet another layer of meaning. As I waited at the light to cross the street back to the Royale, a bald-shaven guy with an earring and a fire department T-shirt pointed down the street to the darkness beyond the city limits, the darkness above the desert, where a massive bolt of lightning split and vanished. "It's a storm coming," he said excitedly. "A big one." Before our light changed, two more bolts split, lighting up the purple sky. This was the real thing, I thought. This might be worth watching. One lightning strike could knock out the lights of this entire city, melt the computer credit-card links, fry the satellite dishes. Even a modest downpour, Julie had told me, and Las Vegas floods. Beside me, an elderly woman snapped a photo as the Mirage's fake volcano erupted.

CHAPTER 15

Another Casualty of the Sixties

July 30—Las Vegas, Nevada

Tomasz wanted to spend a couple of days together in Las Vegas, photographing the Liberace Museum, but I'd already had enough of the place. I had the wild idea that I'd take a bus up Route 95 to Beatty, hitch west along the tiny National Park road through Death Valley, just so I could boast that I had done it (I had the whole thing worked out. I was going to buy an egg, crack it onto the road where I was thumbing, and see if it would fry), then cut north through Yosemite and make for Oakland, where I could crash with Mitzi Porges. I caught a cab to the bus station the next morning.

The cab driver, a transplanted New Yorker, affectionately described Las Vegas as a "friendly little burg." All the same, he went on to say that he worked the 4 a.m. shift because the night shift was too dangerous for his liking. "When they hold you up at night, they have a tendency to kill you." Downtown Las Vegas, I had discovered, is like a barbell, with a glitzy center around the Golden Nugget and a glitzy center around Caesar's Palace with a nasty, decrepit strip running between the two. As we stopped at every light down this strip, the dispatcher put out a call to some apartment building behind the Stratosphere, but nobody answered it. "That's where the druggies hang out. You go in there and you won't come out." Still, he was a cheerful soul and a Boston Bruins hockey fan. It's amazing what will take root in the desert.

The bus station, like most, was not remarkable for its cleanliness or charm. I couldn't see them hiring George Persinger to restore it. Behind me in the line for the Reno bus was a curious couple. She was short, slight, pretty in a tired way. He was a big guy, six three, perhaps 240 pounds; small mustache, long graying black hair slicked back off his forehead and falling down onto his collar; stubbled and gap-toothed, with a deep smoker's cough. He spotted my accent right away, with none of this wishy-washy "English or Australian?" stuff, and told me I reminded him of an English judge in the St. George, Utah, misdemeanor court. "Thirty days," he said, in passable English tones.

They got on the same bus as I did, and sat across the aisle and one row back. "How much do you weigh?" he asked, looking her up and down.

"Hundred and fifteen," she said.

He laughed. "Hell, my leg weighs a hundred and fifteen." I couldn't quite work out their stories, especially hers, since he did most of the talking and had the louder voice. She was going to San Francisco to see her kids, and had been traveling for several days straight. He said something to her about a jail pass, but that might have been a joke. He seemed to have been thrown out of Las Vegas for drunkenness.

"Them girls with the slick pantyhose and the short skirts come around and give you free drinks. I'm not a gambler, but I sat there and fooled around with a dollar, two dollars of nickels for about four hours, had about fifteen drinks...."

He had been in the Army for 18 years, and threw some jokes across the aisle to me about places he'd been stationed in England, about spending most of his time getting off base and getting stoned. "Get out the hashish and fire that baby up!" He said he'd been married "for three years to a bitch from hell," and he'd never do that again.

The bus stopped at Lathrop Wells, Nevada, where a miniature western town—lockup, saloon, gallows, etc.—was just the frontage for a convenience store. Not every convenience store, though, sells postcards of Death Valley tarantulas as big as your hand (which didn't do much for my confidence) or displays a sign saying THEY'RE BACK! BROTHEL T-SHIRTS.

Brothel? A sign outside had said Adult Entertainment, and when I investigated, it seemed to point to a small cuboid building set back from the road calling itself the Cherry Patch Ranch II. I suspected this had little to do with fruit trees, but as everything was closed in the late morning heat, I would never know.

This weird little storefront set me thinking back to *Baghdad Café* again. No wonder outsiders find these desert roadside buildings so compelling. Out in front is the road, the passing of time, the route to the civilized world; out back is the desert. It's as if all of humanity is wedged into those few yards of frontage under the brilliant sun. Anything might happen.

Back on the bus, I noticed that the conversation across the aisle from me had taken on a hint of urgency. He was going to get out at Beatty and try his luck hitching to Reno, or maybe spend the night at Beatty and then try hitching tomorrow; and as we got closer to Beatty he began hitting on her in a gentle—almost courteous—but persistent way, trying to persuade her to get off at Beatty with him. She kept on not quite saying no, talking about her daughter who was expecting her, changing the subject. She asked him what he would do if he won the lottery—buy a Ferrari? He laughed his deep laugh, and perhaps coughed his deep cough, too. "Ferrari? I'd have me a big old black whore about eight feet tall." I liked him. He was loud and coarse, but he spoke his mind and misled nobody. He was a magnificent wreck.

More desert went by, and still more. Every so often a narrow, dusty road would wander away like an ill-advised out-of-stater, to die of thirst somewhere out of sight. It was inconceivable that there was anywhere near here for a road to go to—though somewhere beyond the dry mountains off to the right was Groom Lake, a.k.a. Area 51, the most secret air base in America (that we know of).

The two of them were still talking, but he had half-turned toward her now. Something was going on. "I been reading a lot about the male menopause," he said, "and how once we start realizing that we're not going to live forever after all, we start thinking about what we've done with our lives. And when I look back at it, the fact is, I ain't done a lot with it. I had a lot of fun, but I haven't done much that was any use. My daughters say, 'Look at your grandchildren. They're something.' I tell them, I didn't have anything to do with them. My daughters say, 'We couldn't have had them without you,' but…" He shrugged that argument away. "When I was young, I thought I was going to change the world, but it never happened."

He paused, chewing on what he was about to say. "I'm sorry to get all philosophical on you, but—well, it's been on my mind a lot. Fact is, I know I'm goin' to go to hell."

"Why do you think you're going to hell?" she asked.

"Because I killed a lot of little yellow people." He was young and gung ho and All-American, he told her, and Lyndon Baines Johnson told him to go, so he went. Now one of his few consolations seemed to be that he would meet Lyndon Baines Johnson in hell.

"The worst part of it all," he said somberly, "was that I didn't have any reason to kill them. Hell, the only reason they were shooting at us was because we were in their country. It wasn't like they were in California."

She tried to reassure him, and told him that everyone had committed sins of various kinds. She certainly had. He said, "Yeah, but you didn't kill a lot of little yellow people. Shit, if I were God, I'd send me to hell."

This is the thing that I regret most about the whole trip. I wanted to cross the aisle, sit in the seat in front of them, turn, rest my forearms on the seat backs, and offer some kind of consolation—but I didn't. My own personal theology is still so new and unspoken, and I fell back into that English reserve. So I left him staring into the heart of darkness, his own heart. He had been tested more than many of us will ever be; he had been thrown into a program of accelerated learning—a basic training of the soul.

When I got off at Beatty, they both got off too, though I don't think he even noticed me. When I had set my pack up on Route 374, the side road to Death Valley, he appeared and marched heavily past me on the other side of the road as if heading out of town. He didn't recognize me. After 15 or 20 minutes he reappeared, calling out to me, "Where's the liquor store at?" I spread my arms and shrugged. By the time I went into the hotel-casino to take a break from the sun, they were both at the bar; he was drunk, and it was too late. He was already with his demons, another casualty of the sixties.

Beatty wasn't much more than a bend in Route 95 with a few buildings staggering up into the hot, dry hills surrounding it. The junction where I set up my pack featured a tiny bank on one side—I kept thinking the Beattians pulling over at the ATM were stopping to pick me up— and a tiny Nevada Highways Department depot on the other. A few yards beyond me was a tiny hut, the size of an outhouse, labeled BEATTY MUSEUM, which was closed, and a Death Valley ranger station, which was also closed, but at least offered a map of the region. Beatty fell between Bare Mountain and the Bullfrog Hills, and in the Bullfrogs was Rhyolite, a ghost town where Shorty Harris and Ed Cross had found gold and which, in its heyday, according to the brochure, had three water systems, three train lines, over 50 mines, one daily and two weekly newspapers, an opera house, a symphony, baseball teams, tennis courts, swimming pools, two undertakers, two hospitals, eight physicians, two dentists, 19 lodging houses, 18 grocery stores, over 50 saloons, two churches and Tom Kelly's Bottle House, made entirely of bottles. It sounded wonderful. Somewhere in Death Valley was Zabriskie Point, the Devil's Golf Course, Bad Water, and Salt Creek, which has flowing water and popfish, whatever they are.

I decided against the fried egg. Out here on the fringes of Death Valley, it wasn't that hot—no more than 95 degrees, say. The wind was warm but light, not unpleasant—a yellow wind. All the same,

I was uneasy. The few passersby stared. The sheriff prowled past. "People are strange when you're a stranger," Jim Morrison said.

In order to get past this unease, I tried a tactic I'd never used before: I nodded once, briefly, at everyone who passed. A nod is a simple thing, far less demanding than a smile or a wave, and almost impossible to resist. I nodded, and everyone nodded back: the guys in the Nevada Highways Department pickups, the little old ladies, even the sheriff. After half an hour, I found myself warming to Beatty more than virtually anywhere else I passed through. It was a wonderfully hospitable little town. Everybody nodded.

In more than two hours, I was passed by at most 40 vehicles that were actually going into Death Valley, most of which were expensive out-of-state sport trucks packed to the roof with expensive climbing/running/camping/hiking/orienteering/scuba gear, with mountain bikes hitched to the hatchback and streamlined Thule containers on the roof full of more scuba gear. Maybe it was the heat or the disappointment, but I began to be pestered by a scene that kept rising out of my imagination and wouldn't be dismissed, a scene in which a group of freaks in a VW bus would pull over and yell "Hop in, man!" tossing baggage into a corner to make room, stashing my backpack in the way back. We'd tool over the mountains and down through Death Valley telling stories, laughing outrageously, comparing travelers' tales. We'd all fall silent when we first saw the valley, then breathe "Oh, wow. Far out. Look at that!" We'd look for Zabriskie Point, and someone would say, "No, it's farther over that way, man" and we'd argue over our recollections of the movie, and someone would try to hum the Pink Floyd music from the soundtrack. Then north to Yosemite, where we'd camp out, and from somewhere under the mountain of luggage one of them would haul out a guitar....

No freaks any more, I wrote in my notebook. *No VW buses. I can't afford such dreams. They make me bitter. I need to stay in the present. Stop all this low-percentage stuff. Get some lunch, switch over to 95. Make for Reno.*

Yet no sooner had I thought this—well, no sooner than another 90 minutes of hitching in the midday heat outside a gas station visited solely by Germans going to Las Vegas—than it came true, or at least a version of it came true, translated into the idiom of the late nineties: I was picked up by Hank, an artist from New Mexico driving a Subaru going all the way to Oakland.

I offered to help pay for gas. Sure, he said. "Isn't that what people used to say? Gas, grass, or ass?" His words jarred me like the bow wave of a truck. Once again, I'd stumbled into the traffic in another corridor of time. Is that really what they used to say? Not in England.

"So, you're from New Mexico. Ever seen a UFO?" I said, joking. To me, the whole southwestern desert is an eerie place, the stories of UFO sightings and of top-secret air bases blending in my mind and the public imagination until the flying saucers are next-level Air Force prototypes and the government is run by aliens.

He looked at me as if it was my turn to startle him with a casual comment that arrived like a brick through a window. "As it happens," he said slowly, "I have. Just the other day"—though that encounter turned out to be part of a larger story, a story that seemed to arise from the desert around us and follow us, hovering almost visibly in the hot, dry air.

"I went to a fleamarket in Las Cruces," he began, "and there's this very distinguished-looking old man, 88 years old, selling these wonderful paintings, and he introduces himself and he says that he's the former senator for New Mexico, Joseph Montoya. I'm with the mayor of the town that I live in, and she remembered his name. So we asked him, why was he selling these paintings? Well, he doesn't have his house any more, his wife died, blah blah blah. So we started talking, and I realized that he was the senator from 1945-1949, right during the 1947 Roswell incident. So we wound up buying all of the paintings, because they were great paintings, and we took him to lunch because I wanted to pump him for information about his UFO experiences, because the mayor and I had just had one no more than two weeks before that."

"What? What had happened?"

"Well, we were driving back from Albuquerque at 10:30 at night and a string of white lights on a diagonal line was following us across the desert. It would surge up on us really, really fast—and I had her car going to the floor, I was going about a hundred miles an hour, and this thing would go *whoom!* Just like that. It was a diagonal row of white lights, that's all you could see. And then it would zoom back. It would zoom away."

"Wow. How far off the ground?" I asked.

"The lights looked as if they went right to the ground, but I couldn't tell how high up they were because I couldn't tell how far back it was. There was no way of getting any perspective because it was a dark, dark desert night. But this thing was gaining on us and moving away, gaining on us and moving away. Finally I said, the hell with this, I'm going to stop. And as soon as I took my foot off the accelerator, it just went *whoom!* back, shot out of sight and the lights went out, gone. Then we stopped the car. We were right at the back entrance to White Sands missile base, you know, the proving-grounds base, and within two minutes they scrambled I don't know how many jet planes and helicopters one after another—they scrambled the entire base in the direction that we saw this thing go zooming off in. It was unbelievable. We were pissing in our pants. Then I was afraid to drive the rest of the way. Not one car passed us on that road that night between San Antonio and Saragosa. It's the deadest road in the world."

We turned left at bleak, dusty Tonopah, which I'd always assumed existed only in the mind of the Grateful Dead. Tucson to Tucumcari, Tehachapi to Tonapah—how could these desert names be part of anything but a long, strange trip?

"So then we meet the senator, right? We're at lunch, have a couple of glasses of wine and I had to ask him, 'Joe, you were there at Roswell....' He looked at first a little uneasy, but then he looked at us and figured, well, we're certainly not with the government, and he told us he had been warned not to talk to anybody, over and over again for many, many years, or he would lose his Social Security, he'd go out into a shallow grave in the desert, all this sort of stuff. But he told us that he was there. And saw it, saw the bodies, was in the hangar." The four alien bodies from the UFO that crashed on Mac Brazel's ranch on July 4, 1947, that is, and the fragments of the weird craft made apparently out of tinfoil, collected from the desert hillside and taken to the Air Force base. "Not only did he see it, but a guy around the corner in Truth or Consequences was also on the base as an officer in the R.A.F. who was stationed there, is still alive, now has cancer and wants to talk about it.

"So I go to the Roswell U.F.O. museum, right? and I tell the director this story. He's very, very interested. Very interested. And he wants to speak to Senator Montoya, and this other officer. So I gave him all the information on how to find them, blah blah blah.

"About a month later, a man calls me from Pennsylvania. Pennsylvania, of all places. And he says he's with, quote, the U.F.O.

museum. Gave me some name like Dan Smith. And I had no reason at first to question whether he really was or not. He said 'I'm a researcher and I'm attached to the Roswell thing'—but no one had mentioned his name at that Roswell place. He started asking me all these questions about what happened, what did [Montoya] say, where were you when you had this conversation, and you could tell he was taking all this down, word for word."

Hank broke off to get gas, which I paid for in a small barnboard shack of a gas-station-and-quick-stop, west of Tonopah. In one corner, a crusty old local was holding forth about Clinton's wickedness while the other two or three people squashed into the narrow aisles did their best to ignore him. It was the only time all trip I heard anyone discussing national politics. (The same was true in 1973: I can remember only one person discussing Watergate.) Television, radio, and the newspapers seemed to have their own arena, existing everywhere yet nowhere, in which their own matadors fought their own bulls. For the first time, I understood that this disembodied dimension was what people getting on with their lives out here in America meant when they said "Washington."

He continued when we got back into the car. "The next time I spoke to the people at the Roswell museum," Hank said, "they had contacted Joe Montoya. He'd moved from Truth or Consequences, and he wouldn't talk to anybody because he had been approached by somebody from the government again because of the conversation that we had. Now, how did they find out? The guy at the Roswell UFO place thinks it's his own telephone that the government's tapped. Of course, it sounds totally paranoid, but I wouldn't put anything past this government."

We passed small salt pans amid the sagebrush, and headed toward the chain of mountains at the Nevada-California border.

Hank told me that his wife had died in a car crash; he was very close to his two daughters, now high-powered and magnificent in their own right. He himself lived in what sounded like a high-class condo by a ski area, and did what might be called southwestern art, which was selling rather well at the moment.

Though I didn't know it at the time, that was the last I'd see of the desert, and to my surprise I would come to miss it. My experience of the desert was an oddly social one: I was always in a car or a bus, talking with someone about what I saw, or listening. Now I wish I had spent more time walking, vulnerable to that sense of brilliant and cruel indifference.

At Benton we turned west on Route 120, the most interesting road I traveled all summer and probably one of the most interesting in the country. The first thing that happened, though, was that Hank, who had been complaining of hunger for some time, started muttering, "Hot springs. We'll get something to eat at the hot springs." The sun's got to him, I thought. He's beginning to hallucinate. But the road jumped off the valley floor and suddenly, in a little grove of cottonwood and aspen, appeared a small wooden house surrounded by strange metal carcasses that had once been farm machinery or instruments of multiple torture. This, it turned out, was the town of Benton Hot Springs. Well, this and the tumbledown hotel-and-garage building opposite where someone was mending junk cars by the time-honored method of standing them out in the sun and then retiring for a little nap. Benton Hot Springs' leading citizen seemed to be Uncle Bob Schmidt, droll, semi-shaven proprietor of this antique emporium, ice cream shop, and hot tub spa.

The five hot tubs were out back, each in its own little grove by the little hot stream that, Uncle Bob told us, rises in the canyon above at a scalding 137 degrees, though by the time it runs through his property it is only slightly too hot to take at 124 degrees. (The stream looked innocent enough, though in winter, he said, it steams.) Uncle Bob had jury-rigged a number of hoses, shower-heads, and other miscellaneous adventures in plumbing to draw water from the stream and spray it into the hot tubs, which looked like well-aged whisky barrels. The showerheads were not because bathers liked showers, he said, but because the water was still too hot, and needed more exposure to air to cool it. He'd had the water tested, he said, and claimed it was as pure as any spring water in the world, though high in sodium. "See how it has that slightly greasy feel? That's salt, Mother Nature's water softener."

From this micro-resort, 120 rose into a cradle of hot, dry little hills, turned north, and began skipping along a series of rapid bumps and hollows: driving it was like dry-land powerboat racing. We spent half the time in midair. Then west again through the Inyo National Forest, but almost at once we were cresting a hill and looking in astonishment down to our right at Mono Lake, the strangest body of water I've ever seen.

"In the middle distance," wrote Israel Russell in *Quarternary History of the Mono Valley*, 1889, "there rests upon the desert plain what appears to be a wide sheet of burnished metal, so even and brilliant is its surface. It is Lake Mono. At times, the waters reflect the mountains beyond with strange distinctness and impress one as being in some way peculiar, but usually their ripples gleam and flash in the sunlight like the waves of ordinary lakes. No one would think from a distant view that the water which seems so bright and enticing is in reality so dense and alkaline that it would quickly cause death of a traveler who could find no other with which to quench his thirst."

Russell's "in some way peculiar" might go on to include the fact that the original Paiute residents of the region were known as the Kuzedika'a, or fly-pupae-eaters, because they ate flies—or, more accurately, the grubs of the alkali flies that breed around the lake. Or Russell might have had in mind the strange black cliff of volcanic ash rising down the far shore. Most likely, though, it would be the bizarre gray excrescences rising from the water's edge looking like stalagmites made by dribbling wet sand through your fingers. These are called tufa. The lake is fed by warm underwater streams laced with limestone particles. As the streams hit the cold lake water, they precipitate out, depositing tiny granules of lime that cluster and build up. In past years, when the lake's level was higher, they were invisible; now, as the lake falls in what some see as an environmental catastrophe in the making (caused by the theft of the lake's tributary streams by the Los Angeles Department of Water and Power), the fantastic tufa gardens are exposed like coral at low tide.

You should think of eating at the Mono Inn at Mono Lake, Uncle Bob Schmidt had said, because it is owned and operated by Ansel Adams's granddaughter Sarah. We found the Inn, perched above the lake just north of the oddly named town of Lee Vining. Leroy "Lee" Vining crossed the Sierras in 1852 in search of gold, built a sawmill and sold lumber in Aurora, Nevada, where he came to an odd end: As a shootout developed in the Exchange Saloon, he left the building and started to walk up the street. Somehow his gun went off in his pocket, shot him in the groin, and he bled to death.

The sun was already declining. If we wanted to see Yosemite before dark, we wouldn't have time to wait for dinner. We looked around the room of Adamsiana on sale. We looked around the art gallery, its panoramic window overlooking the lake, while the party ahead of us was waiting for its table. Sarah swept in, tall, beautiful, athletic, to tell the party that their table was ready. This was a magazine moment, a quest moment, one that miraculously granted me access to one of the epic figures of the west, someone who had helped to define America.

But at that instant I suffered what might be called a crisis of time. The past, with its epic photographer, vanished, and in its place I saw a busy woman getting on with her own life. Why should I interrupt her? Besides, I know nothing about Ansel Adams except that when I saw his big show in New York I went the wrong way around it because of my deep revulsion for shuffling along in a crowd. I passed on Uncle Bob's greetings, she smiled, and vanished with her guests down to the dining room.

The sun was barely above the mountains of Yosemite as we climbed up through the switchbacks at the park's eastern gate, crowning the peaks with gold as the shadows crept up from the wooded valleys. We started out giddily, taking turns standing up through the sun roof to shoot photographs while careening under precipices and around blind corners, but after a few miles we reached the first ranger post and were told politely that all the gas stations in the park were closing.

This was when I began to realize that Hank was one of the most anxious people I'd ever met. At once, his high spirits started being nibbled away by the invisible mouse of anxiety. He had a quarter tank. It was at least 20 miles back to the last gas station we had passed. Well, we'd push on. Surely we'd find something. Besides, how far could it be to the other side of the park, anyway?

The first gas pumps we passed were closed. We ran into another ranger. Well, she said, the pumps father west stayed open a little longer, so we might get lucky there. How far were they? Oh, a good 40 miles. *Forty miles?* How big was this park, anyway? Oh, about 120 miles across.

Hank started worrying in earnest—a serious, professional anxiety of the kind that transforms the entire world into one ghastly, undulating threat, and all incoming data just goes to prove that your worst fears were right after all. It was now dusk, and the forest-and-mountain landscapes were dark, winding tunnels. The fuel gauge was just above empty, and we had at least 35 miles to a gas station that might well be closed. To take his mind off all this, I asked him if he had been to Woodstock. To my delight, he had.

"It was a nightmare. Ah, Jesus. The mud. The rain. It was freezing. This black friend of mine, Marianne, bought two tickets, and she forced me to go." He chuckled at himself. "She didn't have a car, and I did....It was our senior year in college. She just laid a guilt trip on me. She said, 'You'd take me if I was white!' And I thought, well, if you're going to go to Woodstock with anybody it should be with this outrageous black woman, with her Afro.

"I don't remember the names of all the bands we heard. Jimi Hendrix. Uh...There was a lot of folk people there too. Joan Baez. You name it. Everybody who had a record at that time was there. Oh, God, who was that black musician?"

I racked my brains rapidly over this faint hint. "Ritchie Havens?"

"That's it, Ritchie Havens. Oh, God, I can't remember who else.... There must have been a hundred bands. I can't remember one. I think I must have Alzheimer's. I wasn't even into that music, that's the weird thing."

"Who were you listening to?"

"I was listening to jazz. I was listening to, like, Stan Getz. I didn't even like the Beatles."

Me, I was 16 and in the wrong country when Woodstock took place, but I remember the British music papers panning the event as musically mediocre and self-indulgent. I asked Hank whether, at the time, it seemed like a significant occasion, or just a mess?

"It was a significant mess. It got so far out of control that the people who thought they could control it finally gave up. Once that happened, it started to be more fun. At first there were signs, there were fences, there were directions, there were guards, there were nurses," he said, as if he were talking about life itself. "There were police, there were all kinds of things. But after a while, it got so out of control that they just gave up. That's when it became a party. And it just went on all night long. Girls on guys' shoulders so they could see the bands, naked or at least topless. It was the era of free love, and there was a lot of that going on. Men and women, women and women, men and men. Of course, the drugs had a lot to do with it, too, but there was a sense of freedom, as if you left the rules of social behavior at the roadside when you entered that farmer's field. Anything went.

"The announcements were funny. 'The blue Pluto acid is no good. Don't take the blue Pluto.' They were warning people about a lot of the, uh, products that were being distributed among the crowd, and acid was a big problem because a lot of people had never tripped before and were freaking out. They had tents set up for people on bad trips, and the tents were filled to overflowing. I wasn't into drugs at the time, thank goodness, or else I'd probably still be there.

"Not everything that happened was good. I heard about people being raped, and being sexually assaulted by strangers because they were passed out facedown in the mud. It wasn't all pretty. For me it was odd, because I was very prudish. This was the most naked people I had ever seen partying at one time. I was from New Mexico, I wasn't used to this kind of thing. Baptist, on top of everything else." He shook his head and grinned ruefully.

"What I liked about it was that it was as out of control as you could get without killing someone, although I think somebody did die of an overdose—of what, I don't know. [Marianne and I] weren't that wild and crazy. I think we were both restraining influences on each other. I was too uptight, she was not going to take off her clothes being with a white guy. She was a black militant woman. If she was with a black guy she might have done it, but here she was with me, this white, blond, Baptist, Nazi-looking guy!"

I asked him what they were talking about as they were going, thinking that they might have been raving over the "three day nation," the sense of love and peace.

He laughed. "Well, we had an argument. She was pissed off because she paid for the motel in advance, and when we got back there finally, of course they wouldn't refund any money just because she didn't show up for the room. They rented the room to somebody else who walked the three miles or whatever it was back to the motel. And it was expensive. This was the closest motel, and they took advantage of that and charged I think about $75 a night, which was a lot back then. She had prepaid that, and she was furious that she didn't get her money back. So we left in a bad state of mind. Terrible hangover. I had slept in the back seat of somebody else's car. It was just parked there. The doors were open. She slept in the front seat. The worst that could happen was that somebody would ask us to get out. I don't know where the owners of the car were. They never showed up. And a lot of cars got stuck in the mud, because people had pulled off the road into the dirt and the grass, and people were helping to get them unstuck.

"If Woodstock were to happen again now, I think there'd be more deaths. We're darker now than we were in the sixties. That was a real innocent time, in many ways. You know, they redid it just a few years ago."

"Did you go?"

"No."

"Did you even think of going?"

"I did. I thought of Marianne—she lives in Buffalo. Woodstock is right near New Paltz. I was in New York at the time. I thought, well, gee, I should call her up. But, you know, the truth is that we were so miserable. We really didn't enjoy it because it rained; it was cold, we were uncomfortable, and I was trying to enjoy myself while drinking Lancer's."

Hank seemed to have drifted somewhere else. "When I see the movie *Woodstock* now, I can't even imagine I was in that. Seeing a movie of Vietnam and being a Vietnam vet, you probably have the same feeling. There's an unreal quality. When I watched the movie, I recognized certain people that I had seen because they were being outrageous, and those were the people they filmed, but looking at it now it's like it never happened. I wasn't there. It was like a dream state, or something."

And my own movie, my recollections of my cross-country trip: If I saw it now, would I even know the lanky, puppyish kid with the chestnut hair?

When we finally reached it, the gas station, a small pool of light among dark trees, was closed. People were inside, sweeping up, but they had turned the pumps off and would not turn them back on. Hank pleaded with them. They swept on. Now he was worrying about bears. This seemed a little excessive to me: We both had sleeping bags, I pointed out, and we could easily sleep in the car. His cell phone even had an automatic distress signal built in that would alert the gendarmes, but he was not soothed. "You don't understand, it's a technique," he said frantically. "If I worry about something, then it won't happen."

Down, down, down, curve after tight curve in the darkness, the headlights falling on countless tree trunks, Hank now convinced that the whole of American society was falling apart, that the kids with their Gothic body-piercings and dark clothing were all main-lining heroin. Then on the right, a patch of light: a little store with a gas pump out front. We fueled up the Subaru and our spirits, and as we broke out of the park and saw the whole of coastal California laid out in front of us in a carpet of tiny lights, Hank asked me shyly if I would mind looking at his poetry.

Who could not love this guy, this world?

~

CHAPTER 16

Between Me and the Basted Egg

July 31—Oakdale, California

Early-morning thoughts, 5:25 a.m.

Any spontaneous decision has about it not only joy and energy but a mysterious kind of truth. Any spontaneous act involves abandoning self-protection.

Oakdale is the home of the basted egg. "It's exactly the same as poached," said Melissa, the waitress. "Don't ask me why we call it that."

I knew right away that I was in California because the roads had become very serious and professional. Oakdale wasn't even on our map, but it had a five-lane street between me and the basted egg. But then anyone's roads seem well-funded after Nevada's.

Hank and I set off westward, through walnut and almond groves, past a ridge of a thousand windmills, their arms churning like a race of stationary swimmers, and it began to sink in that I was back in California again—the name itself still thrilling even though it's one of the few states outside of Vermont where I travel a couple of times a year—and I found myself remembering my arrival in Berkeley in 1973.

For a hip place, Berkeley seemed remarkably ugly. Robin dropped us off on a hot, dusty street of almost identical, charmless houses with address numbers in the tens of thousands. I'd never seen house numbers go that high. We walked several blocks, the numbers mounting in their hundreds like an auction, until we found the number Mitzi had given me.

I haven't the slightest recollection of the guy who opened the door, except that he was young and gave off the air of lived-in slovenliness that was always a good sign. "You don't know us," I began, "but I'm a friend of Mitzi Porges, whose brother Tim used to live in this house, and she said we might be able to stay here." He looked at us. I imagine him scratching his chest through his T-shirt. "Tim who?" We compared domestic genealogies, following the house's recent ancestral descent through its host of transient inhabitants, and came to the conclusion that Tim had moved out before this guy moved in. We waited on the step, he lounged in the doorway. Impasse. Then he caught sight of my guitar. "Hey, you got an axe? Come on in, man! Let's jam."

Richard and I trooped in. The guy picked up his electric guitar, which was lying on the couch like a stoned friend. I took my cheap travelers' classical out of its tartan PVC case. Richard settled in a corner. We tuned, more or less, and began to play.

Musically, the early seventies were a time when virtuosity was beginning to overcome cohesion. It was no longer cool for a band to be tight; individual display was where it was at. Album-length tracks replaced the two-minute single, and In-A-Gada-Da-Vida was born. People would compare concerts by the length of the guitar solo or the drum solo, and nothing was a better sign of artistic integrity than the long, self-indulgent jam session. The next hour and 45 minutes were some of the most boring of my life. I had no idea what he was playing or where he was going, and even if I tried a standard 12-bar chording pattern, he would wander off into keys of his own. I could barely play lead-guitar-style riffs, but it didn't matter: he had no interest in listening to what I was playing anyway. Richard adopted his by now familiar scowl, punctuated with even dirtier looks and jerks of the head to let me know that we had paid our dues and could I please shut up now? But the guy never looked up, and never stopped playing. You might think he was stoned, but I'm sure he wasn't. Narcissistic numbness was a respectable posture of the times; dope was just one way of getting there.

Eventually he stopped. "Far out, man." He told us we could sleep in the walk-in closet behind the front door.

Hank dropped me off in Walnut Grove, a wealthy suburb east of the Bay Area. It looked like the kind of place where the kids of 1973 Berkeley would live when they grew up and started software companies or chic health-food restaurants. One Jaguar driver gave another the finger. In a bookstore, the guy ahead of me in line must have been a lawyer: he was carrying a book titled *Big Deal*, and he had mastered the art of ordering his latte while talking on his cell phone so quietly that nobody else could hear what he said.

I was almost within sight of the Pacific—but how was I going to get there? In 1973 it was easy: Everyone lined up along University Avenue in Berkeley, two dozen, three dozen people in singles or groups with their thumbs out, and by nine in the morning they were all gone as the counterculture rapid-transit system picked them up in ones and twos and took them into the city. In 1998, the only person waiting at the freeway entrance was a ragged man with a sign— "Purple Heart No Income Small Change Anything Will Do Please Help"— calling inaudibly to the cars as they accelerated up the ramp. I was tired, my neck and shoulders still hurt like hell from Las Vegas, and I deserved a break. I was 45, dammit. I walked to the Walnut Grove Marriott, which had its own Avis desk like a baby in a kangaroo's pouch, and rented a little white car. As the computer reeled out the paperwork, another customer swung by and dropped off a couple of posters for the Avis staff. They were an artist's representation of a project under way at the National Ignition Facility. "He works at Lawrence Livermore," the manager explained. "He's making a star."

I zipped out into the traffic, thinking *You're not really in California unless you're driving*, something in me reaching out for that Joan Didion ecstasy, the fast, supple rhythm of the freeways, making for Oakland and Mitzi.

The rhythm of the freeways, though, had changed since Joan Didion's day. Now it was fast, slow, crawl, stop, as the lanes died and the orange barrels squeezed like a sphincter. So it was a few seconds before I realized that the patch of brilliant silver sunlight on the western horizon was the Pacific. It had taken me 11 days to cross America.

CHAPTER 17

Laundry on the Freeway

August 1—Oakland, California

Mitzi and her husband Bill lived in a sunny bungalow perched on the shoulder of a hill in Oakland. Mitzi herself looked completely unchanged after a quarter of a century—though warmer, less like an intellectual hawk—but now asked to be called Maria.

She showed me the little outbuilding she'd converted into a studio and some of her current work. She collects old-fashioned glass bottles, makes molds from them, then recasts them in colored beeswax, so the objects are beautiful, light, slightly unreal-looking. Then she plays with other characteristics of bottles: what they contain, the fact that they're supposed to stand upright, and the very fact that they're supposed to contain something at all. She engraves the bottles—in delicate copperplate gold writing—with the names of their supposed contents, but her bottles are full of abstractions: Fertility, Devotion, Lust. Their shapes, too, defy bottledom. Some have round bottoms, so they can't even stand up, some are joined at the side or bottom like Siamese twins, so the contents of the two would be bound to escape and mingle.

She made me up a bed on the floor of their basement/office/library, and I sank into it. By morning, though, the fear-of-Las-Vegas pain in my shoulders had migrated up to the back of my neck and I could barely turn my head. Maria made an appointment with their friend Doctor Dave, the cool chiropractor, at his office on Lombard. As he went to work with the ultrasound and the manipulations, he told me his own 1973 hitchhiking story.

He had been in Europe. He had $105 in his pocket one day, when he walked past a travel agency in Amsterdam offering a special to New York for $99. He figured he'd better grab it while he could, and flew back. "I called this girl I'd met in Greece, who lived out on Long Island. We'd become really good friends—very platonic, but very good friends. So I went and stayed with her...actually, her mother was dying of cancer, and I think I helped the family a bit because my mother had died from cancer, so we had long talks. Her father ended up really liking me, even though I had long hair and a beard and at first I think he was a bit intimidated by me.

"When I left, he drove me to the George Washington Bridge, and offered to pay for my trip back to San Francisco on an airplane, and I said no. Then he offered to lend me the money for the plane ticket, because he thought I didn't want a handout, and I said no, I'd rather hitchhike. Then he said, Well, at least let me give you some money, and I said no. So I took my five bucks and hitchhiked back across the United States."

Tomasz claims I was nine hours late for our first rendezvous in New York (I deny this) so he walked around the city looking for visionary moments. For him, he said, New York is both a city of gold and a city of the dead, where the future rises glittering above the past (TOP). It's also a conjunction of opposites, though this example (BOTTOM), was an artificial one, part of a TV commercial being filmed downtown.

Photographs by Tomasz Tomaszewski

I found George Persinger and his sons in Toledo, Ohio, working to preserve the faith, not only in the cathedral's statuary (ABOVE) but in its very bricks and mortar. Tomasz was often impressed by the way African-American churches, such as the Second Canaan Missionary Baptist Church in Detroit (OPPOSITE, TOP), played a vital role in holding their communities together. We both saw the family farm, too, as an American icon—though where but in America, Tomasz asked, do you see exhibits, like this one in Woodstock, Vermont (OPPOSITE, BOTTOM), to teach children how apple trees work?

Tomasz arrived in South Dakota a few days before I did, and when he wasn't shooting bikers at the annual Harley-Davidson rally in Sturgis (OPPOSITE, TOP), he was getting up before dawn and driving several hundred miles a day among the state's small towns, finding a panorama of the history of the plains on the main street in Mitchell (OPPOSITE, BOTTOM). Well, not quite the entire history: there doesn't seem to be any sign of the Lakota Sioux. We found them on the Pine Ridge Reservation, where Trevor and Godfrey Chipps improvised a shower on a sweltering day (ABOVE).

"The thing you forget about America," Tomasz said, "is that it's not a country, it's a continent. It has landscapes enough for a dozen countries." Jim Curuchet and Antonio Rodriguez, shepherds from the Basque lands in Spain, were brought over to work under the vast Wyoming sky (OPPOSITE, TOP). Mount Rainier National Park (OPPOSITE, BOTTOM), for Tomasz, was another region not yet cannibalized by progress. Ebenezer Bryce farmed a century ago at the foot of the canyon (ABOVE) that was later named after him. "It's a hell of a place to lose a cow," he said.

I left Las Vegas after less than a day, much to Tomasz's amazement. He couldn't understand why I wasn't drawn to Elvis impersonators on Fremont Street (TOP) or the Liberace Museum. While I saw wings on sale in a sex shop in Chicago, he went one better and found people actually wearing them (BOTTOM): just another day on Castro Street in San Francisco.

He made it in a dozen rides or so, running the usual gamut: a serviceman on a two-day pass driving 1,500 miles to see his girlfriend, a Kansas lawyer who casually pointed out that they were driving past an entire field of pot, a couple who invited him to join them for a threesome, a group of hippies who were so stoned they asked Dave to drive for them ("I drove for six or eight hours, until they came down from whatever they had taken, then they dropped me off, turned round and went back. I think I'd driven them hundreds of miles beyond where they were going"), and a fatherly, blue-collar guy who forced him to accept five dollars. "People in general were pretty darn nice," he concluded, as if it had only just struck him, and I thought, Yes, that's true: As adolescents, we're so self-centered we have no idea how much kindness people show us. That's probably the most significant difference for me: In middle age I no longer take generosity for granted.

"For my last ride, I got picked up by this hippie bus, with three or four people in it, just an old school bus with wooden bunk beds and curtains and posters on the ceiling, and tie-dye stuff, and they were burning incense—pretty colorful, but the thing was so darn slow it drove me nuts. So I saw a girl at a gas station. She had a Chevy Impala convertible. The top was down. I asked her where she was going. She really didn't know; she'd worked for Kodak in Rochester, New York, and just wanted to get away from home for a while. I just said, 'Why don't you come to California and stay at my parents' house?' So she did. No romantic thing between us at all. We slept in the car together in campgrounds. She slept in the front, I slept in the back. We drove for a couple of days, got to my parents' house; I introduced her to them, asked them if she could stay, they said yes and I said goodbye to my parents and went over to my girlfriend's—and didn't come home for two days! She ended up staying with my parents for a few months. She married a guy, and she still lives in California."

Listening to him, I realized how much the word "road" had changed. For me, in 1973, it was an enchanted word. It was the crucible where the elements toughened you up and your encounters changed you into something leaner and wiser, but it was also a kind of circus, full of people from every walk of life who had uprooted themselves and were now, as Cat Stevens put it, "on the road to find out."

Since then, the road has become narrower and harder; a "road warrior" is now a professional business traveler. Everyone travels more than they used to, by whatever means. The lonesome moan of the train whistle and the boats watched from the dock of the bay used to be exotic because nobody left the farm, or the neighborhood. I didn't travel outside England until I was 13. I didn't fly until I was 16, and at that point the longest car journey I had made was less than 200 miles. Hitchhiking was my first real means of travel, period. At 11, my daughter Zoe has crossed the Atlantic a dozen times. But everything is also safer, more convenient, more predictable. Everyone travels, but not everyone explores.

On 101 south all the traffic slowed down, and I couldn't figure out why; then I saw that there was clothing all over the freeway. It looked as though someone had been carrying their laundry in a bag, perhaps on the back of a pickup, which had burst, scattering probably three or four dozen pieces of clothing across the asphalt.

It was bizarre, because it felt as if I was in danger of running over a person—and presumably others felt the same, because we all slowed down to a crawl. A pinkish-red check shirt, probably a woman's size, lay on the road in front of me, and I swerved to avoid it. It was as if the people who lived here, on this place of no people, had vanished, and left only their shapes. Some very deep drama of the road and the city was being enacted in our strange, jittery driving behavior: the freeway is the place where we last expect to see people, and it's disturbing to see even the shapes of people. The clothes represented a strange archaeology, as if here at last was evidence that once people had lived here, before a catastrophe—the building of the highway—had startled them, and they had fled.

Maria and Bill recommended a tiny Mexican restaurant down at the foot of the hill, right beyond the headquarters of the Oakland Hell's Angels. It wasn't a war zone, but it was barely demilitarized. By the time I'd gotten to the bottom of the hill, all the trees had disappeared—had fled, probably—reminding me of the study that found that the fewer trees there are in an area, the higher the crime rate. As I waited for my meal, along with a Mexican family watching a game show in Spanish on the TV and a trio of young African-American women with their kids, a ragged guy came in and tried to bum ten bucks off me until the owner caught sight of him, rolled up her sleeves and threw him out.

As I left, two police cars and a motorbike cop raced past, sirens screaming. Just down the road there had been an accident. Glass was littered everywhere. A crowd had gathered and stared, as if watching television. A couple of blocks farther along, two more motorbike cops peeled down the hill and raced off ahead of me, heading for some other disturbance of the peace.

CHAPTER 18

Don't Start Singing Before the Money Gets Through

August 2—San Francisco, California

"Check. One two two two. Check. One two."

Glide Memorial United Methodist Church on Ellis Street was packed. An usher in a road-crew reflector vest directed me to the far wall. "There's room for two on that windowsill," he said. I waded through a pew to climb onto the sill. It was astonishingly hot in the church—this was San Francisco, after all—and other ushers were passing out purple paper fans with slim wooden handles. On one side, the fans read

REVEREND CECIL WILLIAMS & GLIDE CHURCH

OVER 30 YEARS SERVICE

UNCONDITIONAL LOVE

TRUE DIVERSITY

COMPASSION

On the other, an invitation to "Contribute to Glide and empower us all!" listing a few of the church's 35 programs: Computer Learning Center, Job Training/Placement, Recovery Programs, Feeding the Hungry, Scholarships for Kids, HIV/AIDS Project.

As soon as I reached the Pacific, something had changed. I had done the hard part, the thing that everyone said couldn't be done anymore, and now the tight fist of duty was relaxing. I had a day or so to spare waiting for Tomasz, who had left the Liberace Museum and was somewhere in southern California trying to shoot a single field of 100,000 cows.

I had been longing to see a gospel service, partly because I'd never seen one and partly because of a story Tomasz had told me about shooting a gospel baptism at a Baptist church, a total-immersion service in a river in Florida, during which the congregation had to keep shooing an alligator away.

The band—bass, synth, percussion—warmed up. More people were squeezed into the cracks between the church's bricks. Downstairs, another 250 people were watching the service on live video. *Another* 250. Badgeworth Church, next to the group home for boys from broken homes that my parents ran, was lucky if it saw 250 people a month, even though every Sunday all 40 boys and a half dozen staff trooped in a line through the gate in the high yew hedge, all clean knees and clean handkerchiefs, destined for a boredom close to living death.

A slim, dark-featured man with earrings, close-cropped hair and a shadow of a beard climbed up next to me on my sill. Whatever homophobic dread had seized me in Wyoming seemed to have vanished. We shook hands. I was very happy.

The choir came in, swaying and clapping in their purple-and-gold robes, the most ecumenical choir imaginable, all colors, all races, all ages, everyone cheerful and rocking. Me, too, though whether because this collective spirit was something I'd been missing on my trip or in my life in general, I couldn't tell. Within minutes I was being warned not to jump up and down on the windowsill—not because the usher disapproved of such behavior, but because I was apparently jumping up and down on a heating register set into the sill that might collapse at any second.

Cecil Williams, beaming, rotund, bespectacled, bearded, his hair thinning, called out "Yeah! Oh, yeah! We lurrrrve it when it's hot!" Everyone laughed, cheered, and fanned harder. He called on three members of the congregation to take cordless mikes from the ushers and offer prayers, and the synth player picked up the rhythms of their voices and turned them into quiet and holy songs.

On stage next to him was an interpreter for the deaf, who had a permanent grin installed from ear to ear and interpreted in the visual equivalent of inflected English, or perhaps inflected music, drawing out his signs as Cecil drew out a word, bending them like a harmonica player bending a note. He moved with the music like Joe Cocker.

Badgeworth Church meant ponderous hymns echoing off chilly gray stone, rows of elderly ladies in Sunday best hats, the cassocked vicar, his mouth opening and closing like a sanctimonious oyster, droning "...and Jehosophat begat Temeculah, and Temeculah begat Tempeh, and Hashish, and Hazzamarazzamatazz..."— nothing to do with life as I knew it. At Glide we were holding hands and singing "Amazing Grace" and three or four other songs in succession—the service had more songs that your average CD—ending with "God will take care of you."

Yes, that's it, isn't it? I thought. That kind of reassurance is anxiety's opposite, and its antidote. It's also very, very rare. Where in the modern American urban landscape is the reassurance that anyone will take care of us in this land of competitiveness and greed, with a third of its people in poverty and holes in its safety net the size of small countries? And isn't it precisely the absence of such reassurance that creates most of the anxiety in the first place? "You're at the right place," Cecil said. "You're at the right place to be loved." Yes. Yes.

Announcements: a call for donations to the American Red Cross for tsunami victims in Papua New Guinea. A call for Glide volunteers by a woman who described herself as a Christian lesbian working in a Jewish day school. "Glide is about the only place where I fit in," she chuckled. Then Cecil climbed back up on stage, having been down visiting the 250 in the basement. "Now I want you to listen to this song," he said. "It's the second time we've done it. It's a great song, with great music, great words, and a great soloist. So I want you to listen to it." He paused. "I'm extendin' my conversation so they can finish takin' up the money." Everyone laughed, and he beamed. "I got wisdom enough to know that you don't start singin' before the money gets through."

More wonderful singing, a great trumpet solo by the keyboards player, then Cecil's sermon on spiritual openness and closedness, using the central metaphor of a jar. He had a lot of fun riffing like a jazz player on the qualities of jardom and the word jar (jarring experiences, remaining ajar), he called out, "How'm I doin?" and we all cheered, then more songs, more rocking, more cheering, whistling, jumping up and down and all the other forms of behavior never seen in the precincts of the Church of England. Then we were done, and Cecil was helped off, clearly exhausted. It was the first church service I'd ever been to that was worth it for the clothes alone, or for the beautiful women, or for the great dancing by the handsome young guy on stage at the end. It was empowering, it was wild, it was sexy, it was full of human warmth and compassion, and it was the first place on my trip where I had felt collective hope.

A different prayer of mine was answered, immediately afterward: The San Francisco 49ers were playing a pre-season game against the New England Patriots at home that afternoon. Surely, I thought, this is a benefit of travel: you see in person, things you would see only on TV. And the 49ers are my team. For me, the only cultural artifact of any value to be created during the eighties was the passing of Joe Montana, the outstretched hands of Rice and Taylor appearing like a miracle from the corner of the TV picture to gather in the ball like a sacrament. Besides, this would make a nice echo: The only other time I'd seen a pro football game was on my previous American road trip, when I saw the British Columbia Lions inflict a rare defeat on the Edmonton Eskimos under lights in Vancouver. At the time it was like an astounding circus: Whenever B.C. scored, a pair of motorcycle cops roared around the running track.

So within two hours I found myself in another building for collective worship: 3Com Park, formerly Candlestick Park, and a very odd and contradictory place it was, too. The blunt, massive concrete ramps and walkways suggested a mass-appeal sport, but the $50 ticket price implied the opposite. The whole place, in fact, rebounded back and forth between these contradictions. The concessions stands offered gourmet junk food. I bought a Gordon Biersch Export Ale and a plate of garlic fries that together cost $10. To my surprise, they were both very good. I had another Biersch just to be sure. The vast, ugly concrete rampways offered Internet access. Forty feet above ground, my beer in one hand, I logged on and got the cricket scores: England had won a historic victory over South Africa. The men's room, on the other hand, offered the curiously old-fashioned opportunity to piss in a sloping trough. I could have been a teenager playing club rugby again, except that the walls were clean.

Game time was approaching. I made my way toward my seat, taking care to obey the injunction not to bring in "cans, noise-makers or hard fruit." The first contest was not a game of football but The Bark In The Park, a series of dog obstacle races. I rubbed my eyes and examined my empty Gordon Biersch plastic cup suspiciously. The public address system informed me that the 49ers cheerleaders, the Gold Rush, would be unveiling, if that's the right word, their all-new uniforms at the home opener. "Stay tuned for this exciting new look." Actually, the cheerleaders looked disappointingly fifties, like the Rockettes. Well, if their role hasn't evolved since the game began, it would be hard to expect their dances to have done so. Maybe the new uniforms would help.

The middle-aged guy in front of me heard my accent and decided to turn around and be helpful. He and his wife were from near Sacramento. They made a 280-mile round trip to see every home game, meeting for drinks before, during, and after the long bus trip. "If you have any questions, ask the mouth," he said, gesturing toward his wife. He repeated the information that the announcer had already given us, that the game would feature no Jerry Rice, and several other 49ers and Patriots were injured or being rested. "It's pre-season," he said. "It's a very experimental game. They try a lot of experiments. Like the British did at Dieppe. Sorry. Couldn't resist that."

The Rolling Stones sang judiciously edited excerpts from "Jumpin' Jack Flash" and "Start Me Up" from the digital scoreboard, a plane flew overhead towing a banner reading "Pizza Orgasmica. We Never Fake It," and the game began.

My instructive neighbor yelled a steady barrage of insults at the field, and took great pleasure in calling one of the 49ers team, whose name sprouted vowels and consonants in unexpected combinations, "Alphabet." "Alphabet, you boob!" he yelled, as the guy dropped the ball.

Tomasz arrived from Los Angeles, smiling wearily as he slogged up the concrete steps, still exhausted and anxious about how few pictures he had of me, and how few good pictures altogether. None of us had realized beforehand how slippery serendipity would be. It was like Heisenberg's Uncertainty Principle: Interesting, random things would happen to me only when I was unobserved. Conversely, when he was with me or racing to catch up with me, his own charmed movement halted, and he lost momentum and energy. Heisenberg squared. After our trip, he decided, he would go back around America on his own, to allow his own serendipity a chance to exert its own curious forces.

We gave up on the game just after half time. I was losing interest—in the game, in my team, in football as a whole—and Tomasz was afraid of losing the evening light, now falling through yellow toward the perfect soft pink. He badly wanted to shoot the city and the Golden Gate Bridge. One problem: He couldn't remember where he'd parked the Skylark.

It was hardly surprising. The complex of parking lots, the size of a small town, had its own strange and dangerous laws of nature. One car, an enormous bronze Cadillac, had sprouted a steer's horns above its radiator grille. By one of the fences, I found a dead cat. Someone had written EX PAT FAN on a Styrofoam fast-food box and stuck the box under the cat's head.

The Skylark, meanwhile, was nowhere to be found. Look, I said, we'll find it much more quickly by car. I'll get my rented car, you look for a few more minutes and then I'll meet you by this exit here. I trotted off to get the little white car, but by the time I'd found it, catastrophe had struck: The game had ended, or, more likely, the game had nearly ended and everyone had decided to bag it and leave. The roads now became a one-way system heading away from the parking lots. There was no way to get back to Tomasz.

What saved us was the sock phone, useful at last. I called him. The phone worked, and he answered. He had found the car and was somewhere in the effluent traffic, but he had virtually no gas left. Okay. I would try to get on ahead and scope out some gas and call him. I crawled out into the northbound traffic, which was going nowhere. I called him again. He was somewhere behind me on 101, but his gas needle was looking up at empty. Okay. I'd go on ahead and listen for his call, and if necessary buy a can of gas and come back to him. I managed to fight free of traffic, barreled into the city, and called him again. He had miraculously found gas. Okay. I'd shoot onward to the bridge and see if it was fogbound, and he'd catch up to me. Five or ten minutes passed at lights and stop signs, then he called me. He had fueled up, but was now lost. As it happened, that didn't matter: At that instant I caught sight of the bridge, which was fogbound. We'd have to shoot the city from some other vantage point. Okay. I'll come back and find you, I said—but I was in three lanes of traffic on 101 heading north, barely 200 yards short of the bridge, with no cross streets and three lanes of traffic coming the other way. I took a deep breath and shot into a U-turn, barely avoiding the far curb and a slew of suddenly furious oncoming cars.

This was getting to be fun. I called Tomasz back. He was still lost, somewhere near Van Ness. I know where you are, I said. Hold on. He called back: He had found himself again and would wait for me at the intersection of Van Ness and Market. I called him back barely a minute later, giddy with the power of the communications age, solely to give him my ETA. Zeroing in, I realized he was headed the wrong way up a one-way street, and called him again. The sock phone was blistering. A minute later I slithered to a halt outside a car wash, and five seconds later Tomasz appeared out of a swirl of traffic to pull up behind me. It was technology's finest hour. We dashed in convoy over to an outcrop known to rock climbers as The Crack Above Castro, jumped over the fence, and hiked up to the top, from where the city lay like a perfect idea in the evening sun.

He found a hotel near Chinatown. Back in Oakland, I found that Maria had had enough of this intrusion. I said my goodbyes, packed up, and hauled myself back into the city and a small hotel where the desk clerk turned out to be from Vermont, another young man setting off to find himself and landing for a while in San Francisco. I was delighted. " 'We haven't seen that spirit here/Since 1969,' " I said, quoting the Eagles' "Hotel California," and he laughed.

As I turned out the light in my room, I realized that for some time I had been hearing a steady roar, like a plane standing on a runway one and a half blocks away. I couldn't figure out which direction it was coming from. It was as if the city itself was idling on full throttle; then it abruptly stopped, whatever it was, and all I heard was half a dozen young men and women laughing on the street under my window.

CHAPTER 19

Fundamentally Nomadic

August 3—San Francisco, California

"Oh, shit," Tomasz said. He and I were heaving ourselves up two of San Francisco's steepest long blocks in search of a trolley—he with 15 pounds of camera equipment; I with my pack, my bad knee threatening to collapse.

He shot Chinatown. He shot trolleys. He shot Fisherman's Wharf, half of which was an area of trinket shops, the other half of which was a working dock, rich with the smell of fish. I wandered off among the boats, where tuna was selling for two dollars a pound. The fishermen, a weathered, unromantic crew, and I discussed the possibility of buying a 15-pound tuna, so that every time I got hungry on the roadside I could grab its tail, whip it out of my pack, and take a nibble. "Sell you some ice," one guy in well-worn yellow waders suggested. Looking for Tomasz, I wandered off the dock through a narrow, dark passageway, a wormhole between the universes of the working America and the leisured America, and found myself surrounded by tourists buying T-shirts and sipping latte.

The morning was heating up, but to Tomasz this meant that the fog might be burning away. He had been hoping to shoot the towers of the Golden Gate Bridge rising out of a sea of fog. We grabbed a taxi whose driver told us that Avis had a drop-off right by my hotel, and now everything was haste: back to the hotels, pack up, haul the pack to the garage, rescue the car, clean it out, drop it off, meet Tomasz who had the Skylark muttering by the curb; race through the small streets that I finally understood, driving like a rally crew, me yelling directions, Tomasz hitting 65 mph between one stop sign and the next, diving onto Lombard and in the distance seeing the bridge still in fog, racing out into its cool dampness, then up the little roads that lead to the Marin headlands, guessing where we'd find the best view, rounding a corner and pulling up hard on the sandy overlook knowing we had arrived.

Clouds from the open sea flowed through the bridge and under it, and died in streamers in the San Francisco Bay. The fog rose and fell, changing all the time in a slow, cold boil. Sometimes we could see the cars on the bridge, sometimes just their lights, sometimes just the supports themselves, floating on a pillow of white cloud. Invisible freighters moaned like whales.

The city was vanishing; the past was closing. You were here, but you are not now, the fog said. In future, any vision of this city you have, looking back, will always be misty and perhaps completely obscured. You can be sure only of the here and now, the tawny hillsides of the headlands in bright sunlight, the boy finding a lizard among the rocks, and the hawk circling above the bay, wingtips raised like fingers, and now even that has come and gone back into the mist.

Tomasz and I split up. He would cut inland to shoot Lake Mono and the high plains of Wyoming, I'd follow the coast to Seattle, and we'd meet at Sturgis. Around 2 p.m. he dropped me off just above Sausalito, in the heart of wealthy Marin County, where the traffic came off 101 to take the coast road, the legendary Highway 1, which I hadn't taken in 1973 and had regretted the choice ever since.

I left even more of my baggage in the trunk of the Skylark. Being out on the road not only provided constant novelty, it taught one to adapt to novelty, to thrive on it. I was feeling more and more drawn to Bruce Chatwin's argument that humans are fundamentally nomadic, and the habit of building houses, then cities, cut us off from a crucial range of experience, eating the foods of the season and the place, moving with the buffalo, so to speak. Who in his right mind would spend winters in Vermont? Or summers in Galveston? Civilization was starting to seem like a massive accumulation of weight, an infernally complicated infrastructure to bring goods to us because we wouldn't go to them, and then another infrastructure to carry our wastes away. I thought of the paintings of Columbus or the conquistadors encountering bronzed, feathery natives, and thought how heavy the Europeans looked, as if their armor were already part of their collective soul.

I looked around for somewhere to stick out my thumb, but I didn't like the look of the place. Two sets of traffic were blending at just the wrong spot; it would be hard for them to see me and dangerous to pull over, and I felt scruffy and out of place among the rich. As always my anxieties were unnecessary. I got one short ride in less than ten minutes, and another within five more—but the second guy, a college student going to camp out with his friends on Mount Tamalpais, apologetically left me where Route 1 winds up into the hills, one skinny lane each way between steep grassy banks, with the eucalyptus hanging right over the road and a blind curve every 30 yards. No shoulder; nowhere to stop except tiny passing bays every so often. I started walking—and in a quarter of an hour met my first hippies.

I wasn't even thumbing, as there was nowhere for drivers to stop. A faded blue VW bus—Oregon plates, a bumper sticker with a picture of Einstein and "Imagination Is More Important Than Knowledge" passed me, the vastly underpowered VW engine clattering like eggbeaters against the side of a mixing bowl. It pulled over at once, but the passing bay was so small, the road so narrow and the grassy bank so high, that I couldn't get in the side door. The driver yelled something and pointed to another bay on the opposite side of the road. He puttered over; I ran after and they let me in.

Or perhaps on. The interior was stacked high with boxes, cases, bags, and bundles; and the only way to settle myself was to squeeze my pack into the last remaining floor space and lie on the bed, raising myself on one elbow and jamming my head sideways against the roof.

They called it the Blue Moon Bus, they being Leilea Satori and Aaron Longshore, both young, skinny, and blonde. The Blue Moon was a vintage 1971 with a 1200 cc engine, Aaron fighting it around every corner, pulling into a passing bay every few miles to let all the traffic pass that had built up behind us. Leilea and Aaron loved the bus, but conceded that it was impractical. They'd broken down in

Santa Cruz and had put in a new generator. "You get up close and personal with your Volkswagen," he said. "But it's such a small engine, it's easy to work on." A Westfalia pop-top, sleeping four, would give them more power and more room, but to a true VW buff, the Westfalia might as well be an RV.

He was from Colorado, she was born in Maui. Both of her parents were hippies. Her father sailed to Maui in 1969, lived there for 18 years as a musician, then moved to the mainland and started selling his paintings on the sidewalk in New York; now he has several galleries exhibiting his work, she said. He encouraged her to do whatever she felt was right for her (which turned out not to include going to college), and so far his advice seemed to be working. Leilea and Aaron had a number of shops on the West Coast that took anything they made and sold it out every week. They'd traveled the mainland, and they'd traveled around Europe and Asia together. They set up their studio on Bali, where they rented a house for $340 for the year. They even had Internet access there. They were modern, global hippies. When in the U.S., they were based in Colorado, but for all practical purposes they were living in the bus, just as Ken Kesey would have recommended. When I told a friend about them later, he said, "They can't be hippies, can they? They're imitations." In a sense the past is past; in a sense, though, it merges with what we think of as the present. That's how we should judge an era: not by its eccentricities, which glow in their own strange light and die, but by what survives.

They took me to Point Reyes, where a shop owner who sold tie-dyes and candles and other such sixties paraphernalia had invited them to stop by. I made them unpack the back of the Blue Moon bus and show their wares: blankets with sun-moon-stars and tropical-island designs, pants with diamonds or fishes or colorful

Chinese characters. I bought trousers for Zoe, Barbara, and me. They didn't have small children's sizes for Maddy. It seemed a good idea to have a little of this color and spirit in my life. I'd wear them when I was writing.

So far I'd made only about 40 miles, but for once it didn't matter. I was ahead of schedule (or so I thought). I could look for adventure instead of looking for a 300-mile ride. A short lift up along the shore of long, slender Tomales Bay with a builder—a Marin County builder, who used environmentally sound building techniques—left me opposite an unpretentious little seafood restaurant called Tony's. A gentle onshore breeze carried the smell of fish and the sound of small ripples collapsing on the beach.

A middle-aged woman and a well-seasoned, white-haired guy appeared from a rough driveway just back up the road. She was carrying a bottle of water, he a bottle of Anchor Steam Ale. "We passed you earlier," she said apologetically, "and felt bad about not picking you up. So when you showed up here, we thought you might be thirsty. Would you like water or beer?"

"Well, that's very kind of you," I said. "I've reached the age when if I drink beer on a hot afternoon, I get a headache, I'd be very grateful for some water."

"By the way," she said, handing me the water, "My name's Jan, and this is Ramblin' Jack Elliott."

Yeah, I thought, and I'm Frank Sinatra. But it was. It was Ramblin' Jack Elliott, the man who learned from Woody Guthrie and carried the portfolio of the American folk music tradition to Bob Dylan and to England, where he inspired Mick Jagger, Keith

Richards, and countless other young would-be musicians to pick up a guitar—including, indirectly, me.

We tracked into their pleasantly unmown yard and sat at a rough picnic table under a tree outside Jack and Jan's little house, which was as ordinary a place as you'll ever find a saddle, lariat, and boots tucked away in a corner, or a Grammy next to the TV. How did you end up in England? I asked, and for the next eight hours he told me some of the chapters of the story of his life.

"I've always been in love with the sea, and a lot of it was nurtured by those articles in the NATIONAL GEOGRAPHIC about sailing around the Horn in various square riggers, and around the world in the schooner *Yankee*. Captain Irving Johnson and his wife Electa made about seven trips around the world. The first *Yankee* and the second *Yankee*, about 92 and 96 feet. Then he had a 55-foot ketch that was built in Holland, and he cruised the canals of Europe in that...."

And there it was, that dock-of-the-bay excitement, the thrill of an inconvenient world not yet Frommered and Hiltoned, when people still went around the Horn instead of taking the red-eye. Jack himself was born Elliot Adnopoz in Brooklyn in 1931, a doctor's son, but somehow that assignment seemed to have been a clerical error: As early as he could remember, he was down at the docks.

"You couldn't go anywhere near the boats without permission, but as a youngster I could slip through. I once went on board a Norwegian liner, the *Oslofjord*, without permission. I just pretended to be delivering something. I went up the gangplank when no one was looking and saw all these gorgeous women. I'd never seen gorgeous women before. They didn't have them in Brooklyn, I guess," he chuckled slyly. "They just sort of strolled around as if they owned the place. Norwegian gals. Come to think of it, [the crew had] just unloaded some interesting cargo, including a boat that looked like a miniature Viking ship...."

Somehow this story got supplanted by the story about the seal that had swum up the culvert behind Jack's house and got stuck. Jack had played and sung to it to keep it calm until the official seal-rescuers arrived and scolded Jack saying, incredibly, that you mustn't sing to seals because they're tone deaf and it upsets them. And from there he told me how he first went to England in 1955, though the story, like all good journeys, started out in the opposite direction.

"I got married, having been traveling around with Woody Guthrie through 1951, '52, '53, '54—four years with Woody. Woody brought me out to California on a trip, with two other musicians, Brew Moore and Billy Faier. Brew was a tenor sax, modern jazz bebop player from Miss'sippi. He was a very cool guy. I didn't know him at all before we started the trip.We were introduced as we were getting into the car with Woody. The person who was driving was Billy Faier, my old banjo-player friend from New Orleans. Woody and I were pretty tight by then. I'd spent the better part of 1951 and '52 with him, and '53 intermittently, and then in '54 we got together to go on this trip. We'd made a trip down to Florida in my Model A Ford, which cost $25. Woody spent $50 fixing it on the way down, so I gave him the car and went on my way hitchhiking.

"I was playing guitar and singing. I let Woody write the songs. He was so good at it. In fact, hanging out with Woody Guthrie has prevented me from learning how to write songs. Him and a bunch of other good songwriters I've had the misfortune of meeting," he said dryly, with the courteous manner and the understated humor of the old-school cowboy. "Guy Clarke, for instance. He's such a great writer, I'm intimidated by him. Bob Dylan followed me around after I came back from Europe. We met visiting Woody in the hospital the day after I got off a ship from Europe. The S.S. *Liberté*. Fifty-five thousand tons. Took about seven days to get across the Atlantic. We were held up the first two days by a storm. I was one of three people who lived on deck through the storm. The 2,000 other passengers stayed in their cabins."

By this point, we had at least two stories going: the trip to England and the trip across country with Woody. "We should probably get back to one of the stories," I said.

"Either that, or use two tape recorders," he suggested. "I usually have two or three stories going at once."

He had a way of ending his sentences with a pause, as if it would just be a second or so before he'd think of something else to say. I began to think of what he was saying as not stories but a story, the story of his life and pretty much everyone else's from that time. The story branched like a road, and branched again, or picked up apparently from nowhere. He was wandering around in the deep background of my life, not even in its shadows but in the adjoining rooms, saying things that struck a distant echo, a name or a song title that I hadn't heard in 30 or 40 years, or things that connected to things that connected to things, and suddenly a small light went on under a door. He had met everybody, and people who had always been just names in the music world— Ewan McColl, Peggy Seeger, Seamus Ennis, Big Bill Broonzy, Donovan, John Mayall—now stepped briefly out into the third dimension and said one thing, or did one thing, and for me would never again lie flat. For what it's worth, this is how the brain grows. We are born with all the neurons we'll ever have; intelligence consists of the connections that grow between them, connections that we encourage to grow simply by curiosity and experience. I had the sense that if I stayed there long enough, everybody would connect up with everybody else and it would all make sense.

I asked Jack if he'd ever ridden freights.

"I rode one freight and I didn't like it at all. It was one of the kind of cars that smart hobos would never ride on. It was an empty boxcar, and they bounce. They go up and down about eight inches at a rapid rate, and it's hard to keep your footing. So I sat on my suitcase. It was a beautiful sunny day in Arkansas. Went from Texarkana to Little Rock, and when the train stopped in Little Rock I got off, never to ride again. I hitched a truck. Got a ride in a truck that was going up through the Ozarks to Missouri. That was the last time I ever rode a freight train. I like trucks," he said wistfully. "When the motor home dies, I want a nice big solid Peterbilt truck. Convert the trailer.

"Four days to California in a new Buick," he went on, back with Woody. "A delivery job: We didn't own that car, we were just delivering it for the owner. Woody disappeared a day after we arrived at Topanga Canyon. He had a restless nature, and he felt ill at ease. I think he felt unwelcome because he'd absconded with someone else's wife, a 21-year-old, rather a pretty girl. Her husband was a big handsome man, looked sort of like Gary Cooper. He was an actor named Dave Marshall. Everybody liked Dave, including myself, but somehow his wife fell in love with Woody, who was a tiny little guy with a lot of hair and a beard, just an old hobo, very sun-dried, very rustic, but very poetic. Very romantic...he stole away and they drove to New York in a Terraplane car....So when Woody disappeared from Topanga Canyon, he hitchhiked all the way across America, and was put in a hospital in New Jersey, and he spent the next 13 years just gradually wasting away. Terrible disease.

"After he disappeared, I met June, who was destined to become my wife. We fell in love, we got married in June, and we bought a ticket to go to England."

"Why?"

"NATIONAL GEOGRAPHIC! June was raised on NATIONAL GEO-GRAPHIC too. She became an actress, and traveled all round the country on a truck. She was the navigator. She always wanted to see things...."

I was amazed. The story had linked up—three of the stories had linked up, in fact—but only after touching on a dozen other stories that cried out to be told, and probably would before nightfall.

Jan brought out a guitar, an Epiphone. It was hers; not surprisingly, her own musical career had fallen into the shadow of Jack's, and now she was his fiancée/manager. "When I was a young guitar player," she said, "I went to one of his concerts in 1980 and he said, 'Would you like to run away with me?' I said, 'Can I go home and get my toothbrush and my guitar?' and he said 'No, I'm in a hurry.' So I moped around Los Angeles for six months playing Ramblin' Jack Elliott songs....We got together about six years ago, up here. I thought I was losing my mind. I was working for a newspaper in Sausalito, and I was looking out of a window one night—I'd been working a double shift, 12- and 13-hour days—and, God, I see Ramblin' Jack Elliott looking in through the window at three o'clock in the morning. He was at the ship-yard, 50 yards away from my office, visiting friends, and they set us up on a blind date...."

I had been waiting the whole trip for someone to bring out a guitar. Jack asked me why I hadn't brought my own. I told him I thought nobody would know the songs I sing any more, and felt rather sad about it. Now I had ended up with people who knew almost every song ever written.

We had sung several of them by the time word arrived that Dave and Tamara, neighbors of Jan and Jack's who had built their own trimaran, had sail up, and Jan drove us in the old, old Volvo half a mile to the dock, Jack telling me how at 15 he ran away from Brooklyn ("no place for a cowboy") and joined the rodeo for two dollars a day, slept three feet away from the horses' tails, and learned guitar from the rodeo clown....And somehow that slid into the story of singing the "Mule-Skinner Blues" and other slightly risqué songs at a command performance for Princess Margaret and a hundred of the hipper young members of the British aristocracy.

Dave and Tamara sold organic wine, which we drank along with cheese and crackers, and more stories. Dave, who had a long, bushy, graying beard and the gentleness that often grows in people who work carefully with their hands, had built the trimaran over 15 years; it had been in the water barely a month. The rest of the crew were Jan and Jack's "car czar," Chris, who restored antique wooden speedboats and their engines, Chris's mother Daphne and his daughter Jesse, who at twelve said "I'm working on a equestrian career."

As the sun went down the water was suddenly full of hundreds of medusas, pulsing alongside like small aquatic ghosts, and it was at this point, while it was being generally agreed that swimming was not recommended in Tomales Bay, someone added that the mouth of the bay is one of the West Coast breeding grounds for the Great White Shark. "Remember Tony's," someone asked me, "where you were hitching opposite? Someone caught a 15-footer off their pier a few years ago."

"Ready about!" called Dave.

We picked up an Irish friend of everyone's, who had restored a boat and planned to sail to South America, a born storyteller, roaring with laughter at his own tales, and all the while the three-quarter silver moon rose higher and higher above the bay, above the peninsula where Jesse Colin Young of the Youngbloods had his house before it burned down in a fire that left the whole hillside bald. This was exactly my 1973 feeling, that I could scarcely believe what was happening and felt as if I was constantly blinking in stunned amazement, that all I could do was just grin foolishly and be grateful. The weather was part of this experience, too: The brilliant light and warmth created a haze that was not a haze, just an overflowing of sensations. The impossible was happening. My job was simply to be open to it.

Jack said he wanted to write his memoirs, but he was having trouble, not because of his memory, which was extraordinarily precise, but because one story just sort of rambled off in any three other directions. Later, when people asked me if there was anywhere on my trip I wished I could stay, the only place I was really tempted was Marshall, so I could hang out with Jack and help him write his memoirs, go for a sail every so often, and acquire a taste for Jim Beam.

CHAPTER 20

An Overlapping Assortment of Fantasies

August 4—Marshall, California

The following morning Jack drove me in his motor home— it was like being in a furry brown box—up to Bodega Bay, where *The Birds* was filmed. I wouldn't have recognized the place, but then I barely recognized San Francisco; I must start thinking of memory as being entertaining rather than useful. He told me stories about a fennel forest and a nude beach, about his friends the boatbuilders who seemed to sprout in every crack and cranny of the coastline, and of how he got his limp, which was not an old rodeo accident but, of all things, a skateboarding injury. He dropped me off at a nice straight stretch—a rarity on the coast road—outside a horse ranch, and we wished each other well. I gave him my Union Jack. He seemed touched. "England's been very good to me," he said.

After 20 minutes of watching hawks circle on the updraft from the cliffs, I got picked up by a tall, lean surfer in a wetsuit driving a venerable faded blue VW bus, who was going a few miles up to Salmon Creek. As the beach wound into view we could see surfers in the morning mist. "Gnarly waves!" he cried. The mist was a good sign, he said: the waves get sloppy when the wind picks up.

Five minutes later I got a ride almost all the way to Seattle.

His name was Jay, and he was driving a new Nissan Pathfinder that was, as they say, loaded. Digital thermometer and compass. Global Positioning System (GPS) that told him the heading and distance to any destination he punched in. He was, by all appearances, an American success story: He had retired at 36, had bought himself a boat and a motor home and the Pathfinder and the GPS, had taken up scuba diving, and now he was just tooling around, doing whatever he pleased.

In late 1990, he said, five friends and he, with no money, founded Wizards of the Coast. "We didn't even have a business plan, just six people in the basement of a house." The company designed and sold games, role-playing games. They were, in a sense, professional fantasists. In July 1993, their game Magic: The Gathering was released. "We hocked ourselves to the eyeballs to do Magic. By July '97 sales in 52 countries were well over $100 million a year. We had 500 employees, four overseas offices, the product was being made in ten languages, and the rulebook was being printed in 30 languages. There are Magic leagues, and a professional tour," not to mention one and a half million a year in prize money for seniors and scholarship money for under-18s.

I was immediately a little defensive. It's hard to be a financial failure in America, especially if you're sitting next to someone rich; and although I was eight years older than Jay, I instinctively felt somehow his junior, and started asking him groveling questions about his philosophy of life, as if I were writing for a money magazine.

The road started rising up the cliffs in a series of hairpins. "By the way," he threw over his shoulder to reassure me, "I am a graduate of a number of professional driving schools." Before he got rich, in fact, he was a limo driver. Once, he said, he did a 360 at 40 mph. on a freeway in fog, and managed to keep control of the car. "The client thought it was cool. He wanted to tip me 50 bucks to do it again." The Pacific was invisible, unfortunately, behind a fogbank that hugged the foot of the cliffs. Still, it was one of the most beautiful roads I traveled, skimming the line of the cliffs and then darting inland through groves of pine or eucalyptus, rising and falling as it crossed the innumerable small streams headed for the ocean, surprising a small coastal town and then dodging back into the woods again.

"Why don't you pick out a CD?" he asked, passing me what looked like a thick floppy photograph album. I opened it up. It was a CD book. I had never seen so many CDs in one place outside a record store in my life. They were almost all of music 20 years old: The Beatles, Led Zeppelin, Jethro Tull, Billy Joel; various heavy metal bands whose music I didn't know but whose names I associated with violent pain behind the eyes; Enya (presumably as an antidote) and, of course, Pink Floyd. There was no question. If he had a sound system this good, we were going to listen to *The Dark Side of the Moon*—an album that dates back to 1973 but is still selling several thousand copies a week. I play a couple of the tracks on my guitar, and for some time my daughter's favorite rock song was "Money," which she could name at the age of four from the ringing of the first cash register.

No road trip is complete without a soundtrack. One of my most vivid memories of 1973 is gliding through the cool, dim evergreen forests of the Rockies, while on the eight-track stereo Paul Horn played flute runs into the perfect echo of the Taj Mahal. People stuck in a car together who otherwise have virtually nothing in common can be united simply by listening to the same music—or other shared cultural artifacts. The following day we spent half an hour quizzing each other on Star Trek: Who was the only actor to play four different species in the original TV series? Popular culture is an overlapping assortment of fantasies, some spontaneous, some cultivated. And music can become both the journey and the inhabited space. After a while I stopped seeing the passing landscape, as the music itself had become the scenery.

In a surprisingly literal way. Hearing is, in fact, a specialized form of touch: What we take in are vibrations that strike us in different ways. Jay's was such a good system that after he cranked the volume up more than halfway, the sound didn't seem to get any louder, just more powerful. Every bass note kicked me in the back. Instead of coming out of the speakers, the sound seemed to exist everywhere in the air, and I found myself in the middle of it, each sound having virtually a solid presence and color that nudged me or slid past. It was like swimming among a school of whales. I heard features of composition or orchestration I'd never noticed before. "Look," Jay said, pointing. With each kick from the bass, the rearview mirror twitched. As a teenager I was too self-conscious to be a head-banger, but now I was screaming with the guitar solos, and by the time we reached Fort Bragg, shivers were running from my neck all the way down my legs. "Damn, this is strong stuff!" I yelled to Jay, who nodded happily.

After a while I started to notice that Jay's depiction of himself, as the Man Who Got Rich and Retired Young, was wearing a little thin here and there. For one thing, he had a curious neck-and-shoulder twitch. At first it made me uneasy. We English are taught that it is rude to stare, but in not saying anything about it I couldn't stop looking at it, and looking at it I couldn't help wondering if this was actually a sign of deep-rooted mental illness, and at any moment he might leap across the seat and try to brain me with his GPS. The Bachelard Principle was at work. After a while I started to get annoyed at my own hand-wringing, and asked him about it. He was quite open: He'd been in an accident, and some of the nerve tissue had been damaged. As a result, nerve impulses would fire unpredictably and cause the twitch. It didn't hurt, and he didn't even know it was happening, most of the time. *Pouf!* as they say in France. Another anxiety gone.

All the same, I liked these qualities, which made him more human, more like someone I could travel with. We cut inland through the coastal forest, and by the time we hit Route 101, which runs up through the redwoods, the digital temperature had risen from 59 degrees to 106. Jay had a map that identified dozens of trees that should be visited by any fan of tree giantism, and we started off as if he meant to see all of them. We drove through the Drive-through Tree—officially, the 315-foot Chandelier Tree, thanks to the elbowlike angularity of its branches. We visited huge trees lying down with houses in them and standing up with gift shops in them. There seemed to be no indignity that had not been visited on the silent giants, all of which had to be given names and identities that made them something other than trees. No commodification without representation. Luckily, Jay's determination to obey the guidebook began to flag, and at last I persuaded him to get out of there and head north. Long after dark we hit Coos Bay, Oregon, whose principal feature for me was the cheapest motel room to date: $27.82, and not a roach in sight.

CHAPTER 21

Trodden by Rogues

August 5—Coos Bay, Oregon

At Tillamook, Oregon, which boasted not one but two cheese factories, we went wine tasting. A just-for-show wine bar had been set up at one end of the specialty-products salesroom, and a wealthy blonde sipped from a wineglass with the corners of her mouth down. For a couple of bucks we could sample the local vintages—or rather I could, Jay still being the professional driver. This was clearly to be my next book: *The Hitchhiker's Guide to the Wines of Oregon.*

First, a Secret House White Pinot Noir, which struck me as slightly puppyish and eager to please, but light and fruity. For the hitchhiker, an ideal traveling wine, full of the possibility of getting a hundred-mile ride with a blond cellist in a VW Rabbit convertible.

Next, an Elk Cove '95 Chardonnay, fermented (I'm told) in small oak barrels. Dry and crisp, and existentially rigorous—a wine that knows its place in an uncertain universe. A good wine for a long wait by the road on a cool, windy day with the possibility of rain.

On to the reds. I picked out a Rogue Valley Ashland '95 Merlot, not on the strength of its silver medal or its 87 points in the *Wine Spectator*, but because I liked the sound of Rogue Valley, and grapes trodden by rogues. The wine was dry, inky, and unremarkable, but worst of all it was clearly bad headache material. The thought of hitching at 2 p.m. on a hot afternoon after a bottle of Rogue Valley sent a shudder up my spine. I once hitched west across England after an all-night party where I drank a pint (Imperial, not American) of scotch and ate fried egg sandwiches for breakfast, and I could barely keep my eyes open, let alone my thumb up. I ended up catching a bus the last dozen miles, fell asleep, walked off the bus in Worcester still asleep, and woke up standing in the middle of traffic. That's how hitchhikers get killed.

Finally, dessert wines, at an extra 50 cents per sample. I chose the Hood River Marionberry—19 percent alcohol by volume—solely because I'd never heard of marionberries, or salmonberries for that matter, until the previous day. A port-style wine, said our hostess, making me think fondly of Steinbeck's winos drinking port at Monterey and Brautigan's winos drinking port in San Francisco. The wine came out of the fridge in a long, thin bottle that suggested a seasoned olive oil. This wine can be kept for a year after opening, the hostess added, which should have tipped me off. I sipped. Blood and sand! This stuff was death on wheels! Now I knew why winos drink port: One sip of this, and you can chew on it for days. I could imagine having half a glass of this and waking up seven hours later in a police station with perfect little caps on all of my teeth, made of pink crystallized sugar.

By now I was feeling merry and thoroughly irresponsible, so I bought a packet of salmon jerky because I couldn't imagine what it might taste like, and we rollicked up the highway into the next cheese factory, where the cheese curd was nice. The medium cheddar was nice. The colby jack was nice. The jalapeno pepper jack was nice. I had reached the West Coast, and my cheese trek was over.

Jay asked if I wanted to stay at his place in Tacoma for a few days, or go on to Seattle. I was looking forward to Seattle, partly because I would be able to stay with my first wife, Gail, and her family, but also because of Seattle was another place where I'd had almost a visionary experience in 1973.

We'd spent two days in the city, getting drunk, sightseeing and crashing at the apartment of a girl who stayed up literally all night arguing that Richard Nixon was insane, with the unflagging fervor of someone who herself is completely nuts. When we arrived at the docks, bleary and exhausted, to take the early morning ferry to Vancouver Island, the waterfront was lost in fog. After a few minutes the ferry honked and pulled away from the jetty, and I gradually became aware that everyone on board had stood up and was looking toward the stern, pointing in a concerted fashion that suggested something more than saying farewell to dogs and loved ones. I struggled to my feet and looked back at the docks.

The mist had cleared just enough for the summit of Mount Rainier to appear above the city, an eerie silver-white in the morning sun. Somehow I had managed to be in Seattle for nearly two days without seeing this huge, ghostly, brilliant mountain, apparently floating in midair ten miles, or perhaps a thousand miles away. I left Seattle staring, my mouth open.

When I told Jay I'd prefer to head on right away, he seemed deflated. For all his talk of successful retirement, he seemed lost; he had defined success by work, and he was no longer working. He was divorced ("We got married too young, too quickly, for the wrong reasons, and we didn't work hard enough at it"), but he seemed to miss his marriage, and his former stepdaughter. Since then, he had had a difficult time with women: His uncomplicated background and his all-too-visible money were at odds with each other, and at least once he had been strung along by a woman more in love with the money than the man. Sometimes, he said, he thought of giving away everything he had and going back to some blue-collar job in which he felt more at home. It can't be easy, I thought, to be a fantasist, but no longer a wizard.

We crossed the endless Columbia bridge at Astoria, the Shell station at one end offering little booklets on how to escape from a vehicle that has plunged into deep water, and wound through the river flats and marshes. Jay pointed out espresso stands even in the tiniest damp villages, a sure sign we were nearing Seattle.

As we got closer to Tacoma, slicing through darker and darker woods—where signs by Weyerhauser proudly announced the company's replantings, though were oddly silent about the clear-cuttings that had taken place first—Jay talked more about his house, which had been on the market for nearly a million but which he and his friend Emiel had bought for a quarter of that by shrewd businessmanship. With all the renovations they'd done, it was probably worth $750,000, he said. View of the Puget Sound. Pool room. Games room. Tennis court. Hot tub...He invited me to stay a day, a couple of days. Much as I like playing pool, I couldn't see myself staying: I get uneasy lounging with the rich, and start to feel like a poodle.

The house was as remarkable as he had promised: hardwood floors, cathedral ceilings, deck overlooking the sound. What I hadn't expected was that a band would be cutting a CD in the basement. Kareem, Emiel's younger brother, played sax, and he had hired some local pros to back him up on a selection of his tunes. We tiptoed across the shag carpet, decided to forgo the pool table because of the noise, and ended up with little more than a guided tour and a beer. It was a strange homecoming, in a way: The only part of the house that really seemed to reflect Jay was down in the games room, where he showed me his collection of fantasy-game pieces, not toy soldiers but gorgons and knights and dragons and a whole medieval bestiary, the children of J.R.R. Tolkien.

Kareem and Emiel's mother, who also shared the house, lit the gas fire, the blue flames playing over authentic-looking logs. Kareem finally finished, and reappeared, saying he was pleased, that those guys were really good. Emiel, his brother, had not appeared, apparently still closeted in his room. You should meet him, they said. Emiel's a trip. He owns a .50 magnum Desert Eagle, Jay said, one of those enormous handguns that will stop a horse. Emiel came downstairs and lay down in front of the fire, shirt off, his young body already a little soft from good living. We were introduced.

"I'm curious," he said. "I can't understand the appeal of hitch-hiking. Whenever I travel I go by limo and stay in five-star hotels."

"The problem with that kind of travel," I said, "is that you're never vulnerable."

His eyebrows went up. "Why should I want to be vulnerable?"

"Because otherwise you'll never feel grateful for anything. You've got to make yourself vulnerable before you need something from someone else, and you've got to need something before you can feel gratitude. And unless you allow yourself to be vulnerable, you never have any chance encounters. All the most remarkable people I've met on this trip, I've met by chance."

On consideration he was willing to see the appeal, he said, but he wasn't going to try it any time soon.

He talked blandly about the hurdles involved in opening a casino through a loophole in state law, claimed with a smile that he wasn't afraid of "illegitimate competition"—my euphemism for organized crime—and said he'd always wanted to be in the hospitality business. This struck me as an odd way to describe gambling, which in the next breath he described as "pardon my French, a license to steal."

When he heard I needed to get to Seattle, then to Sturgis as quickly as possible, he swung into the persona of the connected man. He was going into Seattle on business in the morning, he said, so he could take me. And as for Sturgis, he had a friend who owned a plane. And he'd fly me there? I asked, astounded. "He'll do it if I ask him," Emiel said. "I'll make a call."

CHAPTER 22

The Last Don

August 6—Tacoma, Washington

Around 8:30 Emiel drifted downstairs, looking pale, puffy, and fragile. He ate breakfast: coffee and two Pepperidge Farm Selection de Choix cookies from a newly opened box, like a dealer working with a new deck. He disappeared upstairs to shower and dress, and Kareem—lean and eager, young but disciplined—told me about learning from Joshua Redman and Wayne Shorter, Miles Davis and Cannonball Adderly and others whose names I recognized but don't know. He's learned that the important thing is to take something from all kinds of music but to remain himself, he said. He was 19.

Emiel reappeared. "The last don!" Kareem cried. Emiel was dressed for Coppola, wearing a dark-blue suit with a black shirt in the Italian fashion, shades, the beginnings of a goatee. He gave Kareem orders as if talking to the houseboy—do this, clean up that—and then it was time to go. I was expecting a BMW or a

Porsche, but no, Emiel had gone all the way: a brand new Cadillac Eldorado, the sporty model, tinted windows and all. He laid my pack in the open trunk on top of a pump-action shotgun and a saber in a studded leather scabbard. He let the trunk lid fall gently, and it paused a half-inch open as if to show that it could close itself better than any human could, settling with a faint sigh and clicking shut.

We pulled onto the road and at once Emiel was on the phone, setting up a meeting. "Welcome to my life," he moaned when he had finished. "Without a cell phone, a comfortable car, and a pager I'd be a dead man."

He cataloged his real estate interests: he owned several duplexes, and the house in Tacoma....Wait a minute, I said. I thought you and Jay bought it together? He shook his head bluntly. "Jay's money is as good as anyone else's," he said, "but he pays me rent." I felt more sorry for Jay than ever. To think yourself a successful young entrepreneur, and then to wind up living with someone younger and arguably even more successful?

Emiel's last few building purchases had all been of that no-money-down kind I've never understood, with the seller picking up the closing costs. He got into real estate by meeting a mortgage broker, the father of an ex-girlfriend ("dumped the girl, kept the father"), and together with a realtor they formed what he called "a dastardly trio," with him as the finagler and wheeler-dealer. Now they were trying to raise two million to exploit a loophole in the local laws and open a casino, the first in Tacoma. Hell, why not make a quick detour? And he took me to see his palace-to-be, a nice slim four-story brick building on Broadway, across from the theater (convenient for the after-the-show crowd) and a small park (aesthetic and therefore classy). He imagined a New York-style awning out front with a small tree on each side. He wanted to attract an older, more affluent, more respectable crowd than most casinos—which would make him not only a good neighbor in Tacoma but also a guilt-free one. "I don't want people to be spending their welfare checks. I want people who can lose $500 or $1,000 and it's play money. I don't feel bad about skimming the rich."

Then he was back on the phone, talking to a business broker of some kind about the business plan. "You're hired. I'll pay you up front. Check? Hell, I'll give you cash."

He hung up. "I'm having to do a lot of fancy dance steps," he told me. "All I have at the moment is an idea, and to get people to put up two million for this idea is hard to do, especially if you're 21 years old." To illustrate the point, he picked up his business proposal from the floor of the car and flipped it open. The first four pages were devoted to brief biographies and photos of the major players involved. Aha, I said, noticing that many of the faces, even those who looked like bit players, exuded the gravitas and respectability of prosperous middle age. "Exactly," he said. "I'm not stupid."

Something about this reminded me that he had forgotten to follow up on the promise to get me flown across the Cascades. He called his friend Mike and left a message.

Most people's problem is that they don't know how to handle money, he said, and they're afraid of it. His father, he said, though coming from one of the wealthiest families in Iraq, worked as a mechanic all his life making $35,000 a year. Emiel didn't want any part of that. "I hooked up with a bunch of Italians at a very young age, and they taught me how to live good." He grinned. "I tell people I'm Arabic by birth but Italian by choice."

By now we were at Pike Place Market. Emiel hauled my pack out of the trunk, dodged an invitation to explain the shotgun and the sword, promised to follow up on the plane business, shook my hand with genuine warmth, and then, getting back into the car, found he'd been hedged in by the cars behind him. As I hoisted my pack onto one shoulder, I imagined him fuming impatiently behind the tinted glass, and gave him an extra wave. Emiel's either going to go through a cycle of making it and going broke, making it and going broke, said his mother, or he's going to really make it. I've got to do this trip again in ten years' time to see what happens to all these characters, I thought, even if I'm in a wheelchair.

Six weeks later I e-mailed him, half-expecting his "godfather" e-mail address to be a joke. But Emiel is nothing if not serious: He e-mailed me back saying he had his money. Construction would begin in nine months.

At the entrance to the Pike Place Market was the fish stand, fronted by a chunky, aproned guy with a magnificent whisky mustache.

"Clean 'em up, head on!" he yelled to the crew behind the counter, flinging a couple of large fish across the counter.

"Clean 'em up, head on!" they chorused back as the nearest guy caught the fish neatly in waxed paper and wrapped them.

A tall, skinny African-American cyclist with a shaved head, wearing shades, bike shorts, black and yellow sneakers, and an Alcatraz Swim Team sweatshirt, inquired about the smoked salmon. Mustache pointed them out to him, and yelled, "Jail-bird's looking at the smoked!" to alert his colleagues. I decided to take some dinner home to Gail, who had offered me a couch for the night.

"Two pounds king filet!" he called, hurling my fish across Seattle.

"Two pounds king filet!" they called back in unison, catching, cutting, and wrapping. I walked around the cases, admiring rows of crab, an avalanche of shrimp, and a migration of lobsters across the chipped ice, when I heard his voice again, right behind me.

"Three tilapia!"

"Three tilapia!"

I ducked as the fish flew one after another past my right ear.

I found Gail in a small, sunny house in a settled-looking neighborhood of bungalows up on Queen Anne Hill, with plenty of trees, the houses themselves all slightly different, sprouting gables and porches, the sidewalk grass dug up here and there in favor of tiny box-gardens, with pumpkins, rosemary, sage, peas, and tomatoes. Her house was full of light and healthy plants. Two kittens lay asleep in a basket, their paws around each other's necks. Gail and her husband Hal owned an old Mercedes. I was shocked. I thought that anyone who knew me was condemned to a life of poverty.

Gail and I have been in regular contact over the years, and we've formed a collective identity beyond marriage: I think of her as something like a cousin, or perhaps a sister who has gone out to make her way in a different part of the world. She has decided that having been married gives us the right to be honest with each other, and if that had been the only outcome of the marriage, it would have been worthwhile.

Talking about our marriage and my trip, and how things had changed between one and the other, it was only natural that we should come around to the issue of parenthood, and how being a responsible parent affects our freedom and our bravery. When I first knew Gail she had worked in jails as a paralegal, she was becoming a fearless investigative reporter, she had stood up to the Special Branch in London while they smashed everything in her boyfriend the anarchist's flat. Now her priorities were more domestic. Over the clatter of the salad spinner and the percussion of chopping vegetables, she talked of caring for two children in a school system that seemed to be leaderless and vulnerable to copycat crimes. Whether by coincidence or some deep repercussion of a constant, low-level anxiety, she had developed a fear of heights.

Her daughter Gabrielle, she said "is now coming into her fear and vulnerability as a female, in middle school and as a preadolescent. I'm trying to figure out how to help her stay secure and strong. I don't want fear to dictate to her in ways that are destructive, but at the same time I want her to be smart and savvy, which involves a certain exposure to risk. She's asking to watch *Scream 2*, and I'm saying, 'I don't think that's going to help with this issue!' But I think there's a real appeal for girls to watch that stuff because it validates their fears."

She told me a story about a friend of ours named Alice, back in Vermont, a woman with a strong spiritual grounding. "Alice took me to this waterfall," Gail said, "and I asked her if there was anything she wished she had done differently in bringing up her children. She said she wished that early on she had made it clear to them that whatever happened, they were safe. I said 'What do you mean by that?' She said, 'We're all spirits. We're all safe.' That's what it comes down to with Gabrielle. When we play out 'What's the worst that can happen?' we realize that our spirits are always safe. And when Gabrielle looks at things this way, she suddenly feels this enormous inner strength. If you can't do that, you've lost this incredible potential and your reason for being here."

I'd have liked to stay for a couple of days, but it turned out that Jason, the trucker who had recommended I see the Harley rally at Sturgis, had got his dates wrong: the rally ended on August 9. If I didn't leave at once, I'd miss it all—and even now I'd have to cover a thousand miles, a third of the country, in two days, three at the most.

I'd already set up a ride in the cab of a train going east through the Canadian Rockies, and planned to hitch down from Calgary, but now there just wasn't time. I'd have to cut due east and miss western Canada altogether. Which was a pity, because I'd seen little enough of it last time across. After a terrible time on the Trans-Canada Highway in British Columbia, stuck for five hours at a place called Hope, where the slipstream of a semi knocked over and cracked my guitar, we cut south and crept along just above the border. That night, riding in a VW bus owned by a forest ranger who had fallen asleep in the back leaving Richard to drive, I saw one of the most bizarre and frightening sights I've seen. It was well after midnight. We had passed through a small town called Trail and made a right turn by a wheat field when the headlights picked up a post of some kind, perhaps 12 feet tall, just ahead on our right. Whatever was at the top of the post—a sign, presumably— was wrapped in some kind of sacking. Richard started to pick up speed as we approached this pole. It was a slightly odd sight, in an odd place, serving no apparent purpose, and without saying anything we both looked up at it as we got nearer. Just as we passed it, the sacking moved slightly and an arm reached out.

We stared at each other. "Did you see that?" I asked, and Richard nodded, looking white. We said nothing else about it. Nothing would have made us turn round to find out what it was.

The following evening we made it to Calgary and called Ben van de Maele, the farmer, and he said, "Season's starting early, boys. Be here by the first of the month." That was four days away. By our calculations, we needed to make 550 miles a day.

After a sleepless night in the youth hostel, where we shared a stifling bunker of a dormitory with a dozen other guys including the loudest snorer I've ever heard, we were on the Trans Canada at 6 a.m. We made 600 miles the first day, crashing on the floor with some Yorkton kids who insisted on staying up until 3 a.m., drinking and smoking dope, then another 600 miles (including a drenching in Thunder Bay) on the second day; but late on the third, we got stuck at Marathon, Ontario, with 800 miles still to go and nothing in town but a rail junction—closed by a strike— and a gas station. Then a pickup pulled in for gas. Yeah, he'd take us. Where was he going? London, Ontario—right down the road from the tobacco fields. He drove all night and all the next day, and I rode those 900 miles or so sitting in a tire in the back, my own built-in suspension. We got one last ride from Port Burwell (pop. 600) right to Ben's farm, arriving just as the sun went down.

These are the stories hitchhikers tell to each other, reminding ourselves that we once had daring, and that we once found adventure and kindness wherever we went, as if those were the reward for our daring. This was the weird and tragic contradiction of my contemporaries, those I talked to before I left. Given the chance to tell their stories, everyone who had hitchhiked began to soften and melt, to stare away over the horizon and tell me their own epics, eyes glowing, the years falling away, the fire at their core visible, perhaps for the first time in years, telling tales of a lost youth, or the lost youth of a country.

Before I was ready, I was heading back. The idea of backness, of heading East toward the increasingly familiar, depressed me. America would start to repeat itself: I'd start meeting the same people and hearing the same conversations. I was heartily sick of the word Sturgis, and wished I'd never suggested going there.

Only two things kept me going, both of them lessons I'd learned on the trip: a bleak outlook is usually just a sign I'm tired; and whenever I think something will be dull, I'm always wrong.

CHAPTER 23

Idiot A, Idiot B, and the Journey Back East

August 7—Seattle, Washington

Emiel's friend didn't call. There was a bus that went from Seattle through Sturgis, but it was a 29-hour nonstop haul, and I didn't think I could handle that. The following morning, as it happened, Gail and Hal were driving a hundred miles east on I-90 to pick up Gabrielle from camp, so I asked if I could ride with them.

Before we left, Gail took me around Seattle to see what I remembered of it. Virtually nothing. Well, Proust had his blind spots, too, and invented as much as he remembered. Young transients were still drawn to the university, just as Richard and I had been, settling on University Avenue like a small flock of ragged birds: some in dreadlocks, some with piercings, some in Gothic black, some in baggy clothing the colors of dust, hanging out on sidewalks or sitting against walls. They seem so lost, Gail said, and I remembered that Maria had said exactly the same about the young hippies by the freeways around the bay. And our parents probably said just the same about us, all those years ago.

We ended up at Uptown Espresso on Lower Queen Anne Avenue South, Seattle. No Starbucks, this: it had character. Lively chatter on both sides of the serving counter, and their homemade marionberry torte was the best pie I had on the entire continent. Slipping into the local dialect, Gail ordered "a single short wet cap 2 percent."—"If they get it right, they get to keep the change."—I wanted a café au lait, only to discover that Uptown Espresso seemed to have evolved beyond mere coffee. They had reached a quality of life where it was espresso drinks or nothing. I gave in and ordered a cappuccino. She sipped her short wet cap and pronounced it excellent. The trick is to get the foam right, she said. I kidded her that this seemed to me the perfect Seattle remark: We were earnestly discussing something that had style but no substance. No, she argued, but it has texture. Good foam is like velvet.

On the drive east from Seattle, Hal, whom I've never known well and who tends to present the benign cream-of-wheat public face of the professional psychotherapist, began to open up, as if having me dumped on the household was making him revisit his own past. He told us about the commune he had helped to found in Vermont between 1974 and 1977 in a bankrupt girls' summer camp. They lived in the cabins, year round. In the summer it was idyllic, right on the shores of Lake Champlain; in winter it was cold, and they sat around the wood stoves telling stories, playing cards, drinking beer, and getting high. "We had our own paradise, full of energetic, creative people with their own idealism. Anyone who came just stayed because it was so wonderful." Everyone did whatever he or she could—carpentry, farming, cooking—but the collective enterprise evolved, like many other collective enterprises of the time, into an alternative school. This gave the commune purpose and focus, but ultimately destroyed it. Making things up more or less as they went along, they did such a good job with the maladjusted but essentially well-intentioned children of the wealthy that the state started sending them more and more children in state's custody, who had a different set of needs entirely. "We were trying to deal with them based on hippie ideals of togetherness and love and trust, when what they really needed were discipline and locks. That was when I left. I didn't get anything back from my initial investment—it all went to pay off bank loans and debts."

If life in Vermont was an adventure, so was getting there. He was hitching across from the West Coast, making for Hartford, Connecticut, and was picked up in Wyoming by two young guys who turned out to be—or perhaps turned into—robbers. The first inkling of trouble came when they stopped at a topless joint somewhere in the Midwest, where a husband and wife were stripping to music from *The Good, The Bad and The Ugly*. The two young guys got into a fight, and when one of them stormed off to the bathroom, the other grabbed the keys and said, "You'd better come if you're coming, because I'm outta here." Hal went off with him, and after about 15 miles persuaded him to turn round. When they got back to the strip joint, there was his buddy standing outside waiting for him.

Money began to run short. The two had some traveler's checks, but they were headed for New Hampshire, where they planned to live off the checks until they found work or, perhaps, a small rural bank with a geriatric security guard. So they stopped off somewhere in Indiana and robbed a convenience store. One went in and bought beer, using their own money, while the other looked around the place, then they produced a gun and held up the clerk, taking whatever was in the till including their own money. They did this twice while Hal fretted over what he should do. If they were all arrested, he could hardly claim he was just a hitchhiker, and an innocent bystander. On the other hand, he felt a certain responsibility: If he just said, "Drop me off," then these idiots might kill someone sooner or later.

He came up with a fascinating and creative plan. Look, he told the idiots, sooner or later you're going to get caught if you keep holding up convenience stores and gas stations. I know a better way to make the money you need. You (he said to Idiot A, who owned the traveler's checks) give the checks to him (Idiot B, who presumably was sitting with his mouth open wondering what was going on). You (Idiot B) sign them and you both use the money. Then, when we get to Hartford, you (Idiot A) go to the police and tell them your traveler's checks were stolen. They'll see that they were signed by someone else and reimburse you, so you can spend the money now and still have it when you get to New Hampshire.

The idiots thought this was such a good idea (and, apparently, a successful one) that they unanimously elected Hal to be their leader, like a bad *Star Trek* plot, and by the end of the trip they were asking him to make decisions for them—Should we stop here? Should we take this road? Hal went with them as far as southern New England and ended up in Vermont, counseling unmanageable teenagers.

Gail and Hal dropped me off on I-90 in mid-state, feeling as if they were abandoning me to starve in the wilderness. By now, though, the road felt like home. I found myself leaning into the traffic as if this area was my force field, and the cars were passing into it and couldn't help being affected by it.

I was picked up within ten or fifteen minutes by Al Montgomery, a custom builder. A few years previously he and a hired man were working for the U.S.-Canada border commission, clearing a strip of open ground all along the border, the Mason and Dixon of their day. A helicopter would drop them off, they'd work with their chainsaws all day, and their last act would be to cut an open space at the end of the day's strip big enough for the helicopter to land and pick them up again.

Some pretty strange people live right up on the border, he said. One day, he and the hired man were on their lunch break and decided to do a little target practice, shooting off a little bridge that someone had built over a creek. After a few minutes a guy appeared out of the woods and asked them if they'd mind not doing that, as there were children around. Al and his partner immediately obliged, and the man invited them for a drink up to where he lived, which turned out to be a sort of commune, buried in the woods on the border. The newcomers were welcomed into this odd little community, and offered some pot. The hired man accepted; Al declined, feeling there was something strange about the place, wanting to keep his wits about him. He sat with the rifle next to him, while the others lit up.

Looking around, he noticed a newly dug open grave and, next to it, an open copy of Stephen King's *The Dead Zone*. Well, I think we'd better be getting back to work now, he said, picked up the rifle and the hired man and got out of there as quickly as he decently could.

Then another first: I was picked up almost at once by a girl.

Her name was Tove; she had the fresh-air complexion of a skier. Not only was she unafraid to pick me up, she was unafraid to pick me up even though she had all her worldly goods in her Subaru, as she was moving to Mount Hood and then down to Mammoth. No big deal. A lot of my friends hitchhike, she said. She was a true daughter of Title IX: broad-shouldered, self-confident; she looked like someone who could recover from a fall.

The only drawback was that she had to turn off almost at once where 82 split off from 90 and peeled south. I was stuck on the sliver of shoulder between two interstates—never a good spot. After ten minutes of being knocked sideways by the bow wave of every passing truck, certain that I would get hassled by the police, I saw a Washington State Patrol cruiser pulling onto the shoulder toward me. To my surprise, the cop took off his shades and grinned at me. "How're you doing?" he asked.

I had no idea how to answer. I was ready for anything except friendliness. I thought of saying, "Fine until you came along," but that seemed a little churlish, under the circumstances. "Okay," I said cautiously.

"You getting rides?" he asked. Now I was completely off balance, and for want of anything sensible to say, I told him about my trip. He seemed genuinely interested. Almost apologetically, he came round to business. "I guess you got dropped off here by someone going south on 82?" he said sympathetically. I nodded. He took my name down in his log, and I took his—Trooper Mel D. Sterkel—and he allowed as how he'd have to ask me to walk back to the last exit.

"It's one of the best exits around," he said earnestly. "You've got all the traffic coming out of Ellensburg, you've got all the long-haulers...." He sounded like a field reviewer for the *Hitchhiker's Guide to North America*. "Make sure you walk way off to the side," he said in parting. "I want to read that book of yours."

Of course, this meant a two-mile hike over the usual roadside rubble, but even so I wanted to sponsor him for some community policing award. Back in 1973, the police were the enemy.

At the Ellenburg exit, though, the pendulum of police conduct swung back. I was leaning on the sign announcing the entrance to the freeway, and this was apparently too close to trespassing: a jerk in a cruiser coming up the opposite lane screamed something inaudible over the traffic, scowling, making threatening gestures, and pointing back toward the beginning of the ramp. So much for modern policing methods.

I was rescued by Blaine, who had just finished his engineering degree and was working in construction—not a dropout choice but a sound business decision. Housing values in Seattle have gone up 27 percent in the last year, he said, as we passed the strange black river cliffs of the Columbia and then the golden stubble and rippling vanillafudge hills called the Palouse, lying like suede and soft corduroy on the undulating ripples of the land.

He dropped me off at 8 p.m. in Colfax, due south of Spokane. If only I could cover that last 50 miles, I could stay with a friend of Gail's who was writing a book on the Y2K computer threat—but the traffic was failing with the daylight. At the Chevron station across the road, a chubby girl emptied the soapy water from the squeegee tubs and turned out the lights.

CHAPTER 24

Hate Kickin' This Thing out of Cruise Control

August 8—Colfax, Washington

I awoke in Colfax's only motel at 4:30 a.m., anxious to get going, still uneasy from a waking dream: I was back in Vermont again, and Barbara was calling the wife of Redmond O'Hanlon, my favorite travel writer, to ask "Is it always like this?"

"Oh, yes," came the reply, pitched between stoicism and resignation. "He gets home, sleeps for a week, and just when you think he's becoming human again, he says that now he can't wait to start writing about it all, and disappears into his study. You get used to it."

The sun was well up when a teenager pulled over in a pickup, a big old farm boy with fingers like bunches of pink bananas, up early to work on the harvest. Or so I thought: I had to learn again each day that my assumptions about America would always be wrong, as if night healed the gaps that had been torn in the landscape of the mind and it would take the day to break them apart again. Yep, he said, he'd been harvesting all of 'em, wheat, barley, lentils, peas.... Peas? Yes, those were peas on the left there, crawling across the ground rather than climbing up neat little trellises, drying to the same desiccated gold color as wheat and then scooped up and winnowed. Not that he actually knew much about farming; he just drove the truck that took the crop from the combines and drove it down from the fields to the Snake River, where it was floated on barges down to Portland.

So you're not a farm lad, then, I ask, walking into it with my chin out. No, he laughs. All his bulk came not from farm food but from the college weight room: He's a shot-and-discus thrower. He's already got the best discus throw in college this year, and the fifth best in the whole U.S., 211 feet, 5 inches. He hopes to make the Olympic team for Australia in 2000. He's been there already with the U.S. juniors a year ago, he says casually. Give me your name, I say as he drops me off at the Flying J in Post Falls, Idaho, so I can watch out for you. Ian Waltz, he says.

At the Flying J, I asked the manager if she'd make an announcement over the p.a. for me—that I was writing a book about hitchhiking around America, that I needed a ride east on 90. She looked very doubtful, but a couple of truckers standing nearby said sure, why not? Where was I going? Sturgis, I said. Hell, we're going right through there, they said. Just let us grab a bite of breakfast and we'll be on our way.

Over breakfast, unfortunately, they called dispatch (I could have told them this was a bad move) and were told that the principal driver had to be with the company 90 days before they'd let him take a rider, and as he had only 30 days, it was no go.

Still, it might be worth hanging around the truck stop anyway, I thought, and asked a few drivers passing in and out. An ancient, speckled guy with a cane, sitting at a picnic table, told me that the embassy bombings in Kenya and Tanzania the previous day were just the beginning. "A lot of people are sick of the government," he said in disgust. "Soon that'll happen in this country."

"I thought that had already happened in Oklahoma City," I said evenly.

"That was just a little one," he said. "There's going to be a big one."

I gave up on the Flying J, walked across under the interstate, and set up on the bottom of the ramp. After about a quarter of an hour, a well-ridden pickup pulled over, its bed full of storm windows, bicycles, steamer trunks, and all kinds of miscellaneous effects. The driver, who introduced himself as Kevin, was a wild-looking guy in cut-off sweatpants, his blond hair combed back from a receding forehead to fall down over his shoulders, his chest and thighs tattooed, a front tooth missing. He had a curious sidelong look, a cross between a grin and a glower. We threw my pack in among the stuff in back, and as I climbed in I saw two things on my side of the seat: a small, suspicious-looking Dalmatian, who seemed altogether unhappy about having to give up his spot, and a wallet. I handed over the wallet—a great opportunity for a good-faith gesture—and climbed in, the dog turning this way and that to get settled, occasionally digging a claw into my bare thigh.

Kevin spoke in a high-speed mumble, in clusters of words shot out of the corner of his mouth. "Seatbeltsdon'twork," he told me. It took me a second to work out that this was in fact four separate words. "I kinda throw one over my shoulder." He demonstrated, looping the useless belt over his left shoulder and letting it fall down at his side. "Gives the cops something to see."

He had just come from a museum somewhere, he said, selling them a horse-hair bridle. (I thought he said "horse-head bridle"; I had no idea what that was, but he didn't seem to pay much attention to whether I was listening or not anyway.) Two thousand bucks. He'd just sold another one to a different museum, and two to some rich guy for 1,500 apiece. Fifteen thousand bucks so far this year. And he'd only started making them a few months ago. Wow, that sounds like a pretty skilled trade, I said. Where'd you learn that? In jail, he said.

O-kay, I thought. I'm just going to let a suitable amount of time pass before I ask what he was inside for. In the meantime, he was occupied by something else: He inadvertently cut off a woman in a red Mustang, and spent the next ten or twelve miles checking in his mirror to see if she was still behind him. "Jesus," he said, "Maybe I should let her pull up alongside so I can apologize. Shit." I was rather touched by this. For all his wildness, he had an odd, tender streak—actually, he seemed to consist entirely of odd, contradictory streaks. His great-grandfather, he said—and I'm not sure I'd want to try to verify all this, even if I could—donated the land on which Oberlin College was built, and came west with a wagonload of books. Kevin himself seemed to love books. "I got all kinds of books in a foot locker back there," he said, gesturing back toward the bed of the truck. "Longfellow. Whittier. Bibles a foot thick. I gotta Dr. Jekyll an' Mr. Hyde that's so old it hasn't even got a fuckin' date in it." He hadn't read it yet, he said, because he liked just looking at it and feeling the cover.

It was a different ancestor, a grandfather, I think, who came to Yakima, Washington, as a tramp and was treated unkindly by some major figure in town, perhaps the most prominent junkyard owner. "He treated me like dirt," went the family legend. He vowed to break the guy, or die trying, and by the time he died he owned the largest junkyard in central Washington, and his widow became a paper millionaire. Some of this didn't quite add up—if there was so much money, why was his mother working in a Wal-Mart?—but I didn't mind. His parents were divorced, but he clearly adored his mother, and his dad (by which he may have meant his stepfather, I was never sure) often made this trip from Washington to Montana with him. The guy was as deaf as a plank now, and just sat behind his newspaper for the whole trip, "except for one place where he always puts his paper down and just looks at me," Kevin said. "He's sure we're going off the road."

Kevin had been inside, it turned out, for possession of marijuana with intent to sell. "Ten years for possession?" I asked, sympathetically. "Did a year and a half, violated parole, ended up serving nearly six years," he glowered. Actually, he didn't seem to mind: jail had taught him the value of things, he said, though I was never quite clear what values he had learned. He grew up around dope. "My dad had sinsemilla plants seven feet tall, peeking up over the garage," he said. "When he went off to Sturgis one year he said, 'If those plants dry out and die I'll kill you.' By the time he came back they were all lying on the ground from overwatering. I watered them four or five times a day and my sister watered them, too. He'd have killed us if we hadn't."

The road had imperceptibly climbed up to a pass between the Coeur D'Alene mountains on the left and the Bitterroots on the right, and from now on, as they say, it was all downhill. He settled himself in his seat with an expression of grim glee, and set the cruise control on 84. "I used to be a cocaine addict," he said. "Now I'm an adrenaline junkie."

Let me tell you about Montana. Much of the state is wild and beautiful, the interstate running alongside streams and rocky rivers, up between pine-covered mountains and then down to meadows. This section was a genuine mountain pass. On the one side, as Arlo Guthrie sang in "The Motorcycle Song," there was the mountain. On the other side there was nothing.

We wound downhill for several miles, and Kevin passed the time by pointing out how Buddy would've made an amazing surfer, leaning professionally into each turn, and by telling me the story of how his father, who seemed to be a trucker, had not long ago taken a rig, "brand new rig, seven hunnerdnfiftythousand dollar rig, the cab alone was worth a hunnerdnfiftythousand," up over a mountain pass and as soon as he'd started downhill had realized the brakes weren't working properly. Before he was even up to twenny-five, Kevin said, he just opened the door and jumped out. Your heart must've been poundin', Kevin said when his dad told him the story. Not at all, his dad replied calmly. I was just hoping I'd stop tumbling in time to see her go over the edge. And he did: The truck's near-side wheels must have caught in the ditch because she rounded a couple of curves, picking up speed, before breaking free and going over the other side. "Landed in 150 feet of water. They just salvaged the cab. Didn't even bother with the trailer."

So this tale was in the back of my mind as we barreled down into the steepest, tightest curves in the pass. There wasn't much traffic, but every so often Kevin would steam up behind some slowpoke passing some other slowpoke at only 70 or 75, and he'd thump the wheel and say, "Damn! I hate kickin' this thing out of cruise control!"

But there wasn't any traffic worth speaking of when we hit the three curves to end all other curves. The first was a right, so if we flipped we'd just go into the sheer rock face on Kevin's side, which seemed infinitely preferable to me. I braced myself against the g force, and as I was plastered against the door (which, it occurred to me at this very second, was probably in the same shape as the seat belts and might fly open at any pressure), I found Buddy doing the same; his head appeared under my chin.

An insane calm fell over me. At this speed, it didn't matter whether the seat belts worked or not. Everything came down to one roll of the dice. I remembered my friend the psychic, who is always right about the important things, telling me before I left that I wasn't in any danger on this trip, that I was quite safe in cars and with mechanical devices in general; and I thought, *You've just got to let it go.* So I did, and we were around the first bend.

The second bend was a left, the bad kind. The gorge rolled up beneath my window as we hit the curve, the guardrail looking laughable, as flimsy as tin ribbon. For the first time in my life, all the most crucial information in the world—the feel of the road, the grip of the tires—came to me through my buttocks. The truck felt high and loose, the tires impossibly fat and soft. It felt as though the slightest extra pressure, the touch of a toothpick, would flip us over, and then straight over the edge. I realized I was still hanging onto the useless strap of the seat belt. Let it go, I thought. Let it go. Then we were round, and heading back the other way. The third curve, though just as tight, was almost a relief.

"My God!" I breathed, as we straightened out.

"Yeah," he said happily, with his sideways grin. "That's the place where my dad puts down his paper and looks at me. The hard part is, I have to say something to him to show I'm all confident, but I have to turn right round to look at him or else he can't read my fuckin' lips, so I have to stop looking at the road. And meanwhile my heart's pounding. Shit," he added, feeling his chest, "my heart's *still* pounding!"

From then on, he just had time to tell me about his brother being shot—not fatally—by some assholes he threw out of a party, which led to an interesting ethical predicament because he wouldn't give the cops the satisfaction of testifying against the assholes in court. In the end, the assholes copped a plea and ended up doing four and a half years apiece, and we were pulling off the interstate in Missoula, Montana.

I bought him lunch at a chain restaurant. He gave me his card—well, someone else's card, with his name scrawled on the back—so that when I saw his work hanging in some gallery in London next to a Picasso, I could check the name and know that it was his. Oh, yeah...He was struck by a thought, and led me outside to the truck. He rummaged around in the bed, hauled out one trunk, his prison muscles flexing, then another. I thought he was going to show me his beloved books, but he seemed to have forgotten all about them. Instead he threw open the last trunk and produced one of his bridles. It was tightly and expertly woven in what to my untutored eye looked like a series of Navajo designs, tassels on each end, the kind of thing I can readily imagine a rich person wanting to see on a fine horse.

He made a last couple of aslant come-ons to the young waitress, who brushed them off as easily as stray wisps of hair, then he was gone. The place seemed almost unbearably pale and dull without him. I clambered over to the rubble of the work-in-progress interstate exit, where I felt much more at home.

To my amazement, for the first time I had competition. Two hitchhikers, both guys around 20, were already in position; or rather they seemed to have found their position and fallen over it, like a drunken actor looking for his mark. One was sitting on a small, disintegrating vinyl hold-all, surrounded by a raft of plastic one-gallon milk jugs filled to varying degrees with water. The other had given up on verticality and was slumped beside the road—possibly a good move, as it made him less visible, and what there was to see of him was not generally inviting. He was pale and meaty; he had shaved his head; and he was dressed in undershirt, camouflage trousers, and combat boots. Both had large-caliber chains swinging from their pants pockets. They might as well have stuck up a sign saying, "Will Accept Rides Only from Members of White Supremacy Groups."

At first, they put their lack of mobility—it had taken them two days to get a truck ride here from northern Idaho—down to bad luck and other people's fear or hostility, but once we began talking, it became clear that they hadn't a clue about hitchhiking. As soon as they heard how far I'd come, they pressed me for tips. "Well," I said, trying not to sound condescending, "when I'm hitching I never sit down. It makes me look as if I don't care whether I get a ride or not." They nodded and straightened up. How could they not know this? I thought, amazed, but we're at a strange point in history when the idea of hitchhiking has survived but the culture of hitchhiking has not. There was nobody around anymore to set them straight.

We discussed equipment. The senior partner, who was slimmer than his friend and had a buzz-cut, cursed himself for having bought this cheap pack, but at least he'd had the foresight to bring water, he said. This was the half-dozen milk jugs. "I don't know," I said. "I started out carrying water but gave it up. I've never been anywhere yet where I couldn't buy some juice. And all these jugs just make you look messy. You want to look serious about what you're doing."

"Yeah," said the meaty one with surprising bitterness. "When'd you ever see a fat hitchhiker?"

We discussed appearance, and they allowed as how it might be a good idea to put away the chains. They asked me about signs, and whether they should stand facing this way or that way. I asked them if they'd thought of going across the road to the gas station or restaurant and asking for rides. No, this had never occurred to them.

"Where are you trying to get to?" I asked. Alabama, they said. My jaw dropped. The older kid had been visiting his girlfriend, who lived in Idaho, and in a couple of weeks they were going to get married down where he lived. My God, I said, that's the perfect story. Go into that restaurant, over there, where everyone's pulling off the highway for lunch, and tell people you need to make it to Alabama in two weeks for your wedding. Someone's bound to help you out." There was also a Greyhound every day around noon, I told them—it had never occurred to them to take a bus, even though they had money—and it was bound to pull off and stop somewhere around here.

They looked uncertain. They hated this spot, where they had been for four hours, but they hated to give it up. "Okay," I said, "the rules of hitchhiking say that I can't step in front of you, so I'll just go 20 yards farther up." No, no, they said, they wanted a break anyway. I could have their spot; they'd try over at the gas station. We shook hands and wished each other luck. They stumbled off across the rubble. After a few minutes I looked across and saw that they had sat down with their backs to the side wall of the gas station. They didn't go in. They didn't go into the restaurant, either. They seemed to have just given up.

After twenty minutes I was picked up by a young couple—another first for this journey—in a pickup with a cap. He was on his way back from a rodeo; his hobby was steer wrestling.

"Isn't that dangerous?" I asked. Naw, he said in his aw-shucks manner, while his silent girlfriend, sitting between us, leafed through a small horses-for-sale newspaper. "You got a bulldog-ging horse and a hazing horse, one each side of the steer, and you basically get off your horse onto the steer and pull him to the ground." It was his second year, and he was breaking even. In the daytime he worked construction. I had to work hard to get this much out of him, and now he lapsed into silence, a medium in which he was comfortable, and let his girlfriend rest her head on his shoulder. Every so often she would point out a horse, and he'd look at it and smile affectionately at her, and she at him.

They dropped me off shortly before four at a grassy rest area beside a small river, six or seven miles from Garrison. The sun was very hot indeed, and for the first time I was standing on a highway with no speed limit, so half the cars would have needed brake parachutes to stop—but as usual I needn't have been concerned, for within ten minutes I was setting off in a Toyota station wagon heading for Three Forks, at the headwaters of the Missouri. I never learned the driver's name. Each year he set out on his own to follow some of Lewis and Clark's route. He was planning to cycle over some of the mountain passes they crossed, to get some sense of the effort involved.

Around Butte, Montana, the land opened up and dried out into semi-desert. My benefactor had done his own share of hitch-hik-ing, he said, though not in this country: He was in the Peace Corps in Chile from 1968-1971, and anyone would pick you up as long as you didn't mind climbing in the back of the truck or pickup along with whatever or whoever else was in there. He wouldn't do it now. "Thirty years ago I didn't know what I had to lose."

He dropped me off at a little exit in the middle of a broad plain; if it had had corn on each side it could have stood in for Cary Grant's rendezvous with the crop-dusting plane in *North By Northwest*. Almost at once I was picked up by a early middle-aged guy who taught at the university in Bozeman, on his way back from a hiking and climbing trip in Canada. Bozeman was a great little town, he said, a wonderful place to raise children, with a great arts and music festival every summer. And it looked pleasant enough, set in a broad valley between mountain ranges, a leafy spot with a couple from the fire department getting married and running out to the honeymoon fire engine—but the festival had packed every room in town, and just when I was hoping to collapse into a bed, I was out on the highway again, being picked up by a calm, serious young man just out of college who was, I suppose, a traveler himself of a kind, living down by Yellowstone and teaching himself the demanding art of 4" x 5" photography, an Ansel Adams of the future.

I ended up, late in the evening, at Livingston. Outside the Harvey's, a deeply tanned woman wearing a tanktop and peasant skirt, who looked as if she might have been riding a Harley for a few weeks, sat on top of a picnic table with her knee drawn up to her chin, watching the sun set. As I passed her, she lit a cigar.

~

CHAPTER 25

Jeff Bridges Has a Ranch Up Here

August 9—Livingston, Montana

U p and on the ramp by 7 a.m., writing in my journal:
The watchword for the morning is patience. Move calmly. Be here now.

Two mule deer frisk around a junkyard below the interstate ramp, their long tails whisking from side to side.

The sun is in the drivers' eyes. They can barely see me and I can barely see them, with their visors down. I feel no exchange of cheerfulness, no dialogue. By this time yesterday I had already gone 50 miles....No, you can't allow yourself to think like that. Stay in the moment. Look out at the lumber yard below, filling the air with the smell of cut pine. Row upon row, maybe a hundred stacks of plywood sheeting, eight by four foot I expect, a faded cream pickup lurching between them, splashing through puddles as the work day begins. Stacks of weathered pallets, four gray-and-yellow boxcars on a railway siding. Behind them the first ridge of pine-covered mountains, and beyond that the jagged peaks of Yellowstone.

Hitchhiking is starting to look like a spiritual exercise. It fosters patience interspersed with gratitude. It demands faith, hope, and other people's charity, and demands the Buddhist virtues of selflessness and an acceptance of not-knowing. It enforces St. Benedict's principles of poverty, chastity (despite the sexual mythology of the thumb), and obedience— to the rules of the road, and the rules of chance.

I turn the full force of my attention on the cars, and a young guy waves at me with a piece of bread he's chewing.

Minutes later I was picked up by Mike, who was going to Big Timber, another of those vivid and almost hopelessly heroic western town names. He worked for the phone company, he said, but it turned out to be rather more than that. "I'm a farrier—I shoe horses—and I work for the phone company. And I'm a former Mormon bishop. I used to say 'I can shoe your horse, fix your phone, marry you, and bury you,' because I also own a cemetery." He was also a small farmer, with eight head of cattle. "We sell the calves for Christmas money."

I instinctively warmed to this guy. In Vermont, another rural state with almost no major employers, everyone practices this crazy fiscal quilting, patching together an income, no talent unexploited. "If you're making eight or nine dollars an hour in Livingston, you're making good money, and you've got to have a four-wheel-drive in this country."

We cruised on in the quiet, early morning sunlight, following the broad, flat plain of the Yellowstone River, mostly cattle land. "Those mountains over there," Mike said, pointing to a low, barren, angular range away to the left, "are called the Crazy Mountains. Most mountain ranges around here are glaciated, so their ridges and valleys run north to south. The Crazies are volcanic dikes, so their ridges run every which direction." Good hunting up there, he said—ptarmigan, mountain goat, elk, bear— but the fly-fishing was even better, the best in the country. "Tom Brokaw has a ranch on the Boulder River. Jeff Bridges has a ranch up here. Peter Fonda's lived here for 20 years."

We passed a handful of windmills. "This is the third windiest place in the United States. I can remember winds up to 60 miles an hour going across that flat."

He pointed out a sharply pointed mountain on the southern horizon, part of the Beartooth Range running along the top of the Yellowstone National Park. "Big Timber is going to be the home of one of the world's biggest plutonium mines. See the ridge there, with the snow still on it? It's going to be over there. Two hundred jobs. They're going to bring in a big boring machine that'll bore 50 miles through the mountains on a railroad track."

Well, that's what he told me. Afterward I started wondering about the things we tell each other in the confessionals of our own cars, and called the Stillwater Mining Company. Actually the mine is designed to extract palladium, platinum, and rodium; it has two boring machines, the ore is only 18,000 feet into the mountain, and it is expected to create 600 jobs. "Mining," said the mining company's spokesman, "tends to inflame people's imaginations."

But I didn't care whether it was platinum or plutonium or palladium; I liked hearing this man talk about his feeling for this barren, wild country, even if, like most of us, he didn't always get the details right. Like me, he was passionate about trains, and he gestured at the track running alongside the interstate. "Livingston had the biggest rail repair shop west of the Mississippi. Employed about a thousand people. That's what put the town on the map. They did work for the Union Pacific, the Burlington

Northern, the Montana Railroad—they can build a train there. The whole thing. Now they're down to about 200 people. They've got contracts from Germany, Brazil. All of my relatives were railroad people. See the line down there? All those signals are a microwave to Missoula so they can keep track of where the trains are."

Then he was turning off to Big Timber, though I never did find out if he had to fix a phone or shoe a horse. He dropped me off, crossed the interstate, and all traffic at my exit ceased.

It was five minutes before the next car pulled past me onto I-80, and the next was five minutes after that. And this on a day I had to cover nearly 500 miles. I went back to my journal.

Big Timber, maybe. Big traffic, no. Actually, no big timber either, only a few trees along the Yellowstone River, but otherwise grassland, and bare mountains in the distance.

Thinking back to the Flying J in Post Falls and this business of going up to drivers and asking for rides—there's an arm-twisting quality about it I don't like. It changes the emotional equation: the driver may be operating more out of guilt than out of spontaneous generosity, and that isn't always a sound basis for a driving companionship. You're lowering the kindness standard, so you may also be changing the nature of the driver who picks you up. The fact that they're going where you want to go is only one criterion for a good ride.

For me, hitchhiking is a conversation. If the car looks full up, for instance, I acknowledge it by a nod and a wave, they shrug and throw up their hands and grin ruefully and I wave cheerfully to show there are no hard feelings. I greet truckers with something between a wave and a salute, because more often than not, they can't stop: it takes a long time to halt 20,000 pounds, and a lot of diesel to get started again, going up through twenty gears. They give me a signal back, often a more restrained half-wave of the right hand, lifted just off the steering wheel. A salute to the bikers, who always salute back. If I were really cool, I'd give them that bikers' "Further" signal, the index finger pointing up and ahead as if over the horizon. Out here on the bare existential tarmac these are the basic elements of human intercourse.

Just realized it's Sunday. No single guys travelling on business. All families and vacationers.

Patience. In the paddock just south of the exit, three horses toss their tails. In the far distance rise the plutonium mountains, snowy even in August, looking calm and innocent from here.

Should I stay here, or go down onto the interstate itself? The last few yards of the ramp curve to the right. If I walk down it to the highway, neither set of vehicles will see me until the last minute, and both will be at almost full speed. If I stay here at the exit and get only the traffic coming from Big Timber, am I condemning myself to local rides? I can't imagine anyone on a Sunday morning pulling out of this little valley and deciding "Nice day. Reckon I'll make for South Dakota." At 9:30 I'll go down to the freeway.

9:30. Down to the freeway through the long grass, watching for snakes but disturbing only dozens of small grasshoppers.

A new problem: When the traffic's moving very fast, you have to have your arm up so early and so long your shoulder starts to ache. Speed destroys dialogue: we are both just images to each other....

Not a good spot at all. I'll stay here until 10:30, then go back up. You try this, then you try that. Mind you, I don't see any traffic at all coming on at the exit. This is starting to remind me of the Trans-Canada Highway. It's like a zen koan: should you stand beside the road where no traffic will stop, or the road with no traffic at all?

I had barely written this, put my book away in my book pocket, and clicked my pen, when a guy screeched to a stop from 75 mph and took me all the way to Sturgis. The answer to the koan, as to all koans, was to be patient and to trust.

I wasn't going to write anything about this ride—a seven-hour, four-hundred-mile ride—because at the time I thought of the driver as the only guy I met who wasn't interesting. He talked in an expressionless voice I could barely hear; he didn't initiate conversation; he pointed out every KOA (Kampgrounds of America) we passed and his favorite social activity, he said, was singing Neil Diamond songs in a karaoke bar. He told me his name, but I immediately forgot it and never wrote it down. When I described him to my wife, a clinical mental-health counselor, she said "He sounds like that woman, the surgeon with brain damage, we heard on NPR."

This was the clue I had missed. Around Billings he told me that he had served in the military (yet another blue-collar guy who had thumbed home on furlough) in Germany, first "riding at the back of a deuce-and-a-half with an M60," and then as a MP. "I always wanted to be a policeman," he said, which surprised me, coming from this slim, quiet bloke. One dark night a guy he'd previously arrested waited for him in an alley with a metal pipe. He was flown back to hospital in the U.S.; and even though he appeared to recover, he kept suffering from headaches and an inability to concentrate, and his vision was affected for a while. In any event, he couldn't serve as an MP and the Army tried to switch him to a menial desk job, but he hired a lawyer and got himself an honorary medical discharge.

After that, now I come to think of it, he seemed to have lost himself—not entirely, just a little. The pipe had knocked out some of his purpose and direction. He had lived at home in Michigan with his mother, spent several years doing undemanding construction work for a drunken boss, had been dumped by a girlfriend, or a wife, and sang karaoke, even cutting his own karaoke Neil Diamond CD. Then he abruptly decided to see America. I inwardly cheered this; it sounded like a radical act, even a revolutionary one. It was a curious adventure, though: he knew a guy who owned houses in various places all over the map, so he would periodically drive a couple of thousand miles and paint or roof somewhere else, staying in KOA's on the way. He wasn't a hippie: not only did he not have wild and crazy adventures, he didn't seem to want wild and crazy adventures. Yet he was out there on the road—and he had pulled over to pick me up, after all.

We cruised through southeastern Montana, the mild, beautiful grassland rising and falling between the bare hills. No wonder this land could support a hundred million bison. On the southern horizon, there were mountains like the threat of thunder. We drove through Crow lands, the few cheap houses looking dumped in the wilderness as if by government helicopter, as far from white civilization as possible. Before I left home, debate was swirling as to whether Clinton would apologize for slavery on behalf of the American government. Out here in the town lyrically called Crow Agency, it was clear that nobody would ever apologize to the American Indians. If a president accepted responsibility for slavery, he'd face billion-dollar lawsuits for reparation. If he accepted responsibility for the treatment of the Indians, he'd have to hand over the entire bloody country.

And this is bloody country, because this is the site of the Battle of the Little Bighorn. (Monuments to battles where the whites massacred the Indians are, of course, rather less well marked.) Yet it's also heartbreakingly beautiful. The river runs alongside the highway for a while, down on the right, in a valley between the bare hills. Who could have looked down at the grassy meadows and the lush trees clustering on both banks and not seen it as perfect ranching country, imagining a little wooden house down there by the treeline, sheltered from the wind and snow, water at the back door and cattle grazing at the front? And as if to make the point, we passed a large sign: "You're in cow country. Eat Beef."

Across the line into Wyoming, we stopped for lunch at the tiny town of Ranchester, where the only people moving outside on this hot, hot day were the players in the big horseshoe tournament just down from the Silver Spur Bar and Lounge, and a small convoy of bikers coming back west from Sturgis. They were debating whether to turn south and head through the mountains. "There's bears up there, man," said one, shaking his head. "Step out in the road, knock you right off your bike."

We settled back onto the interstate, droning east through country that became progressively flatter and duller. Why did Gillette claim to be the "energy capital of the United States"? "We have, like, 17 coal mines," a lady from the Chamber of Commerce said when I called back later. "We have an awful lot of oil, coal, uranium, that kind of thing." If I had known that, I might not have been fooled by a cloud of smoke that at first, in the distance, I thought was a prairie fire, then a steam train, then a train on fire, but turned out to be a coal train of immense length, with plumes of coal dust blowing off each open wagon. I looked north for the Devil's Tower, but it was too far away, a tiny thumbprint on the horizon. Every few miles we passed a billboard for Wall Drug, the drugstore in Wall, South Dakota, that, in 1936, was the first eatery to serve that most American of drinks—free ice water. It now occupies an entire block.

I finally roused myself out of my stupor and asked him about the culture of karaoke, and whether his mouthing Neil Diamond really turned women on. Without changing his mild demeanor, he moved into a different gear. Sure, he said. He was propositioned all the time. Something about him made me decide he was incapable of lying, or even of boasting. This led to other stories, and then he was back in his youth, before the accident.

He got his first job, cleaning up a topless bar in Indianapolis, when he was 17, he said. He was too young to be in the place legally, so the manager would let him in at 3 a.m. when the place closed, lock him in to do his job and then let him out when the place opened at 7 a.m. He was in teenage heaven. Not only did he have access to unlimited booze, as long as he did a decent cleaning job, but after a while they started letting him in earlier and he'd hang out in the kitchen, which was en route between the stage and the girls' dressing (so to speak) rooms. As soon as they found out that he was a virgin, they were all over him, he said. "Come up to our room, we'll make a real man of you!" He declined; I think he was scared. The most solid evidence he had of the girls' extracurricular activities was that once he was promoted to (unofficial) janitor, he was constantly being asked to fix the sinks in the men's room, which were coming away from the walls, and he'd have to put in bigger and longer bolts to fix them back against the wall. Seems the girls had the guys sit in the sinks in order to give them the best professional attention. There he stopped, for we had reached Sturgis.

Yet even in telling this story he sounded a little distant, as if these events had swirled around him like vapor, leaving him mildly amused but untouched. He remembered and understood them perfectly well, he knew their value as a story, but there was an odd painting-by-numbers quality about his tone. Whatever the incidents had done for him at the time, he was no longer engaged in them—just as he seemed to be no longer engaged in America, taking work here and there that didn't commit him to anyone or anything, gliding back and forth across its freeways and pausing at its campgrounds, where nobody had to take root.

At first glance, the outskirts of Sturgis were as anonymous and dull as any other small plains town, but as I wandered down off the interstate exchange, I heard the first whispers of the heavy metal thunder. A pair of bikes cruised by, then another quartet, then some singles. The show was getting on the road; the circus was leaving town. A young guy slouched on the front porch of a small shanty by the road called out to ask me the time. "Hey, would you like a beer?" he asked.

He was short, stringy, roughly dressed, pasty-faced, and his eyes were still looking for the top line on the chart. He was English, he said, slurring his words slightly, but had been brought up in Ireland. He'd already traveled halfway round the world, had lived in Asia as a heroin addict, now he was hitchhiking mostly by rail across the U.S. "Amazing time. Amazing country." He'd already seen a moose swimming the Columbia River. He'd seen elk, deer, and golden eagles. He'd strolled into Sturgis ten days ago knowing nothing about the rally and someone at this house had offered him a basement to sleep in, beer, and sex. This was his version, at least.

So what was his impression of the rally? "It's funny," he said, after a moment's reflection. It was a bit like the Glastonbury Festival in England (a sort of perennial Woodstock), he said, except that Glastonbury is far more civilized, with theater and ballet, everything. "Here all you've got is hairy aging rockers and Harleys." He laughed.

I asked about the two fresh scars on his forehead. "Fell into a barbed-wire fence," he said casually. "Didn't feel a thing. Absolutely hammered. Booze and grass everywhere."

When the rally was over, he said, he planned to make for Minneapolis to get a job on the barges and make his way down to New Orleans. I saw no reason why he shouldn't make it. In college, I knew a fair number of people who traveled the world like him. The only drawback was that they tended not to remember it. I thanked him for the beer and followed his perfectly cogent directions downtown.

Sturgis was closing down—or rather, like some aging comic-book superhero, it was tugging off its leather costume, and turning back into a mild-mannered small South Dakota town. The tearing-down taking place in the streets and shops was the dark reflection of the setting-up I'd seen at the Indianola fairgrounds, one childlike and wholesome, the other aging and raunchy. A pole-and-awning city was being dismantled. The Road Kill Cafe was closed, but Main Street Tattoo, next door, was still doing business. Two guys were hosing down the sidewalk in front of Millinger's Saloon. A surveillance camera, set up to shoot down Main Street, bore a small sign letting everyone know that the whole shebang was being relayed live on STURGISRALLY.NET. According to the *Sturgis Ratty Rag*, the newspaper of record ("Read internationally by the Rat set"), I'd missed Black Oak Arkansas, Lynyrd Skynyrd, Steppenwolf, Jesse the Human Bomb, the Amature (sic) Short Track race, the Swine Pit's Ladies' World Championship Pickle Lickin' Contest, and possibly TV host Joan Lunden, though the photo caption identified her as "Joan Lundgren," and it wasn't clear if she was really coming to Sturgis or just posing (in leather jacket) with Biker Billy, who in turn may or may not be the same person as Billy Gordon of the Blue Rockers, famous for their CD "Helmet Laws Suck."

I wanted a copy of *The Holy Bible for Bikers*, but the shop had closed. Four enormously fat bikers drove by in a Lincoln Town Car. Across the street, a small, neat building that looked as if it might be a polling station elsewhere in the year had a sign over the door that read Pyramid Presents Venders Penthouse Hooters, and underneath it a smaller handwritten one saying "Lingerie models wanted. Apply within." Next door was the Meade County Law Enforcement Center, which also seemed to have closed. A cop was going in the side door with an armload of stuff, cleaning up.

"How do you cope?" I asked him.

"I was born and bred here," he said looking away over Sturgis, choosing his words carefully, "so I'm used to chaos and confusion. You just do the best you can with what you've got."

How many bikers had turned up this year? He shrugged. "We don't know. Three hundred thousand? Four hundred thousand?" Another cop, passing him toward the same doorway, overheard and laughed. "Three hundred and fifty-seven thousand, two hundred and twelve. There were two hundred and thirteen but one left."

For a week, Sturgis swelled to a population the size of Minneapolis, yet the local paper police reported only 182 arrests for DUI, 281 misdemeanor drug arrests, 39 felony drug arrests, and 10 other felonies. A Minneapolis week: 400 larcenies, 100 car thefts, 60 robberies, 10 arsons, 10 rapes, a murder and a half.

I dug out the sock phone and called Tomasz, who turned out to be two blocks away. I was glad to see him, and this time, for once, he had good news. He had shot trucks with fantastic designs down their paneled sides. He had shot the inventor of the Body Web, the least amount of clothing a woman can wear without being arrested. He had shot the Mayor of Sturgis marrying couples on bikes, and the World's Most Tattooed Man.

We took a break for Indian tacos and Black Hills Gold ice cream at a food stand that was in the process of being converted back to its usual role as a plumbing-supply business. I sat on the curb next to a young dude who had been working in one of the biker-gear tents, and now was taking a break from pushing his dolly around, clearing out. He was from California; it turned out that this was part of a franchise operation selling what he called "sports supplies." They'd had four tents in Sturgis, each with a million dollars of inventory. He figured that they had done $2 million worth of business that week. Then Tomasz was off again, bobbing and ducking along next to a girl carrying what appeared to be an extra head. It was a mannequin she called Electra; she designed hair wraps. She tolerated Tomasz to a degree I found astounding. "If you get tired of him, hit him with the head," I encouraged her. "Give 'im a hooter shot," two bikers suggested amiably.

Tomasz introduced me to a woman biker from Colorado he had met. A fair number of women bikers—the Asphalt Angels—had come here on their own, she said. They bedded down at the Hub Heaven Campground ("a lot of the campgrounds are like cesspools by midweek") and each day went off on their own Harley excursions around the area. Guys could go on these trips, too, but only at the back of the motorcade, "sniffing their exhaust."

We wandered around in a happy daze for a while, then adjourned to a bar, still fairly crowded in the waning of the afternoon, and of the festival. On the sound system was Neil Young singing "Country Girl." This was nothing like Biker-Gang-Takes-Over-Small-

Town; the bikers' vulgar, good-humored shamelessness was rather sweet. Tomasz and I were accepted despite his accent and my odd clothing because for this week, at Sturgis, these guys were inlaws rather than outlaws. At the next table, a dwarf biker and his girl-friend held each other and kissed.

We were on our way back to the car when Tomasz grabbed my arm, said "I must show you something," disappeared into one of the dozens of leather shops that were offering final bargains while being dismantled, and dragged out its resident spokesmodel. She was wearing black leather chaps, a black leather bustier and a sort of black leather fig leaf fore and aft, leaving most of her back and both buttocks naked. She gave us a huge smile involving several ounces of fire-engine-red lipstick. Her name, she said, was Dawna. Tomasz shot us both by one of the dozens of bikes still lining the curb.

"I am thinking she is cool," Tomasz said, looking after her as she ended work for the year and marched off up the street, but-tocks winking.

Another guy, short-haired, clean-shaven, wearing the classic fifties midwestern short-sleeved shirt, stood next to us and stared after her, his mouth open. "So long, Sturgis!" he said, shaking his head.

Tomasz had a double room in a hotel a little way south, at the foot of Mount Rushmore, handy also for the Badlands and the Pine Ridge Reservation, both of which I wanted to see. I drove us there, as he was apparently near death from driving a couple of hundred miles each way every day to Buffalo, Wyoming, where he'd been shooting a parade. "I feel every single part of my body. I could take Ph.D. in anatomy right now."

We had a drink at the Red Garter, a mock-saloon where if we ordered a Red Garter Special—vanilla schnapps and cranberry juice—from the waitress in Victorian western gear, it came with a red garter around the glass.

CHAPTER 26

Where My Dead Lie Buried

August 10—Keystone, Montana

I got up early to have breakfast on my own—if Tomasz had had his way he would have slept until Christmas— down at the Red Garter. Honky-tonk piano was hammering away on the sound system. The place was thoroughly fake, but I appreciated its thoroughness. The walls were wood-paneled, or else papered with Victorian red velvet wallpaper, and covered with paintings—portraits and hunting scenes near the window; dogs and horses above the fireplace, beside the nine antique rifles. The woman at the table next to me was eating a cinnamon bun the size of a soup plate. The doorways were hung with red velvet curtains, the chairs with period red Naugahyde. The black-stocking-and-red-garter outfits the waitresses were wearing the previous evening had gone; it's hard to imagine them being worn first thing in the morning back in Victorian times, either. Next to me was a panel of photographs of the forever unfinished statue of Crazy Horse, the chief's arm pointing, accusing, giving the sad, defiant quote: "My lands are where my dead lie buried."

This morning was the high point of my trip. I had made it to Sturgis on schedule, I had more time than I needed to get back home, and yet I was in no hurry to do so. This scholar-gypsy life was agreeing with me. I was sleeping well. My asthma had vanished. I was eating less and digesting better; I had discovered that, like most Americans, I normally eat twice as much as I need. Above all, I felt lighter, more curious and less afraid, as if by plunging into America I had plunged into life.

I imagined that people who could heal by touch alone might feel this sense of calm, and of available energy. As I walked up to the front desk to pay my bill, the manager and hostess were conferring over some problem, their foreheads furrowed. I made some light remark, I smiled, I don't know what I did; they looked up, relaxed, joked back. We chatted for a moment, and I walked outside—and almost at once, events began to deflate my vanity.

For a start, Tomasz, who was pleased with Sturgis but terribly anxious about his photographs as a whole, told me that the NATIONAL GEOGRAPHIC insisted that I spend a couple of days with him so he'd have some photos of me in a truck, in the West, in the Midwest, in a major midwestern city, and so on. I was to become a passenger rather than a hitchhiker.

Subdued, I got in the Skylark.

Mount Rushmore, just up the road, was smaller than I'd expected, and I had my usual reaction against anything that 250 other people are trying to see at the same time. I really wanted to see Crazy Horse, but by now I was mountain-statued out, and couldn't face doing it again.

We plodded downhill into Rapid City, where Tomasz recovered his spirits over more coffee; we bought Bob Dylan tapes for the car and headed off to the Badlands. Tomasz was thinking of hiring a helicopter to fly over the Badlands to take aerial shots. "Great idea," I said, remembering his helicopter disaster in El Salvador. "I'll watch from the ground."

We sang along with the Dylan tapes at the tops of our lungs. "All those people we used to know/They're an illusion to me now...." One of the radio stations in Warsaw used to play Dylan, he said. The censors were so stupid, he explained, that as long as the DJ prefaced the song with "Here's another illustration of how decadent and worthless western rock-and-roll is," or words to that effect, the station could play anything, especially as almost nobody could understand the words.

The Badlands looked like a Bryce Canyon dripped in wet cement by the devil, a savage landscape under a blinding gray-white glare. A fringe of canyons carved in a thick, putty-colored layer of ash and mud left by a long-extinct volcano, it was the rim of a dry, desolate plain that ran southward into the heat haze. Why on earth did the settlers newly arrived from the East try to farm this awful country? Owning land, and a house, as opposed to feeling owned, must have been a revolutionary act, an act of escaping not only a city, but a social structure that systematically denied everything worthwhile, or parceled it out to favorites—those of the same origin, or color, or religion. Settlers created a new landscape, yes, but also a new political landscape—the West.

We pushed farther south and east into the abandoned volcanic plain, crossing a river white with ash, like the effluent from a cement factory. This was the Pine Ridge Reservation, where the Lakota Sioux were driven more than a century ago following the massacre at Massacre Canyon. If anyone ever doubted that the American government herded the Indians into land that nobody else wanted, this hot, exposed, infertile landscape was proof. Cute little arrowheads framed the route numbers on road signs.

Somewhere around here was Wanblee, South Dakota, which turned out to be a bend in Route 44, where at some point in the recent past a small amount of federal money had paid for a few dozen flimsy project houses. No semiconductor factories, corporate headquarters, or organic farms. No shingles by the road announcing lawyers, doctors, dentists, tax accountants, chiropractors, or homemade preserves for sale. Not even a McDonalds. Pine Ridge is one of the poorest and most isolated communities in the U.S. Unemployment runs at more than 80 percent, and to find work many Sioux have to drive a hundred miles to Rapid City. Per capita annual income averages under $4,000, the lowest in the country. Above-average rates of every kind of illness. The alcoholism-related mortality rate is nine times the national average.

We were looking for Jaylene Quick Bear. Tomasz had met her then-husband Charles Chipps in Nevada. Charles was a Lakota spiritual leader who claimed to be a descendant of Crazy Horse. He traveled the country conducting sun dances and sweat lodges, rituals of celebration and purification.

Jaylene lived in a project that showed the classic signs of struggle in the face of economic abandonment. The houses were cheap and ugly. Children climbed in and out of ground-floor windows;

a board was nailed across one open front door, apparently as a child gate. The yards were mud and stringy grass. A teenage neighbor stuck his head out and asked the kids around him if anyone wanted to go in on a bag of maryjane. I was stunned. Living on the reservation, I'd have fled or gone crazy in a week. It astounded me that people had the resilience to survive such brutal conditions.

Jaylene's house was better cared for than most. Someone had built a rectangular canopy out of pine boughs to shade the front yard. A convenience-store ice machine had been set up along the front wall. Everything was covered with flies.

With our accents and our uncertainty as to who exactly we were looking for or where she lived, several minutes passed with us standing uneasily around the car while several small Lakota children ran around or stared, apparently not understanding us.

After a while, Jaylene came out; she had been making bread, surrounded by children. She was of medium height with a slightly fleshy face; long black hair that might have been beautiful, or wild; jeans, T-shirt, black sneakers. A torrent of laughing, fighting children poured out with her. She was raising 14. The kids all had shaggy black hair and dark skin. They all wore ragged shorts. Everyone had skin blemishes on their arms, chests, and legs. One of the boys hit another, who cried, and then hit one of the girls. Jaylene distractedly reprimanded them, and offered us a snow cone or some water.

Standing in the driveway, talking quietly and without rancor, she sketched us a picture of life on the reservation. There were no jobs. "You've got to be someone's relative to get a job. They want us women to work, but there are no jobs and we don't know what kind of people will take care of our children." The white teachers at the school, from New York and New Jersey, she said, didn't understand Lakota traditions or how to handle Lakota kids, and ended up calling the police on them. The kids ended up embarrassed to be Indian and to talk their own language. There was federal money, but Pine Ridge, she said, was rife with fraud.

She brought out a cheap tape recorder, and a tape of Charles speaking before the most recent sweat lodge. She set it up on a picnic table under the canopy so that we could listen.

"The ceremony will give you a stronger heart, a stronger mind, stronger lungs, and stronger blood," he said.

One of the boys threw a small stone at the other, who burst into exaggerated crying; moments later, they were spitting at each other. A kitchen knife was lying on the table, an accident waiting to happen. Flies landed everywhere, scores of them.

"All we have is our self-esteem," Charles said.

A white girl, Michelle, appeared—a pale, washed-out blonde with peasant clothes and a rather vague look. She was from Kentucky; her husband was from the reservation. She was pregnant, and he had said that it would be easier for the child to be a card-carrier—that is, someone entitled to Indian benefits—if it was born on the reservation. She said, "We want her to know both worlds and both spiritualities." I couldn't imagine willingly bringing a child up on the reservation, with its incredible hardships; but perhaps spiritual strength flourishes in such conditions.

Two-year-old Rochelle was playing with the car doors. "Get away from their car," Jaylene called. "It's locked, anyway."

"The car isn't locked," I said.

"Oh, God," she laughed, "you'd better lock it. This is the reservation."

On the tape player, Charles was preaching forgiveness.

The kids wanted piggybacks; maybe they missed their father. Rochelle walked around on my feet, holding my hands, then asked me to chase her around the car. The boys decided to try a different, less strenuous kind of clowning: Godfrey, 13, climbed into the wheelbarrow on the driveway and Trevor, 14, began playing the hose on him, creating a kind of small-scale bath-cum-shower.

"The pain you will receive in the lodge is a good pain," Charles was saying in his deep, gentle voice, "and it will help you. It's the very next thing to mother's womb. It's going to be hotter than hell." He chuckled.

The older children had scars from the recent sweat lodge: self-wounding is another traditional way to accustom oneself to pain. The kids started piercing at around ten, Jaylene said. Girls pierce on their arms, boys on their chests. When the word got around the reservation school that they'd been doing the sweat lodges, she said, they were taunted for doing witchcraft.

Jaylene wanted to exchange addresses and phone numbers so she could send us information about forthcoming sun dances and sweat lodges. "You know," she said plaintively, "our ancestors used to..." She made a cutting motion across the top of her head.

"Scalp?"

"Yeah, scalp white people. We don't do that any more. I think whites still think we scalp people, and they stay away."

She was 38, and she had no teeth left.

"It's hard to walk on this earth with all these children," she said, "but I'm healthy. I do the sweat lodges. I'll survive."

I didn't feel scalped, I felt gutted. Tomasz wanted to shoot some more of the Badlands, but I was in a foul mood and didn't want to talk to anyone. As I wandered off through some scrub toward a view point, a woman tourist said "Watch out, there's a rattlesnake around. We saw it go over there." I felt like the rattlesnake, ready to bite anybody who came near me.

I was too angry to hitchhike. We drove along dead-straight road after dead-straight road until night fell and we hit Pierre. Throughout the West, I'd seen the destruction of history and the remythication of the past, the steady burning of cultural bridges. No wonder the architecture struck me as phoney: It was trying to fill the gap left by missing pueblos, encampments, and seminomadic seasonal settlements. I thought of wooden Indians outside trading posts, and of their silence.

CHAPTER 27

The Hitchhiker Remains at Large

August 11—Pierre, South Dakota

Next morning, the Sioux Falls *Argus Leader* carried an AP story announcing that although three Americans in ten live in poverty, for most of them it's a condition that doesn't last forever. "Most who are poor pass through poverty," the headline read. Phew. Imagine Jaylene's relief. Just a few more generations and it'll all seem like a bad dream. "Blacks, Hispanics and children are among the poorest groups." No mention of Native Americans.

The same newspaper carried a front-page story of a local five-year-old boy who had been abducted by a hitchhiker. My heart sank. That's all hitchhikers need: more bad publicity. The truth, of course, was far less sensational. The boy was visiting his noncustodial father in California for two weeks, as he did each year. The father, who had picked up a hitchhiker in Utah a couple of days previously, took his son and the hitchhiker to a bee farm in Fresno.

The father went off, leaving the two in the van, and the hitchhiker took the van. He drove it to the bus station in San Francisco and left the boy in the van, quite unharmed. Nobody would read this far in the story, though: Drivers all over South Dakota would load for bear, and anyone standing beside the road was in for a lynching. "The hitchhiker remains at large," the paper said, ominously.

The air seemed damper and thicker; the previous night, when we'd pulled into the motel forecourt, clouds of moths and gnats circled under the lights of the parking lot, the first insects I'd seen in three weeks. I already missed the brilliant clarity of the western weather, and its desert light, especially now we were under scowling skies on a landscape pressed by a steam iron and punctuated only by grain elevators, the cathedrals of the plains. I was gripped by a strange gloom that was somehow made worse by the monomania of straight roads in perfectly rectangular patterns and the torture of the steady *bump-bump-bump* of the tires on the concrete slabs, feeding the urge to drive as fast as hell to the horizon or into some heavy solid object, to go home or just go mad.

A storm was coming up behind us; Tomasz wanted to shoot me hitchhiking in that brilliant purple light called storm light. We stopped.

There are probably dozens of countries in the world where one might see a Buick pull over to the shoulder and disgorge two middle-aged men, one of whom would pretend to be hitchhiking while the other took photographs of him; but only in America would a lobbyist for the Concrete Pavement Association—his name was Bill Brinkmann—stop, ask the two men if they needed any help, recommend the five-cent cup of coffee at Al's Oasis in Chamberlin, South Dakota, and tell them that there was a Stradivarius in Vermilion that was once owned by an Indian.

"All you have to do is get out of the car," I said in wonder, as Tomasz restarted the Skylark. "All you have to do is get out of the car, and things come to you. It never fails. It's just a matter of getting out of the car."

"What do you mean?" Tomasz asked.

I took the plunge, and tried to explain how being "in the car" meant to want to be in control, to be insulated from the world not only physically but mentally. To be out of the car meant to be vulnerable, alert, and spontaneous.

Beyond that, I went on, I can't tell you how many people have told me, "I never pick up hitchhikers"—yet they had picked me up anyway. Something had changed their minds. Beyond that, though I'd begun noticing, how many people had picked me up when, if everything had gone according to plan, they wouldn't even have been on that road, at that time. The KOA camper who took me to Sturgis was supposed to have been traveling a day earlier, with another guy, who had dropped out at the last minute. The guy who took me to Bozeman had left a day later than planned, too. Hank had decided at the last minute to take the desert route through Nevada for no good reason—in fact, he kept wondering aloud why on earth he hadn't driven up the coast as usual. Jay had been as out of the car as anyone in a car can be, just meandering around with no fixed route in mind and no deadline.

I couldn't shake a very strong sense that giving up control exerts some kind of attraction that is, in the language of quantum physics, "non-local": It affects people and even objects in ways and at distances that it shouldn't. It doesn't seem to have much to do with the conscious mind; in fact, our conscious mind seems mostly to get in the way, by second-guessing and worrying too much. Every time I've started worrying about whether I'll get a ride, I told him, it has done me no good. I told him what had happened at Big Timber, the zen koan, and the immediate ride all the way to Sturgis.

I'd come to think of this as the weak force—though I don't mean it in the usual sense, where it describes one of the four elemental forces of the universe. For me the term refers to a paradox: Often what seem to be the weakest connections between people have the most surprising and beneficial results. Many of the people who bring about the greatest changes in our lives are strangers, and, by the same token, many of the most important events seem to arise by sheer coincidence.

The most startling example of the weak force at work had happened a few years previously, during the period right before my mother's death, a time that was full of odd happenstance. The last time I flew over to see her, my plane landed at Heathrow at 5 a.m. on a Sunday. The bus and Underground stations wouldn't be open for hours, so even though it was still dark I decided to walk the mile or so to the M4 motorway and hitchhike to Bath.

It was not an easy hitch: clouds moved in and drizzle began to fall. Cars seemed to have gotten newer and people ruder since my teenage hitchhiking days. By mid-afternoon I finally reached the Bath exit, where I hoped I might be picked up by a student for the last few miles into the city. After five or ten minutes, a small blue car, driven by an elderly woman, passed me and pulled over some 30 yards up the road. As I ran up to it, I realized the woman was my Aunt Barbara.

She was as surprised to see me as I was to see her. Normally she never stops for hitchhikers, she said; it was just that she was heading back to Bath from Cirencester, where she had been visiting friends, and idly listening to the radio, when someone said that we should always be kind to strangers, as any of them might be God in human guise. Almost at once, she crossed over the M4 and saw this hitchhiker, and thought, well....

Later, when I told this story to a grief therapist in Vermont, she took it in stride. "Those who work in hospice from a more spiritual perspective hear stories like that all the time," she said. "We're surprised when something like that doesn't happen."

By now we were in Sioux Falls, looking here and there for the Sioux Empire Fair. The fair turned out to have precious little to do with the Sioux, or their Empire; instead, it featured Spam. We would miss the Spam cook-off, sadly, but the Hormel Foods representative gave me a glossy pamphlet of Spam recipes, featuring Spam Quesadillas, Singapore Spam Salad, Maui Spam Muffins, Spam à la King, Elegant Potato Spam Casserole, Spam Strudels with Mushroom Sauce, Spam Carbonara.

The owner of Nordstrom's Auto Recycling was offering an unusual contest: guess the original make, model, and year of two cars that had been reduced to cubes of crushed metal. Beside them was a motor home that had been thrown, dumped, and crushed by the tornado that without warning had hit a small town nearby a couple of months back and virtually wiped it out. "First the electricity went out, which took out all the sirens, and about a minute later the tornado hit." The motor home was an especially sad story: It had been the property of the most recent owner's brother, who had just passed away out in California. The Dakotan went out to pick it up, drove it back, put $6,000 into it, and then the tornado came along. "Took out his home, his shop, his tools—everything." Only 11 houses were left standing, and they were all damaged.

Amazingly, only five people were killed, though a lot of people were injured by flying debris. "There was a fully loaded semi standing under a grain elevator," he said. "It was picked up, spun around, and dropped down about where that tent is," some 40 yards away.

Tomasz and I, too, seemed to be spinning, plotting routes back East that neither of us really wanted to travel. We wound up in Minneapolis, but we might as well have been anywhere. The only restaurant that seemed to be still open refused to serve me because I was wearing shorts. We'd have to sit at the bar. Quite right, too, Tomasz said unexpectedly. "If I were properly dressed for dinner, I would not want someone in shorts sitting at the table next to me. I would be insulted." We got into a polite but bitter argument in the bar, in which Tomasz was championing the importance of class and I found myself furiously defending the American ideal of classlessness, even though the evidence against me was fawning over wealthy patrons in the next room. On the way through the curiously deserted streets back to the hotel, we passed a beautiful young Asian girl sitting silently in a glass bus shelter, the yellow light from a street lamp falling on her headscarf.

CHAPTER 28

The Lord Said It Was All Right

August 12—Minneapolis, Minnesota

Hitching in a small town, you feel like part of its life. Tomasz drove me across the Mississippi and dropped me off in Prescott, Wisconsin, planning to wander on ahead looking for pictures while I hitched down 35, a slender thread of a road that might take me down the eastern bank of the Mississippi. We'd try to rendezvous in Madison, or far-off Milwaukee.

I settled down at the southern end of Prescott, able to see pretty much all of the old town center: up the broad, old-fashioned main street called Broad Street, with its small, neat brick buildings in the classic American square-top style with the arched Romanesque windows; up to the Steamboat Inn (its name painted in tall, thin, heavily serifed Victorian lettering in the riverboat style), where Route 35 joined Route 10 and the St. Croix joined the Mississippi. I felt like a part of the barge trains nosing bluntly up the river, part of the people crossing the road to the shops, part of the smell of newly mown grass. Who lived here? Who would rent the apartment available on the corner of Kinnikinnis Street?

This is an undervalued virtue of hitchhiking, or of waiting for a bus, or a train: that you spend a lot of time just standing still, looking around, not doing but being. At home, I rarely allow myself such silence: Every moment has to mean something. This enforced surrender, on a warm day with a light breeze, felt like the greatest luxury. Flags lifted and fell back against their poles. Grasshoppers chirped in the undergrowth. Even the little traffic heading south on 35 seemed determined to follow the same slow rhythm for the day, for half of it was dump trucks sauntering down the road to some sand or gravel pit, filling up and heading back; and the other half cruised slowly up to me, pulled a wide, lazy U-turn, and went back to park in a vacant slot in front of the shops.

After I'd been there an hour and a half, though, I started to get concerned that I'd be there all day, and Tomasz would have to turn round and drive a hundred miles back to find me. I pulled out the phone, hit Power, and before I could dial a car pulled over.

It was two retired guys from St. Paul, former employees of the city. As we cruised south through the woods and cornfields, between the river bluffs on our left and the Mississippi on our right, the driver looked around him with a childlike joy. "Diamond Bluff! What d'you think of that! We're from St. Paul. We're just out to kill the day and see the country. We're going to get sweet corn. Maybe ten dozen ears. We've got a friend who owns a farm down here someplace. He says 'I've got more than I can handle. Take some and give it to your friends.' Look, here's the railway!" He had hitchhiked way back when he was in the Army, he told me, from Indiana all the way to Nashville, Tennessee, to see the Grand Ole Opry.

They went five miles or more out of their way to cross back over the Mississippi and drop me on Route 61 in Red Wing, where the boots are made. I wasn't sure I wanted to be on a bigger road, but they were so determined to be kind, I didn't have the heart to say no.

Then, another first: A young couple with four children in an SUV, which I'd have put somewhere below a dyspeptic billionaire in a Rolls-Royce on the Hitchhiker's Scale of Unlikely Rides. They took me a few miles down to Lake City on Lake Pepin, a sort of artificial lagoon of water ballooning on the Mississippi, where they were going to work on their sailboat before the summer ended. They dropped me off at a drive-up hamburger-and-shake stand, because their kids thought it was cool that you could get served right at your window without getting out of the car. I left the car and went over to the counter and chatted amiably with the smiling waitresses, high school girls with healthy Midwest complexions. I asked if they ever wore roller skates, like the drive-in waitresses of the early 1960s. They said they'd like to, but some of the tables were beyond the parking lot, over on the grass, so they couldn't. Still, it'd be kinda cool.

I drank a milkshake, then strolled half a mile down the road through Lake City. Tomasz and I had agreed that small towns were our favorite parts of America. They haven't yet lost their core to office-block-and-parking-garage developers, and their suburbs don't yet straggle away like apathetic teenagers. I also wondered whether I was getting rides from unlikely candidates because these were small towns, and people were simply less afraid here.

I set up shop on the way out of the town center on the lakeside road, opposite the sailboats and the bluffs on the far shore of the Mississippi, and promptly a young girl, perhaps 18 but racy for Lake City with her small tattoo, pulled over in her subcompact and said, "I'm not going very far." That was fine, I said, getting in—I was enjoying this day of short rides between small towns. I settled in my seat, put on my seat belt, and she said. "This is where I turn off." She had taken me all of 400 yards.

It was wonderful. I thanked her and got out, laughing, as she turned into the leafy residential street where she lived. This, for her, was hitching: You did it to get home from the center of town, not to cross the continent. And this is the state of the art, I suppose. A number of my students hitch to the Green Mountains to hike or ski; hikers on the Appalachian Trail often hitch off the trail into a nearby town for supplies, and some people hitch when their cars break down. No, it's the long-distance art, the grand enterprise, that is dormant. Throwing oneself on the mercy of the continent.

A couple of minutes later, a battered van pulled over and an American Indian kid—long shiny black hair, broad shoulders, meaty body—leaped out, beckoning me as I hesitated. I climbed in the front and sat down, surrounded by an amazing collection of sacred trinkets: pipes, bracelets, sticks, stalks of sage twisted into circles to be worn as bracelets or crowns. The driver looked weathered but not exactly Indian. "I'm Bruce," he explained. The artifacts were from a sun dance he'd recently been to, held by Chief Leonard Crow Dog; the children in the back were David, Juddy, and Bo, Anashnase kids from Minneapolis, where there are some 25,000 Anashnase, he said, some in reasonable shape, some not doing so well. "I've sort of adopted them, or they've adopted me." One of them, he said, was the grandson of Dennis Banks, one of the founders of the American Indian Movement.

The kids, who seemed to range from about nine to twelve, sat in the back of the van happily drawing. Bruce was a genuine hippie, a veteran of the Rainbow Gatherings virtually every year since 1973— veteran too of the usual gauntlet of drink and drugs. Some of the time, Bruce told me, he did migrant farm work, some of the time he offered massage therapy. At the moment he was looking for land in Wisconsin, maybe a farm, to set up a kind of sanctuary, a place of respite from the city where the Native kids could learn to hunt and fish, where they could rest and pray and generally dry out from a society that was, at least to them, toxic. "I wanna show these kids that there's a way to live without using. We grow up in an addictive death culture in this capitalist society. Our own cultures have abandoned us. Even we Europeans have lost our tribes and their cultures. In a lot of ways the Native people are in better shape, because they know who they are. They've been genocided for hundreds of years and they turn round and share their most sacred ceremonies with the whole world.

"I'm 45," he continued, "and all my cousins are fuckin' rich. Jewish. Too middle class and materialistic. 'When are you going to get a job?' If I get a job I'll be so busy working I'll forget how to be with people. I'll forget how to be with the earth. Besides, I've got a job. I'm living.

"When I go to see them, the first thing they ask is, 'How's business?' When I see my Native friends, the first thing they ask is, 'How are you? Are you hungry?' It's going to pass. All that stuff about money will pass. I'm going to be patient."

His father, he said, was in an expensive nursing home, learning the dire horror of being alone and helpless in America.

He gave me one of the prayer bracelets from the dashboard. One of the kids in the back called out "Which picture do you like, Bruce, mine, or Dave's?"

"Let me see 'em," he called back over his shoulder. Bo handed Bruce two drawings. He glanced at them. "I like 'em all," he said, sticking them up on the dashboard. "I love 'em all."

Bruce dropped me off just beyond the Mississippi near La Crosse, at the on-ramp for I-90, but in the middle of the usual ugly guardrail architecture, among the dying roadside weeds, I could barely keep my feet on the ground for sheer joy. A good ride is a benediction: in the middle of nowhere, through no virtue of your own, you are blessed with kindness, as cleanly and abruptly as if you are a gong being struck by an unseen hand; and then you are back on your own again, your heart still ringing and astounded, left to recognize that, yes, these are the things that sustain us, even while we're breathing exhaust or being knocked back by the bow wave of a semi, picking up speed for the long haul.

The next person to pick me up, a bio-geneticist named John (in yet another pickup truck) told me two of his own hitchhiking stories, dating back more than 35 years to when he used to hitch regularly back and forth between college, in Utah, and home, in California, making sure he looked like a respectable college student by carrying a suitcase with a BYU sticker on one side and a USC sticker on the other.

On one trip west he got picked up by a wild-looking old character who seemed decent enough, but as they neared the Nevada border, this guy reached across to the glove compartment and took out a handgun. "I was terrified. I was sure he was going to shoot me. He opened his window, leaned out, shot into the air, and told me 'I shoot off whenever I cross a state line.' "

John also told me the story of the guy in Utah who passed John and his brother hitching, pulled up some way farther up the road and stayed there for about ten minutes before coming back for them. "I imagine you noticed I went up there aways and stopped there for some minutes," he told the two lads. "Well, I wasn't sure if it was safe to pick you up. So I stopped and prayed about you, and the Lord said it was all right."

He dropped me off in Baraboo, Wisconsin, birthplace in 1884 of the Ringling Brothers Circus and home of the Circus World Museum, where Tomasz met me and took pictures. I remembered that I really don't like circuses —their garish con games, their abuse of animals. "The exhibiting of trained animals I abhor," wrote Albert Schweitzer. "What an amount of suffering and cruel punishment the poor creatures have to endure in order to give pleasure to men devoid of thought." The tiny town center was a classic, though, with its leafy courthouse square, its field gun, its war memorial—the most perfect, in my day, of small towns.

We climbed back into the Skylark, and headed east. "When I get back to Warsaw," Tomasz said, "I will do several mantras, I will visit several psychotherapists to rebuild my mental condition, which is screwed up, and I will do lots of physical exercise to rebuild my physical condition."

"And you'll eat lots of vegetables, too," I said.

We made for Milwaukee, just because it was there. You'd think that I'd have learned from my day that small towns are more approachable and welcoming to the tired traveler than cities, but apparently not.

CHAPTER 29

Falling by the Wayside

August 13—Milwaukee, Wisconsin

Two consecutive nights of fitful sleep, and my allergies playing up— I'm losing steam. Three weeks ago I couldn't wait to be up and on the road; now I want to sleep, and to let Tomasz drive from one designated photo spot to another. He professes to be utterly exhausted, but this may be a Polishism: under the same circumstances my brother, for example, would use classic English understatement: "I'm a bit knackered, chief."

We slogged down I-94, a wreck of a road, driven to destruction. This was, in essence, the same pleasant Wisconsin landscape I'd seen yesterday, but abused beyond recognition—beyond the point of being a landscape. We might as well have been in a storm drain. The real America seemed to be slipping out of my grasp.

Tomasz told me that Poland introduced a program to encourage hitchhiking in the sxties and seventies, a curiously capitalist enterprise. A potential hitchhiker would buy a coupon book, and hitch by the traditional thumb method or by holding out the book, just as truckers in England will hitch by holding out their log books. When he was picked up, he would give the driver a coupon, which could be redeemed for various goods and prizes. The book also had blank pages in which one could write dates, destinations, and perhaps the drivers' names—a traveler's journal.

I can't see any reason why something along these lines shouldn't be perfectly workable today. In fact, given the GPS technology, the hitchhiker (really a sort of low-impact commuter) could have a credit card that he passes to the driver picking him up, who swipes it through his GPS machine, sending a signal via satellite informing Caltrans (or whomever) who has picked up whom and where, and automatically crediting the driver's gasoline credit card according to the distance he takes the hitchhiker. Safe and environmentally sound.

Tomasz also confided in me, in boyish embarrassment, that on his first trip to America, he had stolen a "Do Not Disturb" sign from every motel they'd stayed in. He had ended up with a collection of several hundred. This is why I like this guy, I thought.

We checked into a Holiday Inn around noon, planning to take the El into Chicago. As we waited for the train at Belmont, two very large guys wearing the black uniforms of National K-9 Security parked themselves beside us and ordered their Rottweilers to lie down. The guys were carrying handcuffs; the dogs were wearing steel muzzles. Tomasz, who has never met a dog he didn't like, tried to engage the humans and dogs in light conversation, and was severely rebuffed. In a whispered aside, he admitted that Rottweilers are the only dogs his wife won't accept in their animal shelter. When the train arrived, a very young couple, she with a nose ring, was sweetly entwined in each other's arms.

Tomasz, still in love with America's love of glitter, was determined to have lunch at Planet Hollywood. Charles, our maitre d', confessed that Planet Hollywood Chicago was smaller than other Planet Hollywoods (or should it be Planets Hollywood?), but claimed that it had more movie paraphernalia, pointing up at deck chairs and life jackets from *Titanic* hanging from the ceiling above us, like escapees from a late Magritte. My seat had a fine view of the Pink and Yellow Power Rangers' backsides, and one of the Teenage Mutant Ninja Turtles, who, on closer inspection, turned out to be Donatello. When my Los Angelean Lasagna arrived, it looked as if it had been designed by Werner von Braun for the 1938 New York World's Fair, all rocket shapes and space-age geometry. It was actually rather good, but it was hard to taste anything because my other senses were working overtime. If the lights and deafening music and constant video clips on the TV monitors, as Tomasz said, reduce a human being to a sort of vegetable, what do they do to vegetables?

We split up to explore the town. I liked Chicago: it has energy without insanity, style without pretense, and people throng the sidewalks without trampling each other. I liked the owl gargoyles on the public library, and the way the El train suddenly appeared between one pair of buildings and vanished between the next like a conjuror's trick. I liked the detail: the fleur-de-lis, the cornices, and mouldings on the old buildings that say that the human hand was there. The new skyscrapers—Tomasz, to my delight, pronounced the word "high-scrappers"—were impossible to take in, though: they seemed like science fiction. I couldn't imagine people inhabiting them; they were more like monuments, or weapons.

My knee has a long memory, however, and soon I needed a place to sit down. No benches. I would either have to find a park, buy a seat at a restaurant, or sit on the sidewalk with my back to a building like a bum—which I often do, out of defiance, but only when I'm wearing clothing dark and heavy enough to take the dirt. I was not equipped, so I limped on, thinking that this lack of benches was interesting: it meant that the sidewalk was not a public space, in the sense of a space actually intended and designed for the public. No public maps; no signposts to the Art Institute or the park. No bus shelters, even though this was the Windy City. Pay phones, yes, but no public emergency phones like we have in Burlington. No push-button crosswalk lights, either, which meant that the traffic was in control of the pedestrian rather than vice versa, and the narrow, dark garbage alleys made part of every block potentially dangerous. It was as if the city needed the public in order to do business, but given its druthers, it would do just fine without us.

When I got to the park, I found the public: a young couple taking photos of each other in front of a fountain, two women (one black, one white) jogging together; a mother pushing her daughter in a stroller, the daughter reaching out in glee at the scattering pigeons; a run-down black guy with his possessions in a plastic bag, reading a magazine; and an even more run-down white guy asleep on a stone bench, his head resting on another model in the perennially popular line of plastic grocery-bag suitcases.

The doorman of a hotel in the shadow of the El hailed a cab with the most spectacular display of whistling I'd ever seen, piercing but also remarkably musical, the Clifton Chenier or Sonny Boy Williamson of the finger whistle. How did you do that? I asked. "Oh, I just did this," he demonstrated with one hand, the fingers in a triangular two-over-one arrangement, the tongue rolled up. "When I was a kid, I couldn't whistle with just my lips," he said cheerfully, making useless blowing sounds to illustrate his point. "So I learned how to whistle with my fingers. Or you can do this," he said, using the index finger of each hand, waggling one to produce vibrato like a harp player, changing pitch with his tongue. "Take it easy." And he strolled back into the lobby.

~

CHAPTER 30

Between Order and Chaos

August 14—Evanston, Illinois

I stole Tomasz a "Do Not Disturb" sign. He seemed quite touched.

On the subway into Chicago I fell in love with the fantastic hair styles African-American women were wearing—the cornrows, the African braids, which I was told can take up to eight hours and cost several hundred dollars, and something I'd never seen called finger waves. A woman on the El had a finger wave that had been dyed to create a two-tone effect, black and a kind of toasted copper color—a stunning effect. In search of a work-in-progress, I went into one salon, and I nearly passed out from the humidity. The receptionist was not interested in my interest. Those fashions, she said, were to be found out in the neighborhoods. "Downtown, we go for the softer look," she said, which I took to mean less Afrocentric, less assertive.

More evidence of the sixties being downgraded to the butt of cool jokes: an ad in the Chicago Reader, which should know better, for Mac University, consisting of a black-and-white photo of a hippie girl with her face painted in stripes and the peace symbol, the stripes presumably red and white and the symbol blue. The caption read, "Back then, self-expression required very little training." No, but it took a certain amount of courage. Besides, what do you mean by self-expression? She may look like a child who has spent the morning face-painting, but she was trying to stop a war.

I went back to look for the whistler of the previous evening. The hotel was the Crown Plaza on Wabash. The morning doorman, Marzette King, identified the virtuoso as Andrew Thomas, but made no big deal of it. "We can all do that. Look, I'll show you." He led me out of the lobby, explaining, "We all did that as kids. We knew each other's code. We'd call each other out of the house—I thought everyone could do that. I thought it was a guy thing." He reached the curb, reached into his mouth, and blew a whistle a little less musical than Andrew's but so loud it set off a car alarm.

At the public library for a buck or two I bought half a dozen books-to-be-tossed, including *The Gentleman in America* (1949) by Edwin Harrison Cody, associate professor of English at Syracuse. "[T]here are still Americans trying to be gentlemen. But the years of the modern in America...have made code and class considerations irrelevant....What is a gentleman? A gentleman is a man whose inner balance of sensibility, good-will, and integrity issues in moral dependability (the instinct to act rightly in a crisis); in courtesy (the instinct to serve other people's physical and psychological needs); and in the excellent performance of some good social function. Or it is anyone who is sincerely trying to be a gentleman." After the trip was over I reminded Tomasz of our argument over gentlemanliness, and he laughed and told me the story of his grandfather, who traveled extensively around Europe and Russia, carrying in his luggage a collapsible rubber bath. At every hotel he had the staff erect it and fill it with hot water.

While I was at it, I bought Tomasz *Talk American: A Practical Guide for Eliminating a German Accent* by Lewis and Marguerite Shalett Herman, published in 1944, and presumably a hot seller among spies. "The American language is inconsistent (*inkonsequent*) in its spelling," said the introduction. "American is spoken with much less energy (*kraftaufwand*) than German.... American speech tends to run its words together in ordinary conversation....Most Americans do not move their mouths as much as Germans do."

By evening, I wanted to hit the town. Tomasz decided to stay at the hotel and work on restoring his lymphocyte count, but he insisted that I call him whatever time I got back. I wasn't sure whether to see Tarkovsky's movie *Andrei Rublev* or the Blue Man Group. Tomasz told me that when he saw the BMG he laughed so hard he fell sideways into the lap of the man next to him and didn't manage to sit back up for 20 minutes. "I had laugh attack, like this," he said, and made those sea gull-like wheezing noises you make when you laugh so hard you can't catch your breath.

The Blue Man Group turned out to be just your basic taiko-drumming mime cabaret satire, performed in blueface and featuring an endoscopy; a Rorschach test, to which the correct answer was "Charlie's Angels"; a vibraphone of illuminated intestines, on which the blue trio played something that reminded me of Tubular Bells, except that it made musical sense, and later "White

Rabbit" by Jefferson Airplane, reinterpreted for the information age. The performance also included some intellectually undeveloped stuff about Mandelbrot sets, in which the faceless announcer pointed out that fractals exist on the frontier between order and chaos. As if to illustrate what this frontier might be like, the show's climax was a sort of happening, a participatory experience involving black light, a strobe, and hundreds of yards of paper in rolls that we passed over our heads down to the stage. But if it was a happening, it was a happening for the nineties—safe and, at 45 dollars, expensive. The Blue Man Show was an electric kool-aid acid test without the acid. "I don't think people nowadays would know how to behave at a happening," Debbie Harry of Blondie recently told *Esquire*. "I think they'd need little instruction booklets."

By now it was dark, and the city night breathed heat and danger. What might I do with the rest of what was, in effect, my first evening off? The bars were stuffed torpid with stiffs drinking beer and watching baseball on TV. No. A sign caught my eye: "Tabou-Tabou. Whips and Paddles for All Occasions." Of course. Here I was, 45 years old and I'd never been in a sex shop.

My first impression was that the sex shop looked surprisingly like any mall store. The two largest signs were

Do Not Crack or Swing Whips in Shop
You Will Be Asked to Leave
and
We No Longer Take Amex

The chrome hangers and racks made most of it look like a lingerie shop, and as for the sex toys and devices...well, they were proof that if you objectify anything, you steal its heat and urgency, and these objects amounted to the ultimate objectification: after all, sex is one of the few human activities for which one needs no objects at all, just people, yet the shop was selling not people but objects. The malling of passion.

Still, I was beset with curiosity, so I put on my best interview manner and approached one of the two girls working the joint. She had short orange hair, shaved eyebrows, and a snake tattoo down her arm. She was wearing black stockings and a faux leopardskin microdress. I didn't ask her name because I assumed she wouldn't want people to know she worked in a sex shop. Afterward, I realized I had learned nothing from my trip: I might have been embarrassed, but she was probably perfectly cool about it.

Handcuffs and whips were the most popular items, she said casually, and bondage chokers, though these were just as likely to be fashion accessories as they were sex accessories. Bondage is chic.

The oddest items in the shop—to me, at least—were pairs of wings, black or white, in various sizes. Did people like to dress up as angels for sex? Oh, they're very popular, she said, especially at bars. Bars? Oh yes, there are some bars where wings are all the rage. Black or white? Both, but mostly black. I shook my head in amazement.

What were her customers' strangest requests? Oh, nothing too bizarre. Gags you can breathe through. Nothing much.

By now several couples, and a small knot of Japanese tourists, were looking at and touching the merchandise without apparent embarrassment; again, it all seemed curiously wholesome and slightly silly. All this stuff laid out so nicely, so well lit—it was hard to take the sign "torture devices" seriously. I left without buying anything, though I was oddly tempted by the wings. Outside, a woman of the streets walked by—but this was a homeless woman of the streets, ragged, talking to herself. Maybe it's because

I'm 45, but I was moved by her more than by the picture of the girl in the satin gag and handcuffs.

Yet as soon as I had my pen out, pad on knee, foot up on windowsill, writing down what I'd seen—"the girl in the satin gag and handcuffs"—the old familiar illicit excitement returned, the dark stirring. More erotic in the writing than the seeing.

In the end, sex remained a mystery to me. Fractals, the Blue Man Group pointed out, exist on the frontier between order and chaos—well, so does sex. Sex lives where mind and body meet, dancing like a flame that is neither the coal nor the air above it.

Back at the hotel, Tomasz insisted on meeting for a beer, which was how we wound up in the strange little hotel bar at nearly midnight, him with camera, me looking for a game of pool.

I put down our four quarters and we met Ezra Becker, who described himself as an MBA student who was doing something in computers. A short, cheerful, stocky guy in his late 20s, his palm full of muscles when I shook his hand, he took it on himself, as a conscientious host, to introduce Tomasz to drinking shots of tequila with the salt thing and the lime thing, then to pay for the games of pool, and finally to show us the only bar in Evanston that was open after hours, Evanston having been dry until 1984 and still being damp only in small spots.

Ezra drove us through the less affluent quarters of Evanston to the Mark II Lounge, where three IDs were required by the doorman, a moderate-size mountain of a guy called Zeno, apparently one of the owners. Zeno greeted Ezra cheerfully—both members of a secret society of zeds, perhaps—and we were in. At once Tomasz pulled off his lens cap and infiltrated himself in the crowd. As always, I expected someone to break a cue over his head, but he was everywhere, his eyes gleaming thoughtfully, shooting young guys playing foosball, saying, "I wonder if I could ask you to...," grinning and ducking toward his viewfinder, at home anywhere.

The television seemed connected to a different time. Some old football game in black and white, then Nixon appeared. Then he vanished. The bar sound system played the Beatles "I've Just Seen A Face." Ezra pretended to be immune to all this sixties debris. The eighties produced much that was just as great, he said scornfully, though he couldn't name it all just at the moment.

The men's room also seemed to be stuck in time past. A slot machine sold a "Love Kit," consisting of Swedish Massage Oil, an Oriental Exciter Ring, an Exotic Condom, and Male Climax Control Creme, all for 50 cents. The condoms themselves might be Bold Black, Mint Scented (Stimulate Her Senses), Ultra Thin (36% Thinner For A More Natural Feeling), or Rough Rider Studded.

When I came back, Sammy Davis, Jr., was on the screen. While Tomasz prowled, Ezra and I played pool (and got thrashed), foosball (and got soundly thrashed), and darts, where my misspent youth had ingrained just enough neural connections for me to be able to win a few games despite the fact that the board had the annoying habit of blurring, like a propeller starting up, just as I was focusing on it to throw. When I finally quit, the TV was showing Olivia Newton-John.

"I admit it," confessed Ezra, now at that intimate stage of drunkenness when you talk to someone by draping yourself on them so they can see how open and pure your heart is. "I was born too late." He promised to show us the sights of Chicago next morning and we sloped out to his car. Before we got in, struck by a thought, he asked "Got a quarter?"

I fumbled in my pocket, squinted at the coins, and held it out on my open palm as directed. "I'm going to grab that quarter out of your hand," he said. "You're going to try to stop me, but you won't. If I snatch it, I get to keep it. If I don't, you get to keep it. Okay?"

What the hell? It was only a quarter. I held my hand out, he poised his own hand about a foot above it, and Tomasz stood by snickering.

Ezra grabbed the quarter. Just like that. I barely had time to move. "Let me try," said Tomasz, like the Polish team in the Drunkards' Olympics. *Bam.* Ezra had his quarter, too. "I put myself through college on that trick," he said, and drove us back to the Holiday Inn.

CHAPTER 31

Bitumen in Their Veins

August 15—Evanston, Illinois

God, my head. Three Tylenol. Up every 45 minutes drinking water. Another three Tylenol. More water....Never again. Just can't metabolize alcohol these days. Worst of all, after Tomasz and I struggled out of our respective beds to meet Ezra at ten, he never turned up; we didn't seem to have his number, and there were about 18 columns of Beckers in the phone book. We gave him an extra 45 minutes and then, in a fit of pique, decided to give up on Chicago altogether and make for Detroit, where I'd cross into Canada and make for London, Ontario, my last scheduled port of call. I wanted to meet Larry van de Maele, the son of the tobacco farmer I worked for in 1973. I navigated Tomasz through the South Side, with its abandoned streets and shuttered stores, and here and there billboards looming over the wreckage, advertising cheap divorces and bankruptcy counseling. He seemed shaken—and he had seen the slums of the Philippines.

Morning fell into afternoon. The sky got more overcast and humid as we went east, as if the air itself were getting more crowded. By now I had actively become allergic to tobacco smoke. Three weeks previously it had merely been annoying; now my sinuses swelled and started watering copiously at the first hint of smoke, and I started sneezing. I think Tomasz was slightly shocked; certainly, he smoked less.

It rained. Tomasz told me about being sent on a shooting assignment to Romania, and seeing room after room full of babies with AIDS. "What can you do for him?" he asked a doctor. "What, this?" demanded the doctor contemptuously, lifting an inert leg. "I saw red," Tomasz said. "They had to drag me off him."

The first truck stop we found—in Dearborn, Michigan, birthplace of Ford Motors and the assembly line—was so primitive and so depressing, we barely recognized it as such. It was more of a truck graveyard. We circled the area as if in a film shot, moving silently from one abandoned building to the next, from one vacant area of cracked pavement to the next, passing a couple of down-at-heel men on a stoop as if they, too, had bitumen in their veins; the camera shot came around to where it started as if to show that there was no way out.

We made for Woodhaven where, we'd been told, there was a bigger truck stop, one of the biggest in the country. The sky was the color of asphalt. The setting sun stuck in it like a rotten orange. Climbing steadily up an overpass, seeing nothing in the smog and low cloud, we might have been driving off the planet. Then the road crested, and we could see around us again—and it was a sight from hell, from a Hieronymous Bosch painting, but a modern Bosch, with no hellish, contorted people, just hellish contorted objects: refinery piping, tanks, high-tension wires. The air was hot and fetid; it smelled like a fume hood.

"This is in a way worse than the south of Chicago," Tomasz said, appalled. The South Side of Chicago was an example of man's inhumanity to man. This was an example of man's inhumanity to everything. "People say that Poland is polluted," he went on. "The worst place in Poland is far better than this."

We found the other truck stop, where Tomasz shot pictures of me in front of a car transporter, its lights on against the gathering dark. While he was changing rolls of film I chatted to the driver, a skinny, cheerful, young southerner, and realized that I had finally found my Alabama truck driver. Even in this forsaken place, it seemed as if a curse had been lifted, as if the past had finally detached itself and was being left behind in the petrol-stained water.

Well, maybe. In the attached restaurant, a trucker was hissing abuses at his wife in a loud whisper, while she stared back at him with steady hatred. Someone had pissed all over the floor of the men's room. "Grab your things. I've got to get out of here," I told Tomasz. I had the sense that a fight was going to break out any moment, or a gas main would explode under the building. He wouldn't go: he had been collared by a broadly smiling clean-cut guy who turned out to be from Cross Road Ministries, a mission from the Metro Baptist Church in Belleville, who was planning to hold a service the following morning in the Drivers' Lounge, followed by a second service in Belleville and a free home cooked meal prepared by "the ladies of the church." I dragged him away.

Just off this ghastly highway under this ghastly sky, we found ourselves in Raymond Chandler country again. A sour desk clerk stared down a young, nervous Japanese man who had a confirmation number from the airport but no room. "That's not my fault," she said. He had nowhere to go, and just stood there. He looked as though he was about to cry. "I got one room left, and that's the Jacuzzi room," she said. He said nothing. "Well, I guess I could find something," she muttered angrily, and gave him a different room. He opened the envelope he had been holding, and gave her three new 20-dollar bills. She offered the next guy the Jacuzzi room for $125. He took it. "The motor's broken," she said. "Don't use it."

It was a shell game. She found us yet another nonexistent room. There were dead insects in the sink, and the room stank of— bizarrely—old apple pie. "It's like a Hitchcock movie," Tomasz said in disbelief. "There is something in the air."

"I need a drink," I said. We dragged ourselves next door for a beer—next door being the next hotel. It was karaoke night. People sat in a windowless room, drank beer, and at the urging of their friends stood up and sang to a television screen.

CHAPTER 32

You Aren't Going to Blow Us Up, Are You?

August 16—Detroit, Michigan

Tomasz and I separated early on Sunday morning as he headed off for the trucker's spiritual breakfast. Later he told me that at 8:30 the Drivers' Lounge was empty except for two bedraggled and startled-looking truckers who seemed to have no idea what the hell was going on, and even the free food wouldn't lure them out to Belleville.

We both loaded up. He made me promise to call him if anything went wrong.

"Watch out for yourself," I said in return. "Before you know it, they'll have made you give up photography and you'll be saving souls in Romania."

"At this point," he said with a weary smile, "anything would be better than continuing this trip."

I didn't take this personally. As always, I was glad to be heading off on my own again, but I knew I'd miss him. Just by appearing every four or five days, he and even the wretched Skylark had acquired a faint hint of the essence of home, and I was always glad to see them. He and I disagreed on almost everything, but he was never furtive or malicious. We had plans to meet in Vermont, but I fully expected them to misfire, like all the rest of our plans, and our friendship to expire in one last cell-phone call: "Tomasz! Where are you?" "Well, I am in this small town in Pencil-vannya, quite charming, I must say, but the light is terrible...."

As it turned out, he would make a second trip around the country to shoot all the photos he had missed. Left to his own devices and directions, he would nearly incinerate in South Dakota and nearly freeze to death in Montana; he would meet a coffin maker who made coffin furniture that you could use around the house and then convert and climb into when your time came; and would be invited to take part in devious and dangerous sexual practices by an obese dominatrix in New Hampshire. Everyone finds the America he is looking for.

The on-ramp to I-75 was one of the nastiest places I've hitched in my life. The roadside was littered with bits of fiberglass, a steel flotsam and jetsam of car parts, a syringe, and a plastic tampon applicator. People in huge American cars stared at me as if I were a hunchback. Worst of all were the mosquitoes, which were many and vicious. The veteran hitchhiker in me completely forgot I had been carrying expensive bug repellant for 8,000 miles and ran back across the highway to a Best Western to have breakfast, soothe my shattered nerves, scratch my bites, and take a cab to the border.

Which turned out to be far easier said than done. The cabbie's name was Pat. "Where are you from?" Vermont, I said. "Montpelier!"

she cried triumphantly. As a kid, she said, she wrote to every one of the state capitals—"That was my little hobby, you know"—and was sent maps and brochures. She was still showing such go-get-'em, still working her way up in the world. She now drove a cab one day a week, instead of seven. Most days she now worked for a courier service, making better money and having her health insurance paid for her. She wore braces on both wrists. "Carpel tunnel syndrome?" I asked. "Yes," she said in disgust. "From driving?" I went on, wrong as usual. "No, from the computer," she said. "Driving doesn't affect me a bit."

Neither she nor the dispatcher had ever heard of anyone walking across the bridge to Canada—or through the tunnel, come to think of it—and had no idea if it were possible. That's ridiculous, I said. How would people without cars cross the border? She couldn't say. People without cars are unknown in Detroit. We decided that she would drive me to the toll booths at the American side of the bridge and see if I could walk across. If so, she'd drop me off; if not, she'd take me over.

That settled, she relaxed into looking around her at the highway which, it turned out, had recently been resurfaced. "God, this is beautiful!" she sighed. I dreaded to think what it had looked like before. Parts of Detroit, she kept telling me, were very pretty. Yeah, I thought sourly, but I don't expect that the line workers, the people who made the cars that made America famous, live in those parts.

As we pulled through the tollbooths on the Detroit side of the bridge, I saw that there was a sidewalk, as common sense would expect, running over the bridge, and no signs prohibited crossing by foot, so I paid Pat for the ride and the bridge toll, thanked her, and she headed off to cross the bridge and return to Detroit. I threw on my pack and set off along the sidewalk, passing a large metal sign (lying down) that read "Handguns PROHIBITED in Canada."

Within seconds, I heard yelling behind me, and a shortish, middle-aged guy in uniform was bouncing after me. "No walking on the bridge!" he yelled. "You can't walk on the bridge!"

"Why not?" I asked. "There's a sidewalk."

"Yeah, but you can't use it."

"How am I supposed to get across, then?"

"If you haven't got a car, you'll have to call a cab."

I explained that I had just gotten out of a cab, and that Pat was by now crossing back on the other side of the bridge in search of more of Detroit's magnificent new roads. He was stumped, but adamant. They couldn't let me walk.

"Why not?"

"This is a private bridge. We're not allowed to let walkers on it."

"A private bridge? But this is an international border. You mean this is a privately owned border crossing?"

And so it was. The toll guard, whose name was Joe, took me into the bridge supervisor's office as the intercom was screeching "We got a walker on the bridge! We got a walker on the bridge!" The bridge supervisor, whose name was Ralph, explained that the bridge was the property of one Maddy Moroun, who owned not only a major share in the company that owned the bridge but a substantial share in the tunnel, the only other means of crossing between Detroit and Windsor, Ontario. In fact, he owned the American side of the bridge through an American company and the Canadian side through a Canadian company. His companies also owned duty-free stores on both sides of the border, and a number of trucking companies that regularly crossed over the bridge or through the tunnel. But as to why I couldn't walk across, they had no answer.

Joe and Ralph came up with a compromise: I could hitch on the American side, on the approach to the tollbooths, and, if I was still there when their shift ended, they'd give me a ride over. This was very kind of them, but it must be said that standing on the verge of eight lanes of traffic, all sorting itself out and searching its pockets for change, is not the easiest place to hitch. An enormous black Cadillac pulled up with a front vanity plate that read YES BLACK WOMAN. One of the female toll workers asked me warily if I'd been threatened or attacked, and when I told her that everyone who'd picked me up had been kind and friendly, she replied "Those are the ones I'm afraid of—the kind ones. They lure you."

No sooner had I started to worry that I'd be there until Ralph's shift ended when a big American car pulled over and I got a ride all the way to London. With a communist.

His name was John Foley. He was stocky, medium height, with dark hair swept across his forehead, making him look younger than his 55 years. He kept strong hands on the wheel of his big, American, union-built car. He worked at the GM Delphi plant in Rochester, working in a machining area, deburring fuel rails, a part that brings fuel to the combustion chambers in the engines.

He was on his way back to Rochester from a meeting in Detroit. "I'm with a group called New Directions [for the UAW]. Which is really Old Directions: there's still labor, there's still management." While I'd been on the road, I realized, I'd missed the outcome of the big GM strike over relocating jobs to Mexico, and asked him what the result had been. He shook his head, as if the outcome had been not only unsatisfactory but predictable and all too familiar. The union had sold out. Leadership had caved in, made concessions, made a big show of cooperation with management in their common interest, and the workers had ended up losing yet more ground, another small step backward.

Wait a moment. This condemnation of the union leadership—specifically of the United Auto Workers Union, sounded familiar. Wasn't that what Michael Moore had implied in his documentary *Roger and Me*, which showed General Motors stripping and abandoning his home town of Flint, Michigan? He chuckled. "Michael Moore is hated by the UAW. *Hated.*"

He talked about the sad, bitter history of American labor, from its initial sell-out a hundred years ago when the American Federation of Labor became the first procapitalist national labor organization; through the brutalities of 1918-1938, when strikers were attacked by Pinkerton men, police, the Army and hired thugs; to the Cold War, when the more enlightened industrialists realized they could live with unions as long as they were guaranteed to be docile, and agreed to recognize unions' right to exist in return for the unions agreeing to throw out their radical members, not to criticize Cold War policy and to refrain from social analysis and comment—in short, to castrate themselves as a political force in order to become "business unions."

I was curious: How had he become politicized in a country that is so conservative that the Democrats are regarded as left of center? And how had he stayed radical when the rest of us were wimping out?

It was probably in his family roots, he said. One grandfather had worked on the docks in Boston, the other was a fireman, and his parents were in the restaurant business. He spent a year at Bard College, dropped out, went into the Army from 1963-66, then worked in construction, in a textile plant, and finally at GM.

"In college, I was a liberal Democrat. I dropped out after a year; went into the Army, then into construction. It was the trade union stuff that got me to the left. The fella I worked for had a fairly extensive library. He was close to being political. He'd gone to Cornell Labor Studies School after World War II. I started to read about the early CIO and began to realize, 'Huh. There were a lot of left people around in the trade union movement,' even though they never elected anybody.

"When I was an organizer for the Service Employees International in Syracuse and Rochester we were organizing, but we were going around in suits. This was service model unionism: The workers voted in the union, and then the union sent in the suits to talk to the boss suits. Somehow this didn't seem right. We were like the gas company: you hired the gas company to take care of running gas through your house. Hire the union to run the union through your plant. You didn't create anything in the workers. If they had a question about the boss, they'd say to me 'You're in the union,' because they knew I was on the Education Committee, or this or that. In the end I gave up saying 'No, we're all in the union...,' because by that time less than 2 percent of the people were coming to meetings.

"The first two UAW presidents, when I got there in the mid-seventies had somewhat of a socialist or social democratic background. They still talked about workers taking control of the plants, about the sit-down strikes of 1936, 1937. Social unionism was still around in the UAW: you had a women's committee, a civil rights committee...."

By "social unionism," I took him to mean a sense of universal sister-and-brotherhood, a concern for all working Americans and indeed workers of the world, rather than uniting merely to protect one's own job. As soon as he started talking in this vein I knew that this was the last, uncharted territory on my trip, the missing Left side of the country, as misunderstood and misdescribed as the Louisiana territory, left of the Mississippi, in 1799.

"The UAW still had summer schools. You'd still hear people saying 'These corporations don't care about jobs, cars, or people; they just care about profits.' You'd still hear that kind of statement from a course instructor at the UAW Cornell Summer School. They still had political economists in their research department, people who could use words like 'capitalism.' They didn't use the word 'socialism' very much, but many of them came from a socialist background."

And now? "Social unionism is dead. They've internalized the corporate agenda. Everything that comes down from management is a joint statement. A change in the hours —they're now going to butt the shifts instead of overlapping them, which means we effectively have to work an extra half hour—that will probably come down as a business decision that the shop committee has signed on to. I'm sure that the young [workers] can't tell you where the union begins and where the company ends."

Ironically, this sounds just like the way unions were co-opted in eastern European countries under Stalin: They chose power instead of principles. "So they're aiming for a frictionless relationship?" I asked.

"Right. Which is, of course, bullshit. There are strikes, sure, when work is outsourced or sent to a Mexican plant, but there's no social vision or trade union vision any more in the United Auto Workers leadership." One leader recently said "Well, even if they go to nonunion plants, we want them to be American non-union plants," which is straying dangerously close to right-wing nationalism.

Despite his opposition to the UAW, he was still prounion. "Unions do left things: They redistribute wealth and power at the point of production or service. You don't pass the overtime out to whoever you want; you pass it out on an equalized basis." I found myself thinking of Bob, the trucker who never got a load going to Texas because dispatch hated him. I was coming full circle. "There are objective reasons why someone gets a promotion, it's not subjective. And if the objective criteria are equal, then seniority prevails. Workers do still have some power through their union to control what happens to them, but that's slipping away. In 1982 the union started concessionary movements, saying that workers had to cooperate with management to fight off foreign competition—the Japs, as they called them. As soon as that stuff started, everything else went."

I asked John when he joined the Communist Party. "In the mid-eighties, I was working with an unemployment council in upstate New York. Some of the people who were doing the best work with agencies in the area were communists, and that's when I got recruited into the CP. And I enjoyed all the people I met—it was as much social as political. I was looking for some place on the left to hang my hat. Since I was an industrial worker, they were very happy to have me, since most of the party members were middle class—teachers, government employees.

"I was around for effectively five or six years, and then a group of us walked out. Angela Davis left. In spite of what they said, they were still Stalinists." At one big, successful meeting of a thousand labor people from the broad left, "this old party hack showed up" and starting talking about taking the conference over. "I looked across at this guy who was the vice-president from Local 1199, we were in the party together, I was on the state committee for New York, and it was like 'Jesus Christ!' But that's the way those old left people talk. It's hard enough talking about the left to workers who have had no exposure without Stalinists talking about 'We're going to take this over....' "

He continued to work as a rank-and-file activist, running the education committee, but it was an uphill struggle. "Most union workers' level of vision was 'Let's get Bill Clinton elected.' My God! The first thing he did was to push NAFTA!" John was always more committed and more radical than the majority of union men around him, even those on the education committee. "One guy would literally walk out of the room when I talked about this stuff, and now he's a lobbyist for the Professional Employees' Federation."

Hearing this story of the decay of radical sentiment, I asked him what happened to the so-called new left that arose with the Civil Rights marches, the free speech movement, and opposition to the Vietnam War—the youthful energy and commitment of my generation?

"The activism of the sixties was basically self-interest. There was nothing underneath the new left politics that required permanent change. Everyone could still go to college. Income was still going to be distributed the way it had always been. Power was still going to reside in the government, with a few adjustments. There was no class analysis in the new left. People going off to live in the hills weren't going to change anything."

In our defense, I couldn't help adding that thanks to McCarthy, when the radical generation finally arrived it had no exposure to left ideas and no left organizations to call on as allies. Everything had to start from scratch, from ignorance, among middle-class members of the new left who didn't feel personal, day-by-day class injustice.

"There were working-class people in the new left," he agreed, "but once it was over, it was over. The war was stopped, and that was good, but after that there was no reason why those people [from different backgrounds] would meet each other on a daily basis."

Meanwhile, the manufacturing economy began to dwindle just as minorities were beginning to get into steel, say, so they were pushed out into the growing service industry, the least unionized sector in the country. "There was an article in the paper yesterday about a messenger on Wall Street who carries piles of money—checks, obviously, nothing he could steal—around all day for $5.50 an hour and lives in a homeless shelter. And an African-American who had a job as a cook in a restaurant on Long Island who was living in a homeless shelter."

At the same time, the history and memory of the American left has fallen into a willful oblivion. "People [aren't] disloyal to capitalism because they [don't] know how to be disloyal to capitalism. The thousands of socialist newspapers that had been published by the foreign language societies [have] gone because the people were Americanized. I was carrying a copy of the *Monthly Review*, the Independent Socialists' magazine, and this electrician said, 'You aren't going to blow us up, are you?' The only time he'd ever heard of anyone being a socialist was some kind of radical bomb-thrower. The Italian syndicalists—even most Italian-Americans don't know about them. Wonderful tradition. Very important in the Lowell and Lawrence strikes. But what kid who lives in that town knows about them?"

Like Bruce, the hippie befriended by the Anashnase, John had had his battle with drink. It's hard to imagine anyone swimming against a current as broad and strong as mainstream American capitalism without suffering some damage. "How do you manage to sustain yourself?" I asked.

"Psychological profile. I'm an oppositional figure. This is how I get to be a pain in the ass. Maybe only certain people can do it because they're used to going right where everyone else goes left, and vice versa. It may be something you can't do if you want to get on with people. There may be people who could tell you the same things I've told you and have learned the same things I've learned, but they wouldn't want the alienation that came with it." He's used to a solitary life. He doesn't go deer hunting; he goes up into Canada to see movies and listen to jazz.

Did he see signs of hope anywhere? "The Saturn workers have just thrown out their UAW leadership for agreeing to take nonunion parts," he said. Mind you, the news from Saturn wasn't all good. "An African-American worker came and spoke to us who had gone down to Saturn headquarters near Spring Hill, and management said to him 'Don't you want to see the plantation?' They'd built a model plantation, with slave quarters and everything! He said, 'No, thank you. I'd just like to leave Tennessee.'"

He was the best-read, most thoughtful person who picked me up, and the first thing he did after dropping me off on the outskirts of London was to drive sixty yards down to the on-ramp and pick up a couple more hitchhikers.

Let's see, I thought, looking around the stores and businesses clustered around the interstate exit. How would I know I was now in

Canada? By the United Furniture Warehouse? Superstore Mall? Giant Carpet? Discovery Zone? McDonald's? Costco? Burger King? Arby's? Ah, yes, there was my evidence: the Amoco gas station. It proudly bore signs saying, "All Canadian Independent."

Yet the place was different, despite the superficial glaze of American commercial culture. As I was eating a fish sandwich in the McDonalds, a couple in late middle age came over to me and asked me if I was hitchhiking, and if so, would I like a ride to Toronto? When I declined, grateful and astonished, but said that I planned to head on in that direction in a day or two, they gave me a list of places to stay and things to see. A young couple with a child asked me the same question as I was leaving. This was the hitchhiking I remembered: ordinary, simply part of the landscape. I wondered if it had anything to do with the fact—well, the rumor, I suppose, as I haven't been able to find anyone in office with a memory long enough to verify it—that in the early 1970s the Canadian government, concerned about Quebec separatism and rumblings of dissent from the West, decided that it was vital for the future of the nation that young Canadians think of the nation as a whole, and came up with a brilliant and visionary plan. They would appropriate a small amount of money to beef up the country's youth hostel system and start a propaganda campaign to encourage hitchhiking, and to encourage people to pick up hitchhikers. If this is what actually happened, never in human history has a government so neatly caught and used the spirit of the age; and never has $6 million in federal money had such widespread and long-lasting effect that it was still being felt 25 years later in a fast-food joint.

When Larry and his wife Josie arrived in the family van, we didn't recognize each other. Of course, last time that I saw him, he had a full, stringy beard and long hair piled under a baseball cap, and

I'd forgotten his large, piercing eyes. But then I hadn't really known him at all: I had no idea he loved sailing, and had bummed his way down to and around the Caribbean for a year. I'd forgotten that his first child had already been born by that harvest summer; I didn't know he had divorced his first wife and remarried....All I remembered, really, was him showing me the opening to "Stairway to Heaven," the smell of exhaust as he backed his '55 Chevrolet out of the garage that was the other half of the bunkhouse where we pickers lived, and his passionate wish not to follow his father into the tobacco.

Oh, and one other thing: I remembered that he had a high school friend called John Bentley who appeared halfway through the season and asked for a job, becoming our sixth picker. John had long hair, loose, old clothes and spoke slowly, half to you and half to the middle distance. He had spent the previous three or four months riding up and down the Rockies on a horse. He declined a place in the bunkhouse and slept in his sleeping bag out on the grass, where I couldn't stand for a minute without being devoured by mosquitoes.

"John, how do you do it?" I asked him after a while.

"Well," he explained slowly, with his knowing grin, "you've heard that all living things give out vibrations?" All right, I thought, I'll take this and see where it leads, and I nodded. "Well," he said, his grin slowly growing wider, "if you're really, really in tune with Nature, you don't give out any vibrations. Then the mosquitoes can't find you."

Later that day, I ran this explanation by Larry. He snorted. "If I'd spent the last three months on a horse, would you want to bite me?"

We drove out to Larry and Josie's neat little suburban house. Since I'd last seen him, he had fulfilled his greatest ambition and got out of the tobacco. "Eighty was my last crop, or eighty-one." He retrained in electronics repair, putting himself through tech school by playing in a country band at night, and ended up owning his own repair business in London. A lot of people are following him out of the tobacco: The total yield is down 30 percent since 1973, and the number of farms in the area has halved.

Ben had died after two heart attacks. Larry visited him in hospital after one collapse and Ben said "I've been flying." Flying? asked Larry quizzically. Yes, said Ben, the most sensible and phlegmatic man you'd ever meet, and described the classic near-death experience of floating around the room, then the hospital, then out around a tree there in the grounds—and of course Larry realized that from the bed where Ben had been lying, he couldn't see that part of the grounds, or have known that there was a tree out there, just where he described it. By the time Ben died he had sold off portions of land, then the farms and one of the houses, leaving his financial fields in good order and his family well provided for.

When we got home, Josie's sons, Jordan and Brandon, were in the den watching...wait for it...*The Monkees*. "This is Tim," she said. "He's a traveler," and out of the blue, or the black, or whatever color we ascribe to forgetting, came a memory: when I came home after my trip to America in 1973 my little sister Jennie, then nine, had stuck a homemade sign on my bedroom door saying, "Welcome Home Traviller." I've still got it.

Tonight was a billiards night: Josie and two of the boys were in a local league: small prizes for weekly winners, and the one in each category with the most wins gets a trip for two to Las Vegas. She changed into her pool shark's-gear: lamé top that left her midriff bare, and denim shorts. "I'd always been competitive at baseball and volleyball," she said. "When I turned 40, I looked around for something else to be competitive at, and I found pool." She had won the local event once, Larry Ben three times, Jordan twice. The boys already had their own cues, and she had just ordered herself a custom cue, too, which would cost $350. We pulled back the cover, brushed off the baize, and played a few warm-up games. I played a couple of times and managed some good runs, but while I was fading, trying too hard, the others were moving up through the gears. She bought the table, she said, so the kids would have something to do at home, something that would keep the family together. Now the family was heading out into town like a trio of gunfighters.

Larry and I climbed into the van in search of the past. Many of my most vivid memories of that summer were from the tobacco: Ben leaning in the bunkhouse door, switching on what he called "the hydro" and calling "Time to empty a kil', boys." Mary's enormous breakfasts, huge plates domed high with scrambled eggs, pancakes, sausages, bacon. Struggling into waterproofs, as the plants were always wet with a vicious dew that had soaked up nicotine: One drop in your eye and you were blinded for two or three minutes until the stinging passed and you stopped cursing. The hard-edged metal framework of the picker that crawled the rows, and the boxes into which you slapped the leaves, and the fact that the slightest knock against that metal left a gouge or cut that wouldn't heal for weeks, the scab getting soaked and softened by each morning's dew. Then stripping off the waterproofs by 9 a.m. as the sun rose, and from then on every leaf you broke off at the stem threw a drop of sap onto your hands, or your forearm, or your hair, or anywhere nearby; and as it dried it formed a tiny speck of black tar. I've got a photo of myself in among the leaves, and there's a black smudge on the tip of my nose.

And after work, taking a shower in the greenhouse, where the water was cold on cold days and scalding on hot ones. There was nothing to do in the evening but drink beer, so every couple of nights we walked two or three miles along a dirt road into Vienna (population: 450) whose only hotel had not only a bar but a pool table. The sun had just gone down at the end of an other cloudless day, and for the first time I noticed that between the dusty orange at the horizon and the purple of the night the sky managed to be green, a color that was beyond my comprehension. This was not the breezy, nimble English evening sky I knew; it was the motionless, hermetic nightfall of the mid-continent, where the universe seems to have been painted on the inside of a vast glass ball in which the sounds of insects and of a footfall scuffing dirt might travel forever, and anything could be about to happen.

Larry drove me out to see his mother, and to look at the old farm after all these years. It was dusk. The old hotel had burned down; the new Vienna was just a half-lit crossroads scrawled on the evening landscape. Down the road, the tobacco plants were smaller than they seemed when I was bent double underneath them, picking the leaves from the ground up, and were now gray in the twilight, row on row vanishing into the darkness. The new owner must have consolidated farms, for the buildings were silent and empty, the wooden kilns stood open and the yard was full of nothing but moonshadow.

Mary lived in a small, well-kept house; she and Larry greeted each other with affectionate courtesy. She offered us boys a beer, and then she and Larry remembered all those pickers from years ago: a Barbadian, some Floridians, the kids from northern Ontario who worked alongside me. Mary couldn't picture Boots, the one who told me that he had been expelled from high school for sniffing gasoline;

she didn't like Weeds at all, and Lonnie was forever combing his long blond hair and wrapping it carefully in a T-shirt so that when the sap dried the tobacco tar wouldn't cake on it and ruin it. Ben was forever cursing Lonnie, she remembered, saying "Goddamn that boy, he's always the last in the trailer!"

Now she kept busy as best she could, took calls from her children, had just come back from a trip to Grand Bend "with four other widows," she added, a little caustically. She was dreading the coming winter. She had pulled her shoulder out bringing in firewood when Ben was sick and despite physiotherapy, chiropractic, and massage, she said, "I don't think it'll ever be completely better." She had a cabin in the woods, but out there she felt even more isolated; she often thought she might sell it, but then changed her mind.

Larry was the last of my revisits. It had been a curious experience, meeting figures from so far back in my life that I no longer knew them; and in any case my memory had played its card game on them, shuffling the facts and picking out only the details it wanted. Simply confirming that the experience had happened seemed to be a tonic. Even the odious Richard resurfaced: I discovered from one of his distant relatives in Canada that he was married and living in Norway, and to my amazement, I found myself feeling glad that he was still alive and doing well. The fact that a person had entered my life at all was apparently something to be grateful for. It was like Bell's theorem—that once two elementary particles have been in contact, it's impossible for them to remain unaffected by each other, no matter how far estranged by distance or time. As if love were simply the warmth created by brushing up against each other.

I came to believe that we are an aggregate of the personalities we have been in our lives (and, some would say, our previous lives), but instead of collecting selves we tend to abandon them, afraid that they will embarrass us in public, or get us in trouble. As any parent knows, having a child encourages us to be a child again, and a self that had been put away in the attic with the toys now rushes out to meet us with open arms, in all its rolling-on-the-floor impishness and delight. Finding these people also involved finding the part of myself that had set out to explore the world, and realizing that that self was still available, if I wanted him. Life is not just consumption and decay: We can blow on the embers of the past to rekindle the present.

CHAPTER 33

Dowsing for Kindness

August 17—London, Ontario

Next morning found me looking for a bus stop, walking through a neat little development of bungalows and two-story houses in brick, in the English fashion, with neat lawns and flower beds. It seemed to be a sensible mid-Atlantic compromise, like so many things Canadian. In America, each house and its land would take up at least twice as much space; in England, slightly less. The bus was prompt and clean, the driver courteous. Downtown was in good repair; the population was ethnically diverse; nobody looked lost or broken. The buildings were modest in scale and ambition, and there was no sense of waste. I felt as if I'd just spent the previous four weeks in a Third World nation, or at least a post-apocalyptic First World one.

Life in America seemed plagued by both fears of crisis and unrealistic hopes. In America, teenagers might or might not be taking drugs, Christ was wrestling with Satan, the Stock Market might boom or bust, the President might shrug it all off or be impeached, the U.S. Cavalry might save the world or destroy it, and your local public radio station would go broke without your contribution, so call now.

On the other hand, the landscape of the United States, so scruffy by contrast—cheap slotted utility poles at every angle but the vertical, untrimmed hedgerows, cracked paving, traffic lights swinging on absurd little wires—gives me, at least, a perverse sense of value. We don't want America to grow up and be sensible; we want it to be forever risky, the place to live on the edge, to take chances, the place to sharpen our edge. In trim and tidy Canada, as in England, I feel as if everything has already been taken care of by someone else, things are going on very nicely without my help. In the U.S. there is work to be done, a country still to be built. Heroes needed: apply at the third window on the left.

I caught a second bus, which dropped me off by 401, dragged myself to the on-ramp, and put my thumb out. I wanted to go home, but I didn't want to give up this trip: I hadn't gotten enough out of it, yet, to let it go. I'd hitch to Toronto, I thought, then catch a train to Montreal—I love trains—and a bus down to Burlington, but it felt like giving up.

After 20 minutes, I was picked up by a young guy selling $2,000 vacuum cleaners, the kind that vacuum even the air.

"I hope you don't mind if I drive fast," he said.

"Just as long as we get there alive," I said, my usual answer, intended to perch in the back of his mind like a macaw speaking the voice of reason, but this time it didn't work. He hit 99 mph, in traffic, on 401 just west of Woodstock. At that speed, tires feel as if they're melting: The car starts to lose its grip on the road and you feel it starting to float from side to side over the tires. By the time

I got out I was shaking and my nerve had gone. *That's it,* I thought. *I've had enough. I'm too old for this kind of thing.* I couldn't even bring myself to stick my thumb out. From the rubble beside the shoulder, the cars and trucks looked not like opportunities but lethal weapons—a deer's-eye view.

Yet as I was standing there ten feet back from the highway, feeling small and beaten, not even hitching, I got picked up. A Volvo pulled over—another first—driven by Walter Bak, a roly-poly young Polish guy, the son of a machinist who had one day packed his suitcase and walked to Austria to escape communism. (He was a tool-and-die worker, but when he reached Canada the government sent him to Saskatchewan, where there's nothing but wheat. It's not only communism that produces daft bureaucracies.) After Walter dropped me off at Kitchener, I was wandering reluctantly through stringy grass toward the on-ramp, thinking, *I still don't want to do this,* when a car pulled over and another young guy called out, "Are you hitchhiking?"

"Uh...yeah," I said uncertainly.

"Where are you going?"

"Toronto."

"I'm going to....ah, what the hell, I'll take you to Toronto." His name was John Ouzas, he was just about to leave for a year at the University of Glasgow. Having nothing much to do he drove me 50 miles out of his way to Toronto, and I knew that somehow, I was being taken care of. If I wasn't going to the drivers, they would come to me.

Oddly, I had been half-expecting something like this to happen. Even before I set out from home, I wanted to know what would happen once I relaxed my usual vigilant, slightly anxious grip on my life, and allowed other forces to come into play—forces I couldn't name or explain, let alone control. Would things fall apart, or would I be, in some strange way, helped? And for me this led to a broader question, one that underlay everything: how does our life turn out the way it does? Luck? Hard work? Or is there sometimes an invisible hand on the wheel, whose light touch affects our course only if we're not gripping too tightly, too desperately?

I wanted to know because that's what seemed to have happened in 1973. After the tobacco season was over, I had three weeks of vacation left and, apart from the need to be in New York on October 3 to fly back to England, I had no particular place to go. I thought I might make for Boston, as I'd heard it was a cool city, but in the back of my mind I had a far more ambitious destination: I wanted to find a way to stay in America.

I was on the New York State Thruway east of Buffalo when a black Porsche stopped. I've never had a ride in a Porsche, before or since. The driver said he was going onto the Mass Pike, but then he'd have to let me off, as he was turning south and going to New Haven. All right, I thought, I'll go to New Haven. Mitzi was there—she had transferred to Yale—so I could crash with her. As we pulled into New Haven, though, I realized I didn't know her address, and I had no means of finding her. The driver dropped me off on a corner downtown, I put down my holdall and guitar, stretched, looked around, and there was Mitzi, standing right next to me.

So I slept on her couch for a few days, got to meet her housemates, and that Friday one of them told me he was going up to his parents' place in Vermont, and did I want to come? Sure, I said. Why not? I'd heard it was a pretty place. So we drove up, climbed one of the Green Mountains, ended up drinking beer in a bowling alley, went back down to New Haven, and the following day I got on the bus for New York, and the plane back home.

So when I applied for teaching jobs in the U.S., the University of Vermont was on my short, naive list; and even though my sooty letters of application were hand-typed on an old manual typewriter, and were so badly spaced that they either ran one line onto a second page or were squashed onto one page by typing in the top and bottom margins, UVM offered me a job.

Looking back down the forking path that left me in Vermont, it now seems an impossibly fragile twig. I never understood the choices I faced, never made informed decisions, and yet I ended up in a place that, although entirely unfamiliar, would come to feel more like home than anywhere else I'd lived.

So that was the lasting discovery of my journey, not so much a creed as a set of metaphysical possibilities to spell out and spend the rest of my life testing: that thoughts, when fed with passion or with energy, are also forces that may subtly affect others who are on a similar wavelength. That we are cared for, and can sometimes draw to ourselves the very people we need, or who need us. That living spontaneously can bypass the constricting effects of anxiety and give us access to astonishing inspiration and energy. That hitchhiking is, in effect, a sort of prayer, and the better part of me is the part that can let go, as if it were hitchhiking, thumb held out like a hazel twig, dowsing for kindness.

Downtown Toronto was full of miracles of steel and glass, but I'd had enough of miracles of steel and glass. I was tired. I just wanted to be home.

The VIA train left a slender footprint on the land, slipping quickly and quietly through the woods and fields of Ontario, spreading little exhaust and delaying almost nobody else. The car, by contrast, drags an entire paraphernalia of commuting out into the countryside, like a honeymoon car dragging a string of ever bigger tin cans: first the road, like string, then knotted onto it gas stations, quick-stops, fast-food joints, supermarkets, chunks of asphalt, Coke cans, cigarette packets, pieces of metal trim, drive-in ATMs, golden arches, cappuccino stands, car dealerships, Styrofoam coffee cups, parking lots, billboards, gasoline dregs in puddles, outlet centers, stop signs, and minute particles of pulverized rubber and brake linings— the entire nowhere landscape of the car that we had seen everywhere and had driven Tomasz insane.

On the train I met Gwendoline, a chic French-Canadian girl with oval glasses and her hair pulled back into four stainless-steel clips, the spray of hair over her eyes dyed blue. She was 15, though she looked four years older. She was returning from a stint as a live-in nanny for an American family, having hated it, but she was determined to keep practicing her English, even if it meant borrowing my English newspaper and reading about cricket. We started talking; she asked me searching questions about my trip, and after some time announced that she, too, was going to start hitchhiking. In fact, next summer she and a girlfriend were going to South America. What did I think of that idea?

Well, I thought, that's asking me to put my money where my mouth is, isn't it?

Plenty of women, I told her, have hitchhiked safely and successfully, and some still do. One of my UVM students whose car had broken down somewhere in Colorado wound up leaving it there and hitching to the West Coast and up through Oregon to Washington, climbing mountains, having wonderful experiences. (She carried a knife, though she never used it.) At the same time I was making my road trip, Jen Knops, the daughter of a friend of mine, set off across country with her boyfriend, slept in caves in the Black Hills, drove out to Seattle where she dumped him—another casualty of cross-country travel— then spent several months hitchhiking and riding freight trains up and down the West Coast with friends she'd met en route, picking up odd jobs. She was away six months in all.

"Did you ever feel at a disadvantage because you're a woman?" I asked.

She laughed and shook her head dismissively. "The only time was when I went into manpower agencies looking for work. 'Sorry,' they'd say, 'we've got nothing clerical.' I'd say, 'Give me a break. I've worked on trail crews; I've worked as a cook; I can handle hard work.' 'Okay,' they'd say, and they'd offer me some guy work, but say 'Sorry, we can only pay you $5.50 an hour because you're a girl....'"

All the same, going off to South America, where Gwendoline wouldn't speak the language, at 16, sounded a bit ambitious for anyone, boy or girl. I suggested she do as many small, safer trips as possible first, to learn how to cope: what to do if you fall ill, or run out of money, or the car breaks down, or there's nowhere to spend the night. How to get people to help you rather than take advantage of you; how to shrug off misfortune. The problem with imagined catastrophe is that it is absolute: In our nightmares we are helpless, our enemies superhuman—and we assume that, when confronted by the drunk or the thug there's nothing we'd be able to do. In fact, the outcome is in our own hands to a remarkable extent, but those may be untutored hands; making the best of a difficult situation is a learned skill, or a thousand learned skills. A *New York Times* columnist recently wrote about a 65-year-old Brooklyn woman who had driven through all 48 contiguous states. Almost all her encounters were not only safe but deeply affecting.

Once, though, she was harassed by a drunken man shouting obscenities at her while she used a pay phone at a campsite.

"I had been given mountain-lion training because a mountain lion had swiped a woman and her child," she reported. "We were told if we saw one, keep your ground, act big and make a lot of noise. I never saw a mountain lion, but that's what I gave this guy. I never shouted so loud in public."

Peggy Bradley, commenting in the *Los Angeles Times* in 1970 from the perspective of a woman who had been hitching for four years without ever being assaulted, said, "When you hitch it is important to feel relaxed and in control of your body. Once this feeling of confidence is mastered you will grow to love being on the road and constantly meeting new people." When she wrote "your body" she may have been thinking of the female body, with its supposed vulnerability, but it's true for all of us. Anyone can look like a target; anyone can look robust and self-reliant.

Gwendoline was clearly not your average 15-year-old. She had lived abroad, where she had to speak her second language, and she struck me as wary, yet curious, intelligent, well-read—she might go far. When I shook hands with her to say goodbye, her grip was surprisingly strong, and she looked me straight in the eye.

Meanwhile, another teenager had been chipping in on our conversation—Joe, a bright kid just about to start college at Vassar, coming back from Detroit where he and his mother had been helping relatives work on their house.

Joe, speaking with a slight lisp because of his pierced tongue, asked me if I wanted a ride—hitchhiking was determined not to let me give up. I was being offered rides even when I was on a train!—as his father would be meeting them at Cornwall, Ontario, and taking them home to the village where they lived in upstate

New York. Next morning they had to go into Plattsburgh; if I wanted, they could drive me to the ferry that ran across Lake Champlain to Vermont.

His father, Larry, who worked as a prison chaplain, picked us up at the train and drove us back to the tiny village of Churubusco, where over a late dinner he talked about the strange events following his father's death.

"We weren't doing that well financially," he began. "He died around Christmas, and I went down to be with my mother. She asked me to go through all his clothes and take anything I could use. I knew my dad: he was off and on, losing weight, gaining weight, losing weight, gaining weight. I knew there was nothing that was going to fit me. But something kept coming to me in the night: 'Your mom says, "Check the clothes."' Finally, about two days before I left, I went through his entire closet, and all ten different sizes, everything fit. Including shoes marked size seven and a half. I wear a size nine. I still have those seven-and-a-halfs.

"After that, I started feeling his presence a whole lot. I talked to a priest about it, because [in the Catholic religion] there is a warning: You don't speak to the dead. I told him, 'This is getting too strange.' He said, 'Wait a minute, Larry. Do you think your father went to heaven?' I said, 'Yeah, I think he went or he's on his way.' 'Then he is with the communion of saints?'

"Anyway. I'd be at work, and I'd get dizzy and disoriented. It was like I was floating through a channel. I would lose my train of thought. Finally, the revelation—and I feel it was a revelation—came to me. 'I've lived for 77 years in this physical presence. I'm in transition right now. I'm going from the known to the unknown. I need a link so I don't lose my way.' For whatever reason, my father chose me as that link."

His father "said" that he needed to resolve certain conflicts before he could let go and move on. "I remember feeling often that he was just drifting, and that he needed to feel, to hold on to what had become normal [to him] over 77 human years. I knew that he was reaching out to me. He and I weren't that close, but during that period I knew I was being used, willingly, by him to help with that transition from the physical life to the spiritual. It was incredibly powerful, to the point where if I was at work I'd have to sit down, and say, 'Okay, Dad, what are you spinning about right now?' "

Larry said he was the youngest of three brothers. "In theory it should fall to the oldest, but it came to me: 'Larry, you may be the youngest but now you are the patriarch of the family.' That was scary. I was given the care of my mother, for sure. Dad really had to talk to me. We talked about the fact that growing up he never said he loved me, or was proud of me. One night [during this transitional period] we had, oh, it must have been an hour-long conversation, and he made it quite plain that he did love me deeply, and was proud of me. "Apart from the personal matters, it was mainly 'I'm uncomfortable. This doesn't feel right. It's not what I'm used to!' It was confusing to him. Maybe he had a preconceived notion of what it was going to be after [death], and it wasn't the way he thought it was going to be!"

As time went on, the contact became less powerful and less frequent. "I remember saying 'How long is this supposed to last? This is really starting to affect my work, it's starting to affect everything.' And it came to me: 'How long did it take for the Master to go through his transition [in the wilderness]?' Well, 40 days. 'It will not be as long as the Master.' And that was it. On the 37th day the cloud lifted, the fog lifted. It was weird. It was really weird.

"Do I believe in the afterlife? After that, you bet I do."

For some reason, I lay awake that night thinking of my grand-mother. Widowed in middle age, she moved to the south coast of England and lived in the same village for her last 30 years, but her life was seldom dull. Not only was she a great walker, like her daughter, my mother, but she kept a kind of global open house. Whenever my Aunt Ruth, who emigrated to New Zealand, heard of a student heading for England, or my Aunt Barbara set off on one of her vagabond trips to North Africa or the Middle East or China, they would pass out my grandmother's name, address, and phone number; and as a result, the doorbell of the little house in East Dean was rung day and night by an unpredictable cascade of visitors, some having barely arrived in the country and speaking almost no English, who signed her visitors' book and slept in her spare bedroom. They kept her on her toes; they may have kept her young, for she lived to be a spry 92. I found myself thinking of her as the inventor of stationary hitchhiking.

CHAPTER 34

We Should Do All Right

August 18—Churubusco, New York

I n the morning it was drizzling. For the first time in a month I pulled on my jeans, borrowed an umbrella, and walked around the dripping maples, the three dozen fading, white wooden houses, and a stone Catholic church around a single hollow square that is the village of Churubusco.

Larry drove us down to Plattsburgh, a somber trip in the drizzle: The trees on both sides were bent or shattered from January's catastrophic ice storm; and those that were still upright now lacked most of their upper branches, so they looked as if they'd been given a buzz-cut. "I hadn't seen that kind of devastation since Vietnam," Larry said.

Joe pointed out Lyon Mountain, where they mined the iron that made the Golden Gate Bridge, though the mines are long closed. Both of them talked about the difficulties of living in a small impoverished town in upstate New York, especially, Joe said, if you're a teenager with long hair and a pierced tongue, or in fact any kind of independence of thought.

"A lot of kids in our class have never made it out of Clinton County," Joe said. Most of the students he graduated with would stay around town, and many of those who went away to college typically returned after a few weeks, finding the outside world too much for them. "We're so secluded that people lose the desire to do anything that involves leaving the town," Joe said. "It's very sad."

The drive was somber also because I was almost home. I wished I had been able to spend longer away; I wished I'd been able to spend more time on back roads—but then part of me might never have returned. At the end of *Trio's Trek*, the story of three women's hitchhiking trip from England via France, Spain, the North African Coast, Egypt, the Sudan, Uganda, and Belgian Congo to Kenya, Mary Jacques-Aldridge wrote: "Now the three of us would settle down to ordinary, mundane lives again; the freedom, the camaraderie, the novelty, the open road would become only memories...." I dreaded that fall back to earth, and with it the loss of my solitary certainty, my sense of direction.

On a bright day, the view from the Lake Champlain ferries is spectacular, with the wooded shorelines, the Green Mountains rippling down the eastern horizon and the younger, taller, and more rocky Adirondacks to the west. Today was was gray and cold. Nobody from the boat picked me up on the far shore, even though I was in my home state, even though I was passed by cars with University of Vermont stickers. I walked a mile, thumbing, thinking that for the first time, I could conceivably walk the 20 miles home if I didn't get a ride, though it would take me until dark and my knee would probably be wrecked. Then a well-ridden pickup—

God bless pickups!—being driven in the opposite direction by a typical old Vermont farmer, made a U-turn and stopped.

He wasn't a farmer, of course, and he wasn't from Vermont. This was my final reminder that reality would always be more complex and interesting than I expected. His name was Robert Stowell. He was born and brought up in small towns near Syracuse, New York. He used to hitchhike a lot when he was in high school, he said, never thought twice about it. Only time anything scary happened was when he and his friend Jimmy were hitching after dark and a friend of theirs came by on his motorbike and picked them both up. They had a close encounter with a tractor-trailer on a curve that straightened them right up as it passed, and halfway home there were headlights behind them, and the friend up front said, "Oh my God, it's the cops! If they catch me with three on a bike I'll lose my license!" So he went tearing around these little country roads at 80, 85 miles an hour. When they finally got into Clyde, New York, and Robert went to get off the bike, he found that Jimmy, behind him, was still clutching onto his jacket for dear life. "It's okay, Jimmy, we're home. You can let go now," he said, but poor Jimmy was so petrified it was several minutes before he could bring himself to unclench his fingers.

Robert had worked as an engineer for 26 years and was now retired, he said, living in Huntington, Vermont, just doing odd jobs here and there. He was pretty comfortable around fixing things; he only drew the line at jobs that would take two fellows. Then he said, "Well, you'll just have to find someone else to do that for you." He was supposed to paint someone's porch, but with the rain and the cold wind off the lake he thought, well, he might have to take it easy today, and I knew I was back in Vermont just by his dry wit. Only later did I notice that this was yet another instance of being picked up by someone whose plans had been changed for them, whom circumstance had diverted toward me.

"I'm a garden freak," he said. He and his dad used to have an acre garden, a couple of hundred tomato plants, three hundred peppers, lettuce, kohlrabi....The garden in Huntington hadn't done well, too much shade in the autumn; and he and his wife weren't so keen on winter, so they were thinking that they might move down to the western part of North Carolina some day.

"We're kind of reserved. She does her crocheting or her knitting. I'm independent. She lets me do what I like, cooking, baking, cleaning up around the house. I play around with the computer, or I work in this little wood shop I've set up."

Now I think about it, there was something very English about the life he described. Pottering around in the garden, tinkering in his shed—it's straight out of "When I'm 64." And that Englishness is increasingly important to me, as it is to many expatriates passing through middle age like the arch of the parabola. Wanting to spend less time and energy constantly remaking ourselves, keeping up with the adopted idiom, the second language.

Robert was 59, and when he turned 62 he'd have a couple—actually, three or four—pensions coming in, from the Navy, and the company he worked at for 26 years, and all that time he was doing work for the local school board. "My wife'll have her Post Office pension, too, so we should do all right. We don't smoke, we don't drink, we mostly eat in, though I like to go out for a buffet breakfast on Sundays now and then."

Maybe it was just because I was tired, but by now everything was starting to seem very simple. Journeys, like days and lives, are parabolic: We blaze away full of ambition, then slowly our energies dim and we fall back to earth. At the end of each journey, when ambition and vanity are burned away, we're left with the qualities that work for all times. Kindness. Gratitude. Everything beyond that is just a matter of working out the details.

As for how America has changed in the last quarter-century, I can barely even conceive of America as a single place, having seen so much of it, and its vast contradictions. Instead, it seems to be me who has changed. I think I once read that in the time of the Crusades a knight would go to the Holy Land twice, once as a young man, to conquer; once late in life, as a pilgrim, to ask forgiveness for the sins of his youth.

Robert drove 15 miles out of his way—"Heck, I didn't have anything better to do today anyway"—and dropped me off right at the top of my driveway, where the old Volvo had been sitting idle for too long, and everything needed a good weeding.

A Short History of Hitchhiking

One of the great charms of hitchhiking is that it never sold out. Nobody ever got a grant from the Pentagon to study the tactics of hitchhiking, or from NASA to study sweat loss under zero traffic conditions in New Mexico. No hitchhiker ever made it onto the cover of *Time* or *Newsweek*. There was never a Hitchhiking Channel, nor a Hitchhiking Hall of Fame. No daily mileages were ever published in the *Wall Street Journal*, no rankings in *Sports Illustrated*. Nobody ever sold giant hitchhiking thumbs inscribed with "We're #1" at roadside stands. No specialist hitchhiking clothing in the L.L. Bean catalog, no websites, no *Hitchhiking for Dummies*, no OBE's or knighthoods for services to hitchhiking.

Not surprisingly, then, nobody has ever published an authoritative history of hitchhiking. People must have been begging rides ever since one person had transport and another didn't. Hitchhiking as we understand it, though, seems to have been born with, or shortly after, the automobile. John T. Schlebecker, writing in *The Historian* in 1958 said, "Hitchhiking probably began during the First World War [among soldiers], but the art apparently declined immediately thereafter. It was taken up again in the 1920's, with strong overtones of adventure. In 1921, J. K. Christian won membership in the Chicago Adventurer's Club by hitchhiking 3,023 miles in 27 days," an astonishing rate of progress considering the roads of the time, and the small number of cars.

In the twenties, Schlebecker suggests, a slight depression, the land boom in Florida, and the growing number of cars spurred a rapid increase in the number of hitchhikers, who were now being noticed by the police, the press and by self-appointed keepers of public morals. In 1925 the *New York Times* editorialized, "Most of these people...are not dangerous. They are simply immeasurably impudent." The *New Republic* estimated in 1931 that 300 miles a day in the West and 250 in the East were considered average—not a bad rate of progress even today. I've done 600 miles in a day, but it was a long, long day.

A remarkable number of these early references mention women. As early as 1927 the *New Masses* wrote, "Most young janes have their heads full of a trip to Paris, or a hitchhike through New England." In a series of short stories for *the Saturday Evening Post*, Booth Jameson chose as heroines a pair of girl hitchhikers who worked as waitresses up and down the coast between New York and Florida. Claudette Colbert and Clark Gable hitched in the 1934 movie *It Happened One Night*. The Baltimore *Sun* reported in 1933 that "New England...is filled with young men and young women who are continually thumbing their way from one camp to another," like early Grateful Dead fans.

The Great Depression forced hordes onto the roads. As part of the New Deal, a Transient Bureau between 1933 and 1936 established and ran some 300 centers for the care and shelter of transients—the infrastructure of hitchhiking. Still a mix, though: hobos, people looking for work or relatives, college students out for adventure, children hitching to places of recreation. "In fact, during this decade, college men seem to have considered any other form of travel as slightly reprehensible," suggests Schlebecker. By 1937 one writer estimated that at least one man in ten had hitchhiked once in his life.

As the popularity of hitchhiking rose, so did the number of stories of crimes by and against hitchhikers. "Every imaginable type of nastiness, cruelty and brutality was perpetrated by hikers," writes Schlebecker, adding perceptively that such crimes were thought particularly despicable—and therefore particularly newsworthy—because they had been committed by those who had been befriended. The new laws prohibiting hitchhiking were supposed to protect motorists, but were actually heavily supported by public-transport companies: one electric railway claimed to have lost more than $50,000 from hitchhikers in only one year.

Hitchhiking was officially prohibited by the Army and the Air Force in orders going as far back as 1936 for being "unmilitary" and "a discredit to the service." All the same, during and after WW II the Defense Victory Ride Program, organized under the auspices of the Good Neighbor Association, aimed to enlist "an army of civilian motorists engaged in giving the uniformed men a lift, to and from their destination, whenever possible," and if they couldn't offer a lift, giving the V for Victory sign to boost the GI's morale. By 1944, more hitchhikers were on the road than ever before, especially because of gasoline rationing. Even Emily Post, mistress of manners, approved of female defense plant workers hitching to and from work.

In the conservative fifties, hitching came under sustained public attack from newspapers, magazines, automobile clubs, and the FBI. In this climate, some hitchhikers may have abandoned their art but others, typically, simply took it farther. Andrew Tangelos, a retired diplomat, told me that when he graduated from high school in 1953 and went down to interview at Harvard, he hitched there and, following his usual practice, found a used car lot and slept in the backseat of a car. The same decade saw a boom in hitchhiking memoirs, such as Joseph Bormel's *Around the World on Fifty Dollars*, Donald Knies's *Walk the Wide World*, and *Harvard Interlude*, in which Charles Stone Borden writes about his travels with his friend Paul Southwick across the U.S. in 1941. "The most obvious conclusion to draw from our experiences on the road is that the proletariat is our friend, the Good Samaritan, while the bourgeoisie are implacable enemies. The latter fly by in their shiny cars and look at us, if at all, with curiosity, animosity, or at best, indifference."

In *Black Like Me* (1960), John Howard Griffin, a middle-class white sociologist who had his skin turned black in a series of surgical maneuvers, wrote about hitching through the South. "In a car at night visibility is reduced. A man will reveal himself in the dark, which gives an illusion of anonymity, more than he will in the bright light." (He went on: "Some were shamelessly open, some shamelessly subtle. All showed morbid curiosity about the sexual life of the Negro.")

I don't know when the hitchhiking boom of the sixties began, nor why, nor how many people were on the roads at any given moment. In 1970, the *New York Times* reported that each summer at least three to four million hitchhikers were on the European roads; but in 1970, I was on the roads, and nobody counted me or anyone else I know. Here's one thought, though. Hitchhiking has always offered a chance for young adults to prove ourselves. If at any given period the way to personhood and respect is to get a steady job or start a family, then working in a bank is a way of proving ourselves. Hitchhiking rose rapidly at a time, and in a constituency, when we needed to prove that we were *not* good citizens, capable wage earners, good parents, good team players, loyal employees, because those qualities seemed to lead to the problem, not the solution. We proved ourselves on the opposite scale—as travelers and individualists, paupers and outsiders.

Yet hitchhiking was always as pragmatic as it was romantic. In 1973 the city of Fort Collins, Colorado, adopted a legalized and controlled hitchhiking system, and after nine months the hitchhiking co-op had 2,600 members, with no reported complaints. Marin County, California devised a similar plan, and something along the same lines was included in a report produced by the University of Colorado-Denver for the U.S. Department of Commerce.

The Denver report, by the way, tried to assess just how dangerous hitchhiking was. The Los Angeles Police Department announced that 22.6 percent of rapes involved hitchhikers, even though no official statistics on violent crime include under what circumstances the crime was committed. The California Highway Patrol concluded that hitchhiking contributed to .6 percent of all crime in California. When researchers pinned down the District Attorney of Adams County, though, he had to admit that in ten years as a D. A. he had come across only two cases of violence involving hitchhikers, both of which involved a driver robbing someone he had picked up.

Countless novels and nonfiction works included hitchhiking in a glamorous or casual way. An anthology of poems about hitchhiking was published in 1969. There was even a comic for and about hitchhiking called *Hit The Road*, published in 1971 in—not surprisingly—Berkeley.

But a boom in hitchhiking always seems to be accompanied by a backlash of warnings. From the early 1970s on, an almost constant stream of anti-hitching propaganda appeared in newspapers and magazines and on television: "Hitchhiking: Road to Rape"; "Hitchhiking—Too Often the Last Ride"; "Hitchhiking: The Road to Rape and Murder"; "Thumbs Down." In 1977, the Los Angeles City Schools produced a pamphlet called "The free rider: hitchhiking, can you afford the risk?" The Walt Disney company seems to have been especially alarmed. In one of the most bizarre anthologies imaginable, Disney released the cautionary after-school special *Andrea's Story—A Hitchhiking Tragedy* on the same video-cassette as *20,000 Leagues Under the Sea*, the latter presumably intended as a warning not to hitchhike by submarine.

Most astonishing is the way hitchhiking was lumped together with a hair-raising list of social deviations. In 1973 the sociologists Greenley and Rice of the University of Wisconsin wrote that women hitchhiking constituted "quasi-deviant behavior," even though two-thirds of the female university students they surveyed had hitchhiked, which would seem to imply that *not* hitchhiking was the deviant form. None of the respondents reported ever having been raped, attacked, or kidnapped. In 1986, the McGruff drug-prevention and child-protection program (format: 2 sound cassettes, 1 hand puppet, 1 teacher's guide) lumped hitchhiking together with child molestation, child abuse, alcohol, drugs, vandalism, robbery and burglary, marijuana, gangs, shoplifting, inhalants, arson, cocaine, and crack.

I don't know why hitchhiking fell out of fashion. All the aforementioned propaganda can't have helped, but I suspect it's also because the eighties destroyed the solidarity of misfortune: no self-respecting student wanted to look poor, to be thought a loser. Nowadays, when we do hear of a hitchhiker, it's almost always in terms of disaster: nothing is more reassuring, in a twisted way, than something that confirms our opinions, even if what it reinforces is fear. Perhaps the most famous recent American hitchhiker is Chris McCandless, in Jon Krakauer's *Into The Wild* (1996), who had so imperfect a sense of danger and his own limits that he froze to death in Alaska.

~

Product Testing
Notes

By the end of the trip, the equipment and clothing I was using regularly had been whittled down to the following items, indispensible for the next generation of hitchhikers:

Sandals: Teva Terradactyl. In Canada after a long wait on a hot day, I put my feet up on the dash and caught of whiff of the most nauseating rancid stench, which I thought was the Tevas decomposing. Turned out to be my feet. $65. Eastern Mountain Sports, South Burlington (EMS).

Pants: Ex Officio microfiber parachute pants. Light, cool, dry instantly, Velcro cargo pocket the right size for notebook. $59. EMS.

Pen: Dr. Grip by Pilot. People seem to either like chubby pens or hate them, but it felt companionable and never leaked. Only shortcoming: hard to keep it behind your ear. $5.99. Staples.

Notebook: *The Small Travel Journal* by Graphic Image, Inc. Best notebook I've ever owned—beautiful, light, well-bound, the perfect balance between suppleness and stiffness—but at $19.95 it should be. Barnes & Noble.

Tape recorder: Wretched, battered old Panasonic. Made everyone sound as if they're being interviewed while pacing about in a huge revolving drum of corn flakes, but good portable cassette recorders seem to be a thing of the past. Paid $80 or so for it. Can't remember where.

Shorts: for dry weather, Royal Robbins heavy cotton. Backside pocket (with Velcro) so deep it'll hold a road map. $48. EMS. For wet weather, Columbia nylon. Dry quickly, double as swim trunks. $15. Pre-season sale, Phil's Trading Post, Essex Junction, Vermont.

Belt: Patagonia nylon webbing. Never let me down in times of crisis. Light, washable. $10, plus or minus. EMS.

Backpack: EMS 3000LT. Worked remarkably well considering it was being used by someone (a) with a history of back problems and (b) who stuffed far too much into it. Imagine how amazing it would have been if I'd gone back and had all the straps tuned up. $99.50. EMS.

Rain jacket: EMS Gore-Tex. A wonderful piece of contemporary clothing technology, but I can't help thinking that if I'd needed to, I could have found something half as good for a tenth the price. $300. EMS.

Jeans: Wrangler. $13. 2-for-1 sale, Ames, Essex Junction.

Shirt: Gramicci microfiber. Took other shirts, but gave up wearing them. Of all my high-tech equipment, the most worthwhile. $54. EMS.

Sneakers: Nike Air. Light and comfortable. Survived the trip, then blew out both sides on the tennis court. $5. Tent sale at Mills & Greer, South Burlington.

Antihistamine: Allegra.

ACKNOWLEGMENTS

This trip and this book would not have been possible without the self-lessness of my wife, Barbara, who kept home and family running when I was away. There should be a Guild of Travel Writers' Wives, who are awarded royalties of their own. Thanks also to two editors, Gail Hudson, who asked tough questions, and Oliver Payne at NATIONAL GEOGRAPHIC, who was not just an honest, encouraging, and intelligent editor, but a partner in crime. Tomasz Tomaszewski suggested the title, Chris Pedler and Seth Martin contributed valuable research, and Andrew Hendrickson recovered the first five chapters after they'd vanished off my hard drive.

ABOUT THE AUTHOR

TIM BROOKES was born in London, but now lives on a dirt road in Vermont with his wife and daughters. He is the author of two previous books, *Catching My Breath: An Asthmatic Explores his Illness* and *Signs of Life: A Memoir of Dying and Discovery*. He is currently working on a subjective geography of Lake Champlain. He teaches at the University of Vermont, and if he had any sense he'd hitchhike to work.